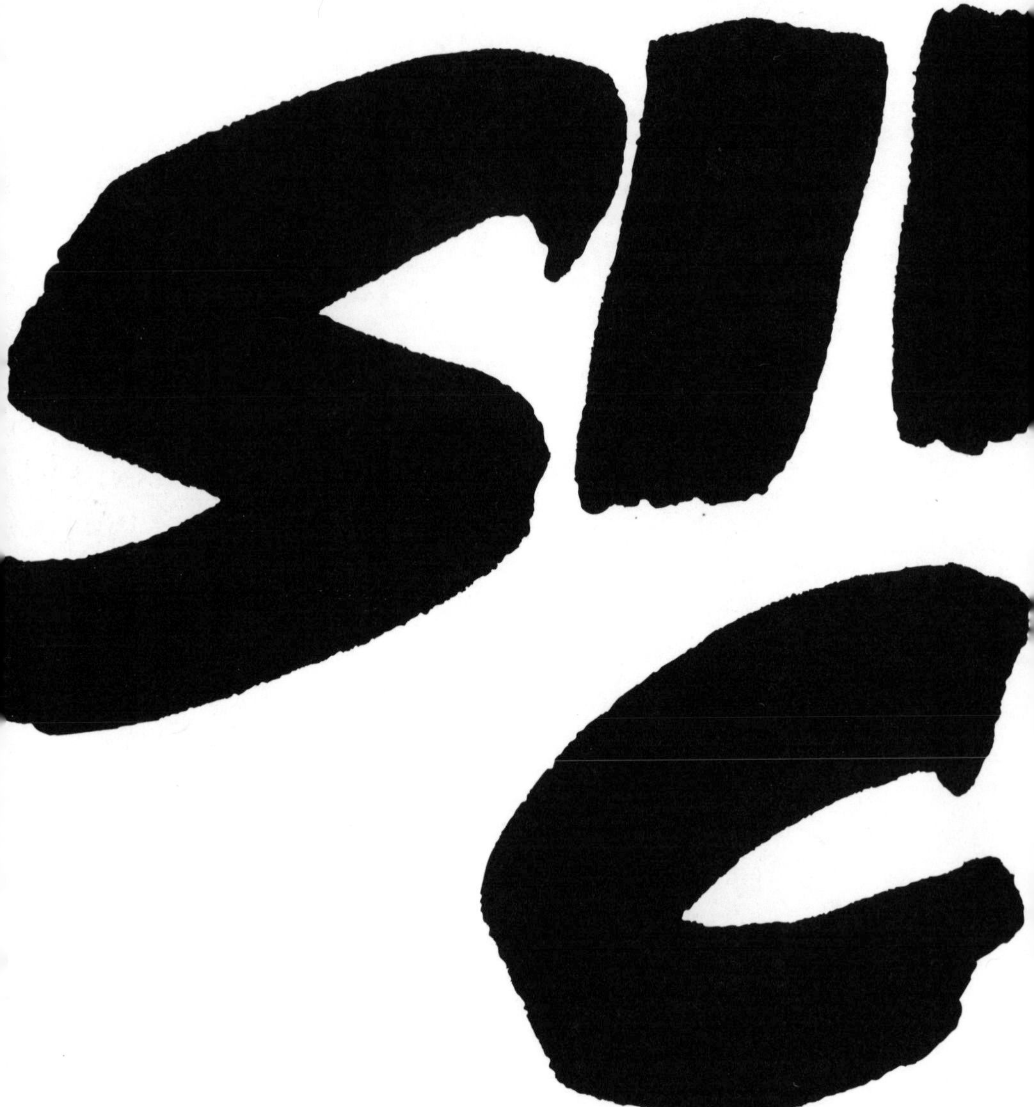

CONTENTS

*All stories written and illustrated by **FRANK MILLER***

The Babe Wore Red and Other Stories
Silent Night
A Decade of Dark Horse
Lost, Lonely, & Lethal
Sex & Violence
Just Another Saturday Night

Cover color for *Sin City: Silent Night* and *A Decade of Dark Horse* by Lynn Varley

Original stories edited by Bob Schreck, Randy Stradley, Peet Janes, Kris Young, Barbara Kesel, and Diana Schutz

Booze, Broads, & Bullets **FRANK MILLER**

DARK HORSE BOOKS®

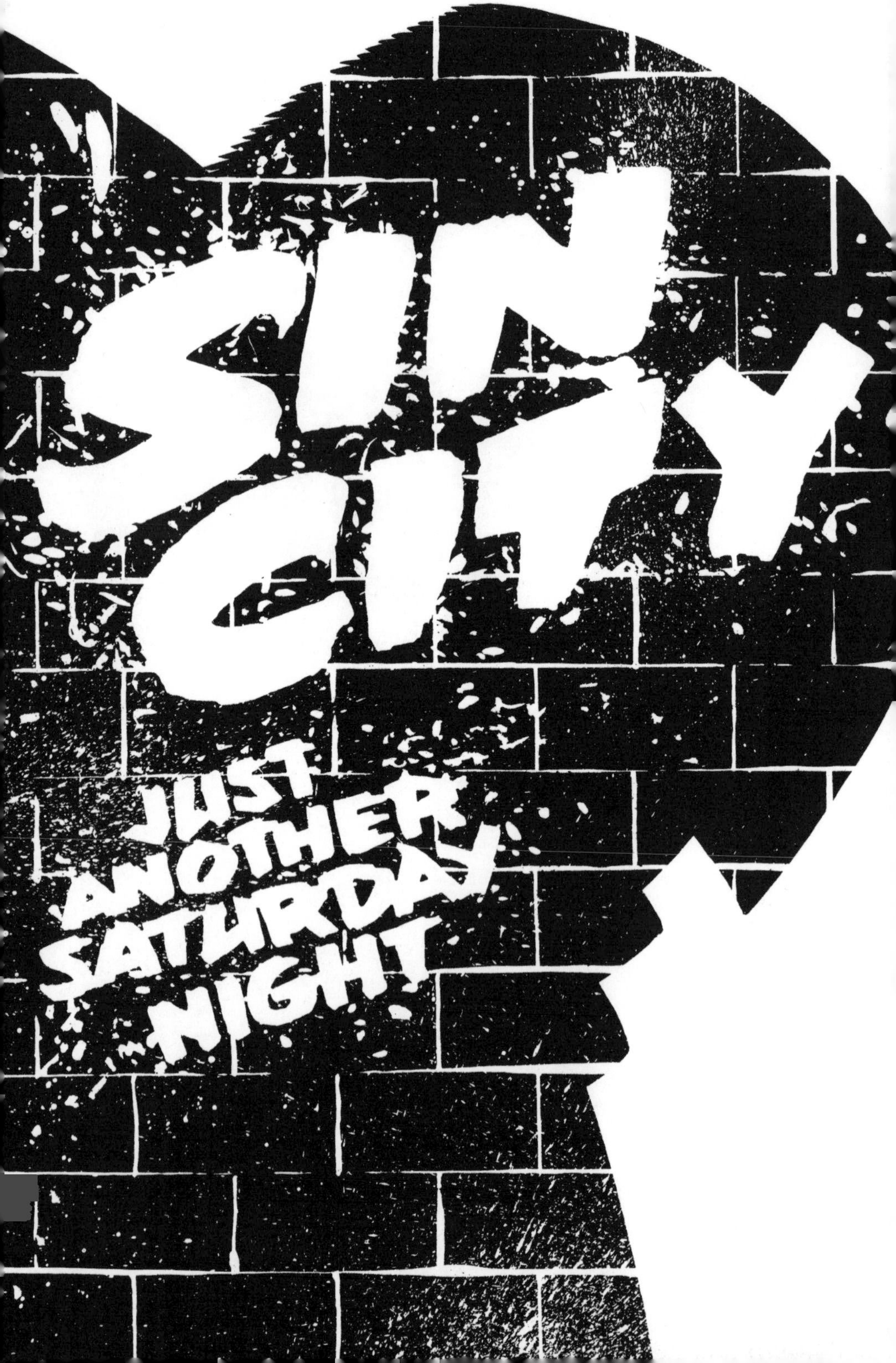
SIN CITY
JUST ANOTHER SATURDAY NIGHT

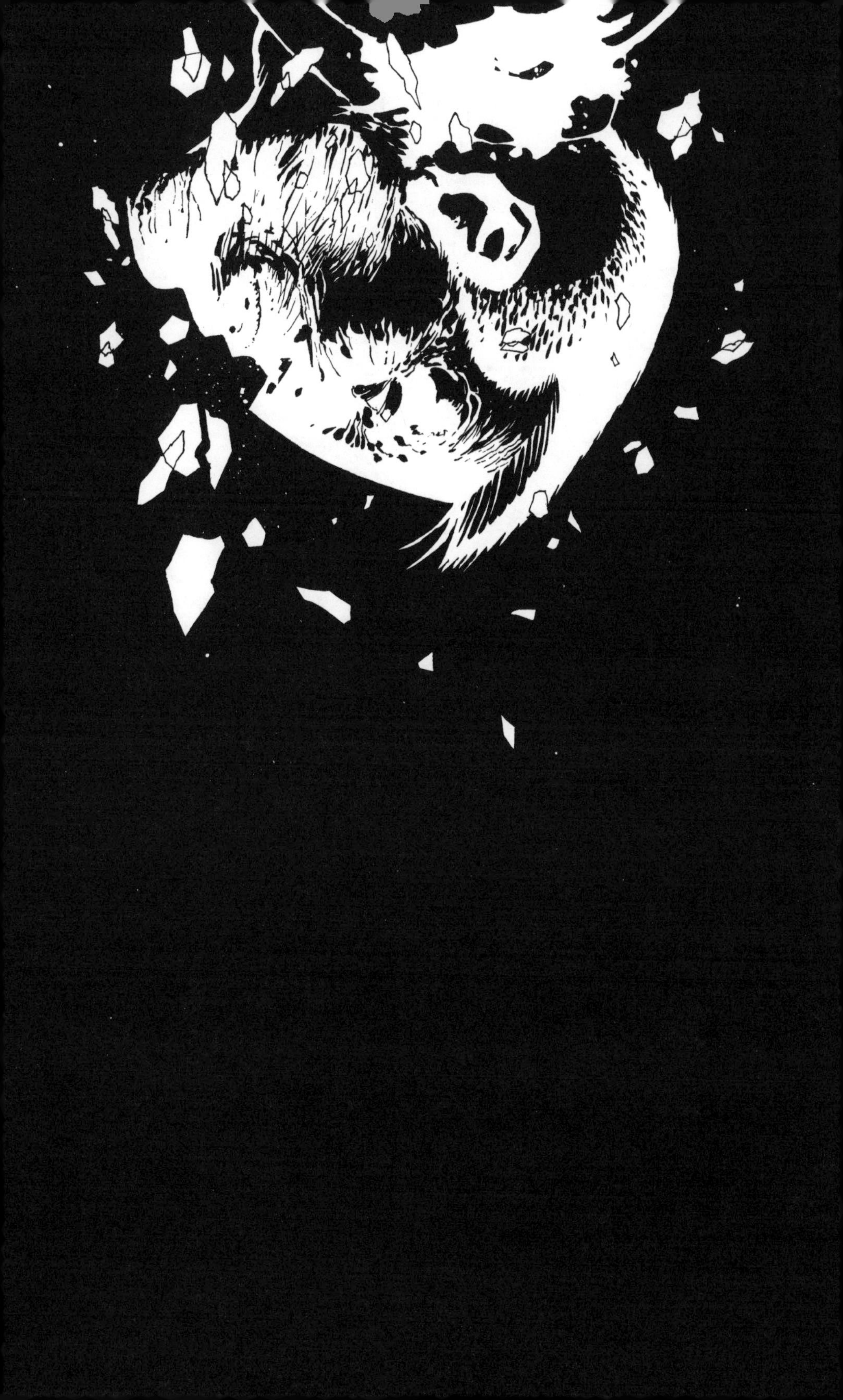

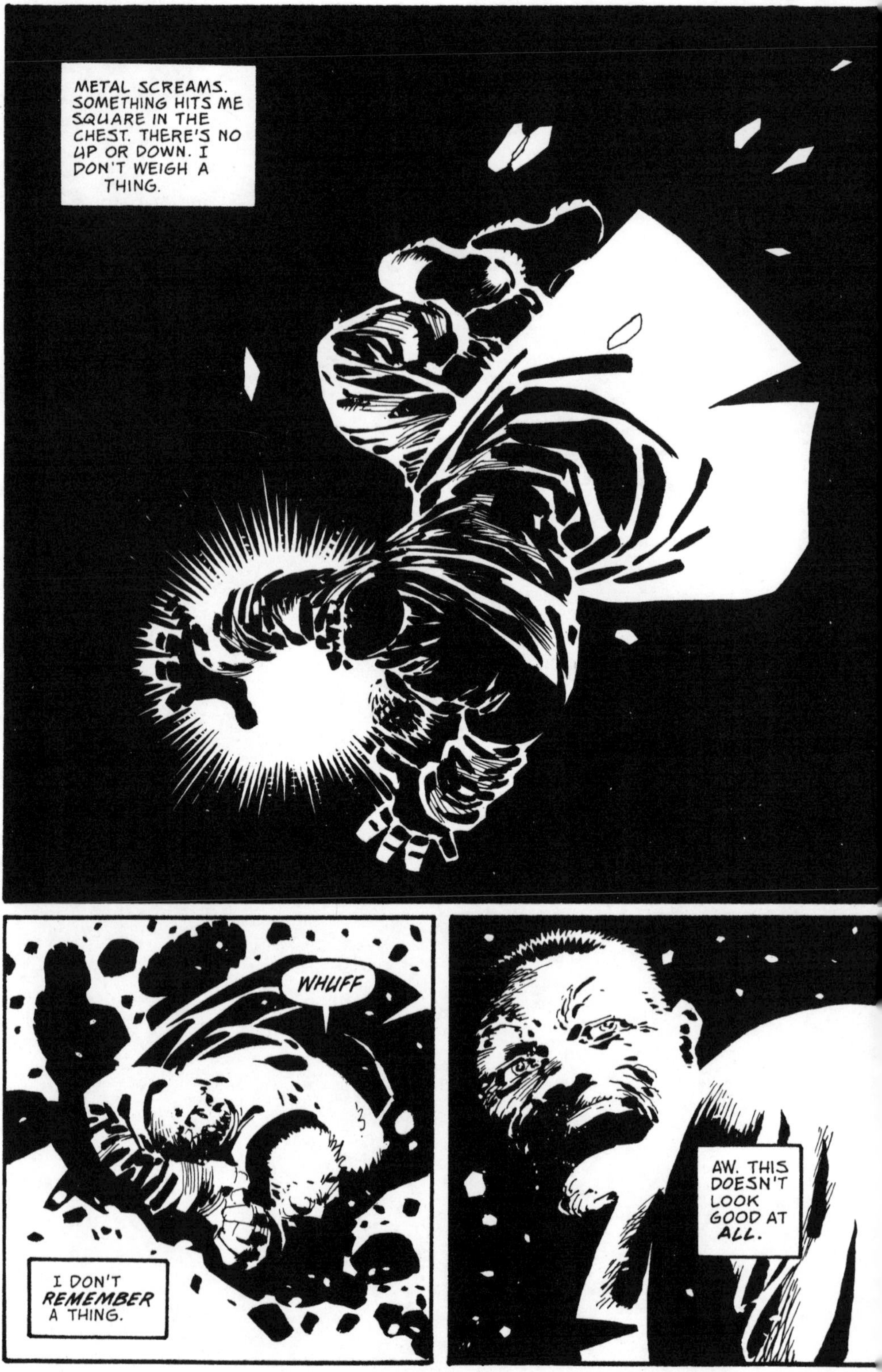
METAL SCREAMS. SOMETHING HITS ME SQUARE IN THE CHEST. THERE'S NO UP OR DOWN. I DON'T WEIGH A THING.
WHUFF
I DON'T REMEMBER A THING.
AW. THIS DOESN'T LOOK GOOD AT ALL.

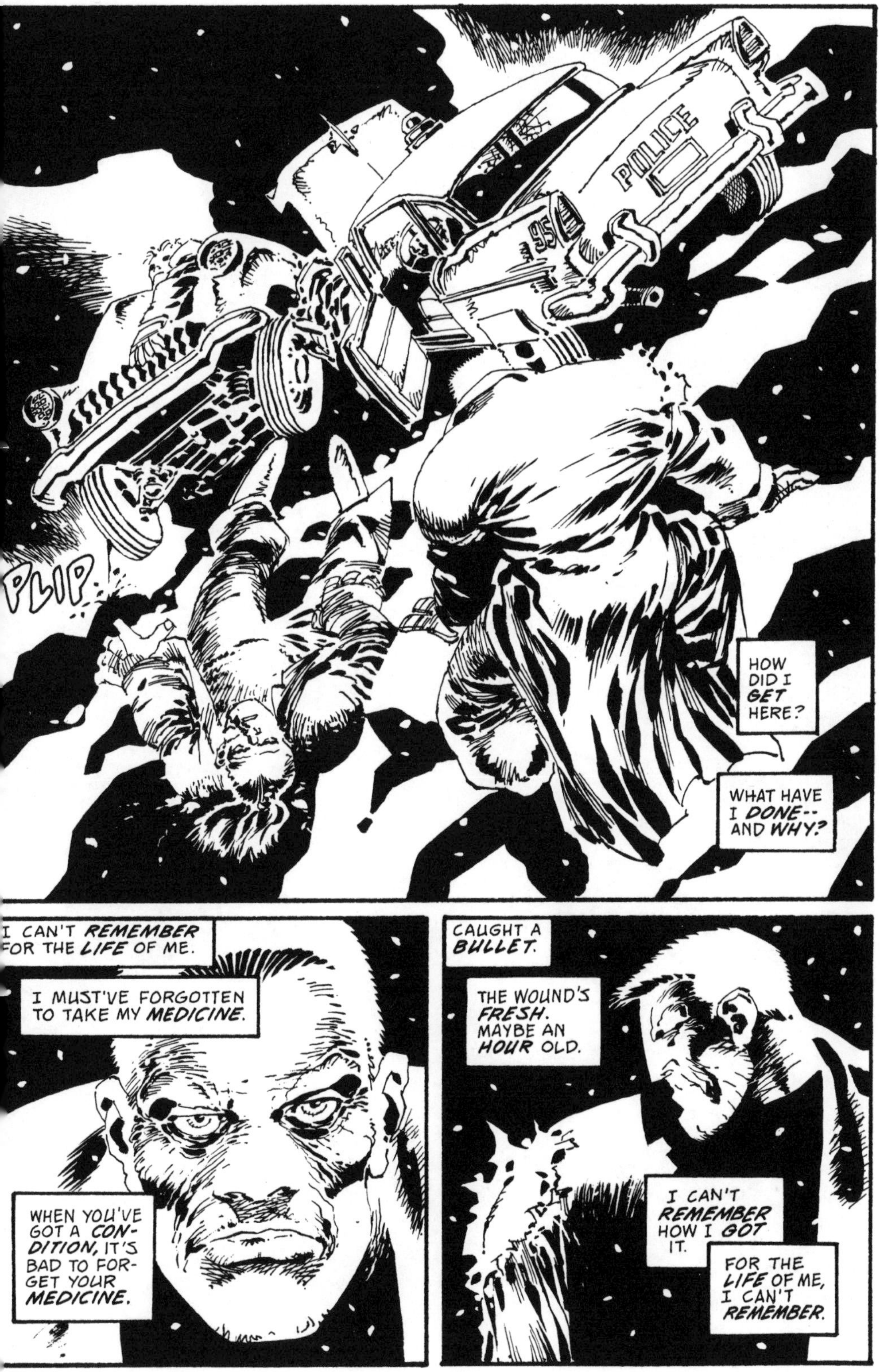
PLIP
HOW DID I GET HERE?
WHAT HAVE I DONE-- AND WHY?
I CAN'T REMEMBER FOR THE LIFE OF ME.
I MUST'VE FORGOTTEN TO TAKE MY MEDICINE.
WHEN YOU'VE GOT A CON-DITION, IT'S BAD TO FOR-GET YOUR MEDICINE.
CAUGHT A BULLET.
THE WOUND'S FRESH. MAYBE AN HOUR OLD.
I CAN'T REMEMBER HOW I GOT IT.
FOR THE LIFE OF ME, I CAN'T REMEMBER.

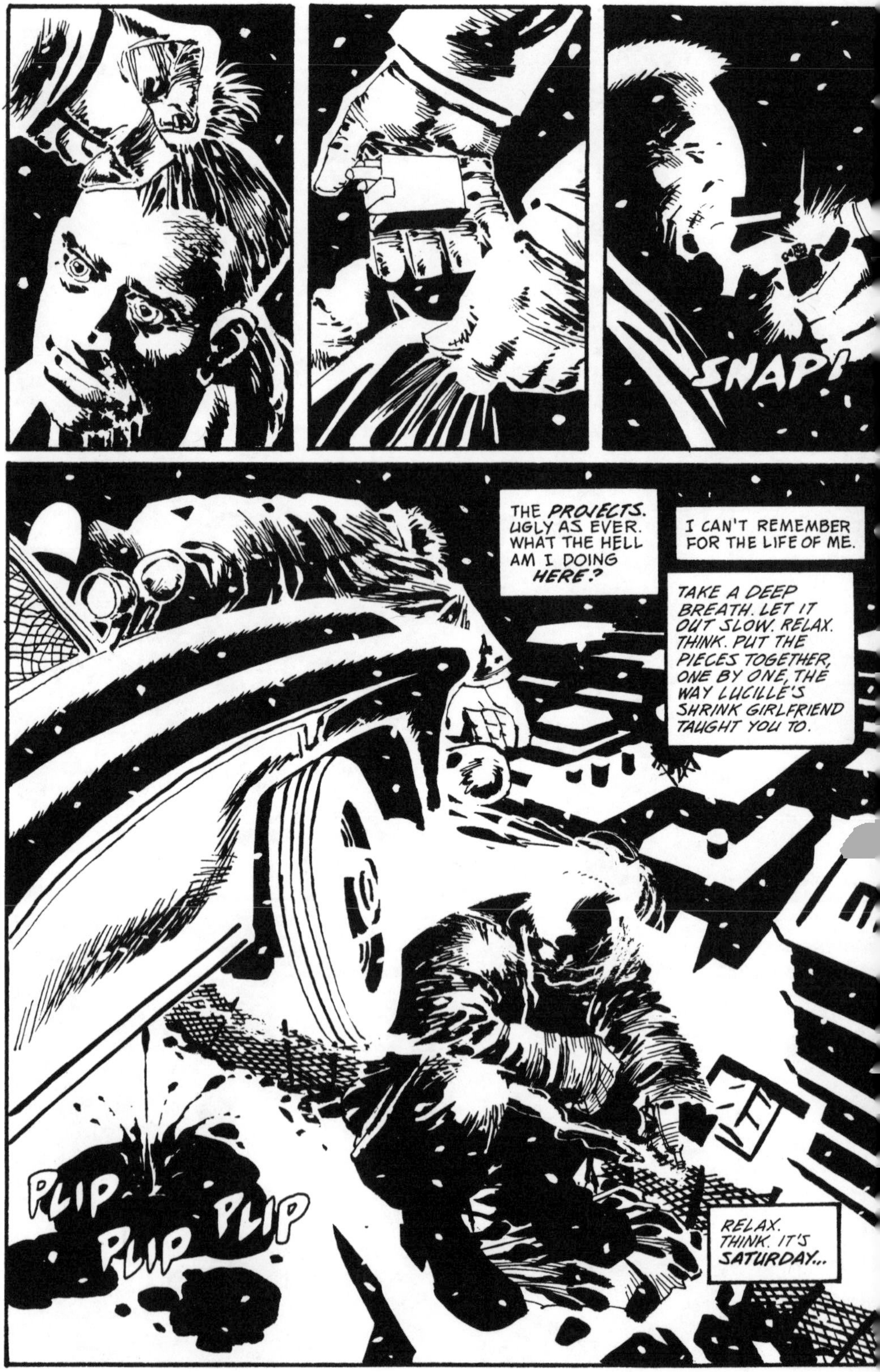
SNAP!
THE PROJECTS. UGLY AS EVER. WHAT THE HELL AM I DOING HERE?
I CAN'T REMEMBER FOR THE LIFE OF ME.
TAKE A DEEP BREATH. LET IT OUT SLOW. RELAX. THINK. PUT THE PIECES TOGETHER, ONE BY ONE, THE WAY LUCILLE'S SHRINK GIRLFRIEND TAUGHT YOU TO.
PLIP PLIP PLIP
RELAX. THINK. IT'S SATURDAY...

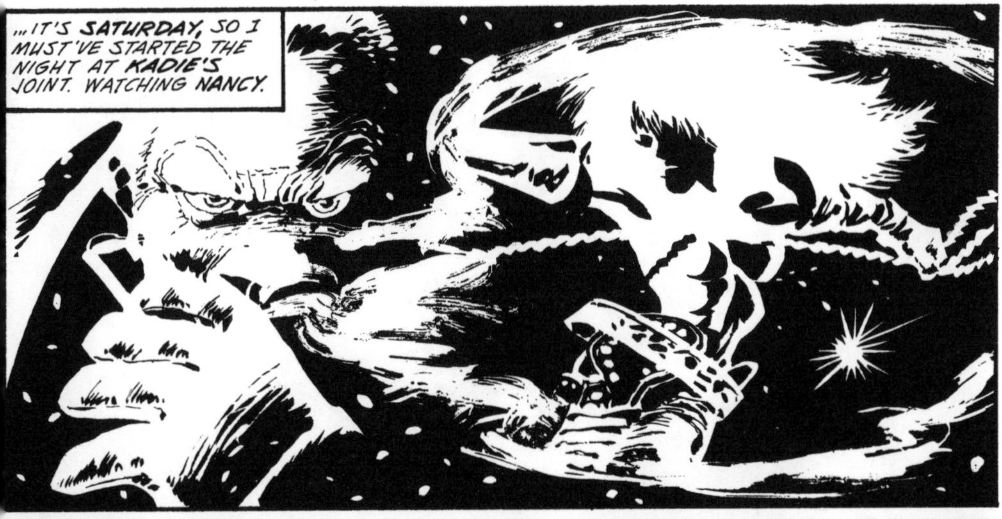
...IT'S SATURDAY, SO I MUST'VE STARTED THE NIGHT AT KADIE'S JOINT. WATCHING NANCY.

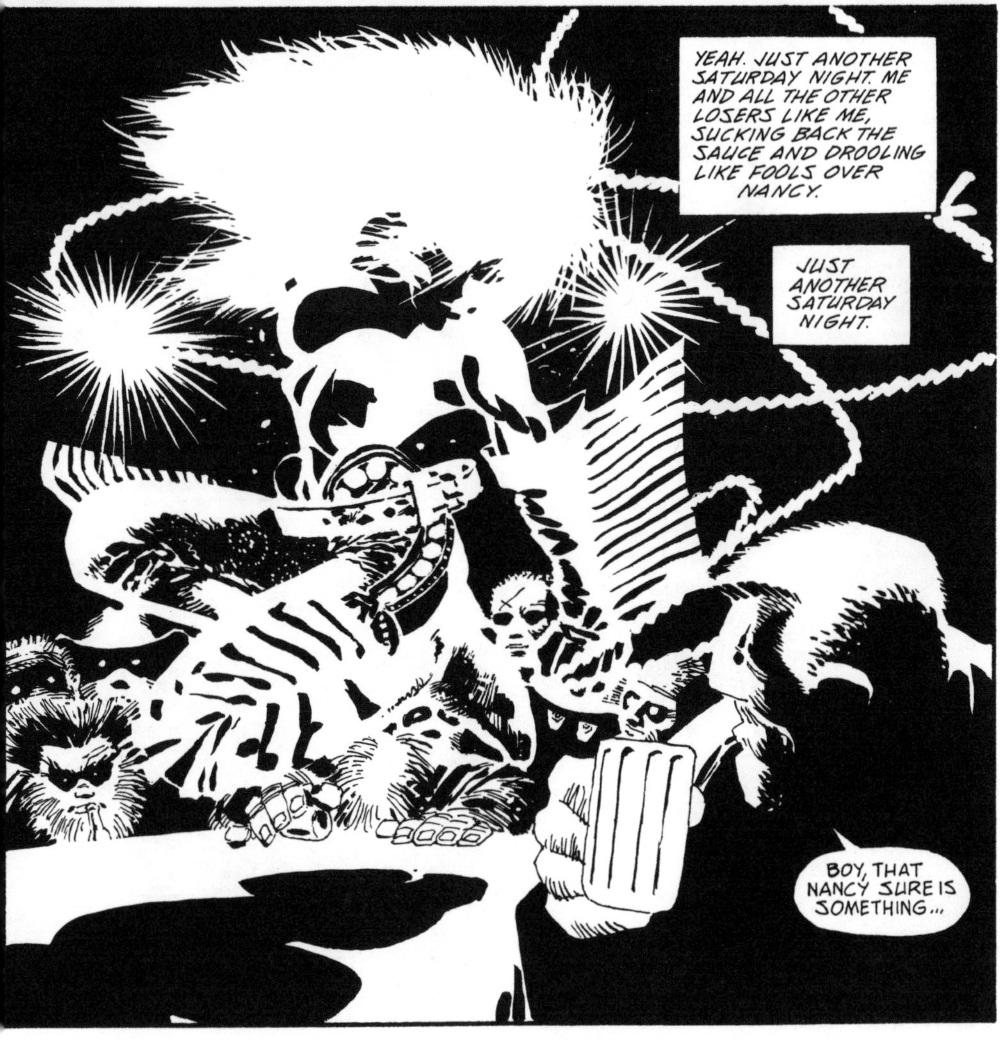
YEAH. JUST ANOTHER SATURDAY NIGHT. ME AND ALL THE OTHER LOSERS LIKE ME, SUCKING BACK THE SAUCE AND DROOLING LIKE FOOLS OVER NANCY.
JUST ANOTHER SATURDAY NIGHT.
BOY, THAT NANCY SURE IS SOMETHING...

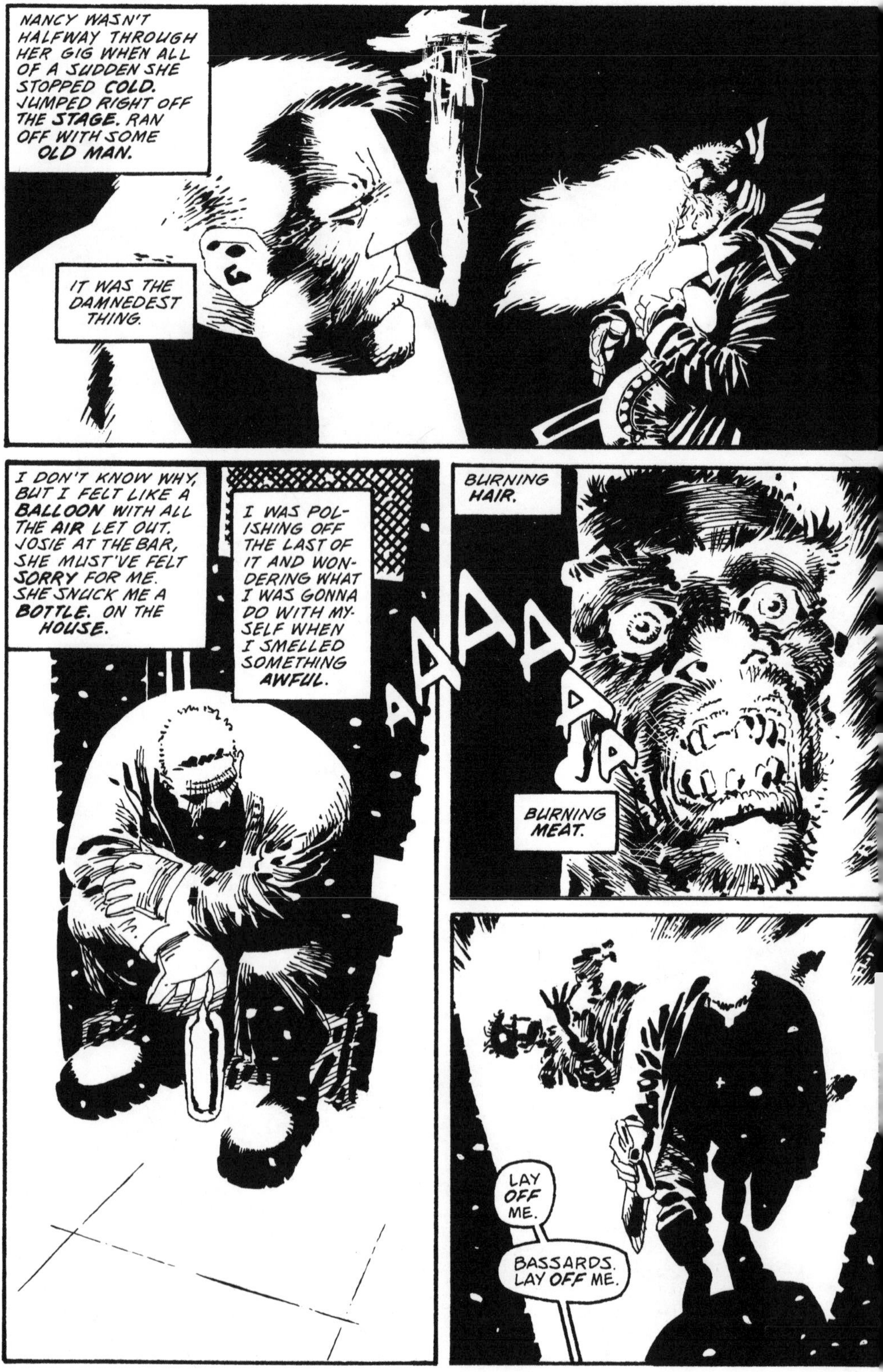
NANCY WASN'T HALFWAY THROUGH HER GIG WHEN ALL OF A SUDDEN SHE STOPPED COLD. JUMPED RIGHT OFF THE STAGE. RAN OFF WITH SOME OLD MAN.
IT WAS THE DAMNEDEST THING.
I DON'T KNOW WHY, BUT I FELT LIKE A BALLOON WITH ALL THE AIR LET OUT. JOSIE AT THE BAR, SHE MUST'VE FELT SORRY FOR ME. SHE SNUCK ME A BOTTLE. ON THE HOUSE.
I WAS POLISHING OFF THE LAST OF IT AND WONDERING WHAT I WAS GONNA DO WITH MYSELF WHEN I SMELLED SOMETHING AWFUL.
BURNING HAIR.
AAAAAA
BURNING MEAT.
LAY OFF ME.
BASSARDS. LAY OFF ME.

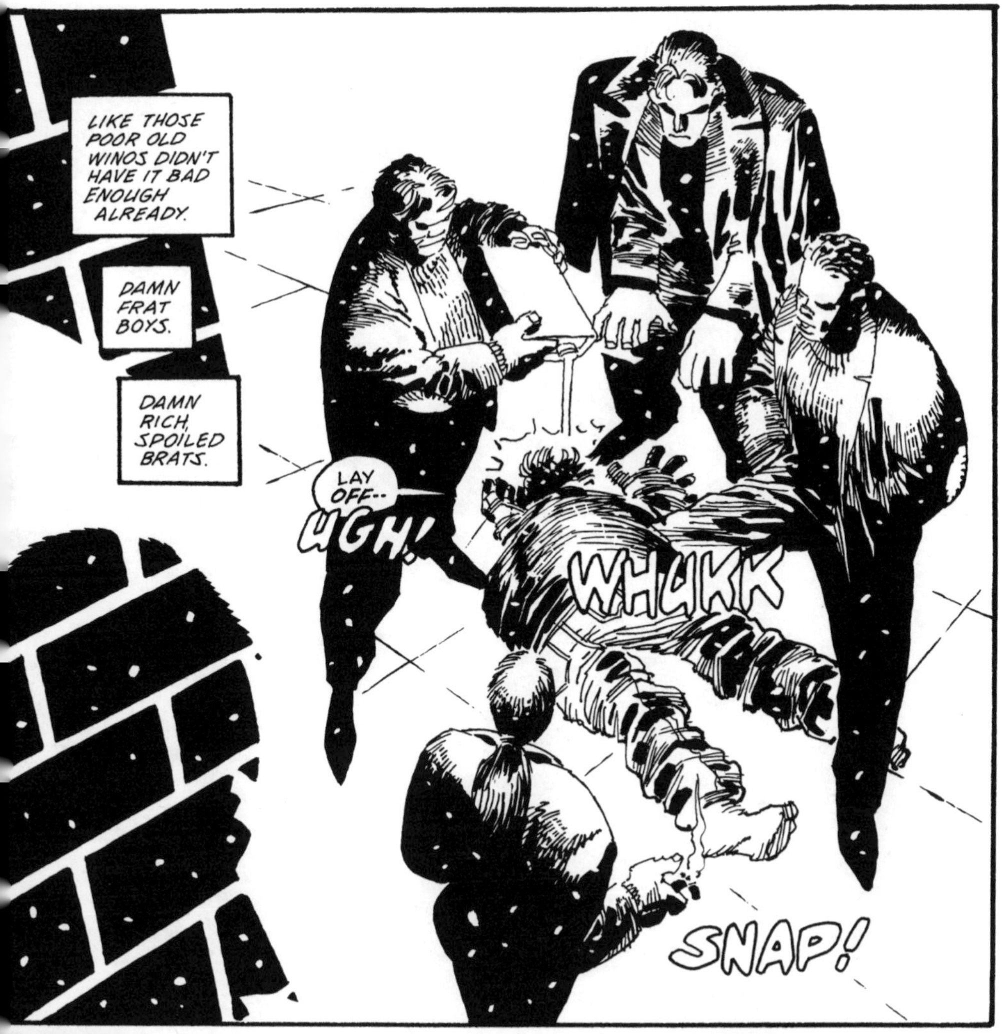
LIKE THOSE POOR OLD WINOS DIDN'T HAVE IT BAD ENOUGH ALREADY.
DAMN FRAT BOYS.
DAMN RICH, SPOILED BRATS.
LAY OFF-- UGH!
WHUKK
SNAP!
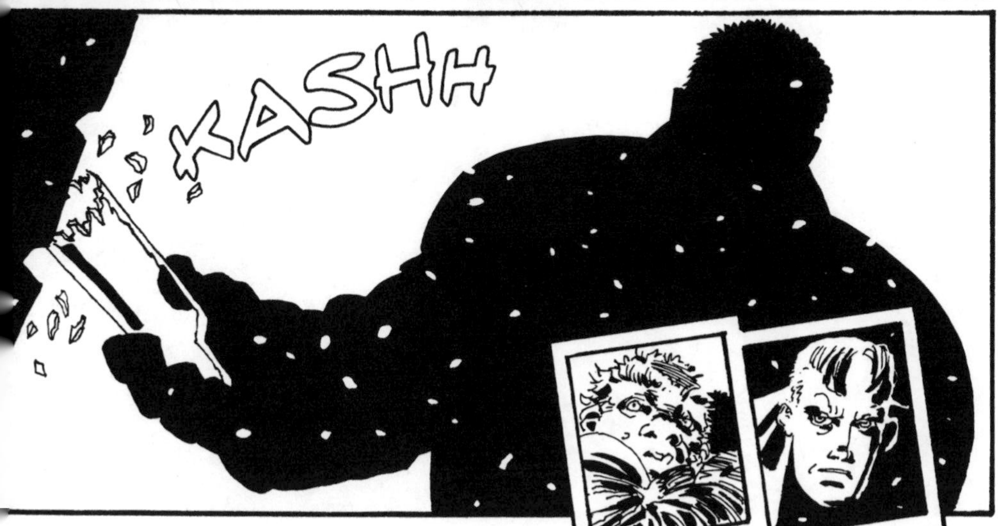
KASHH

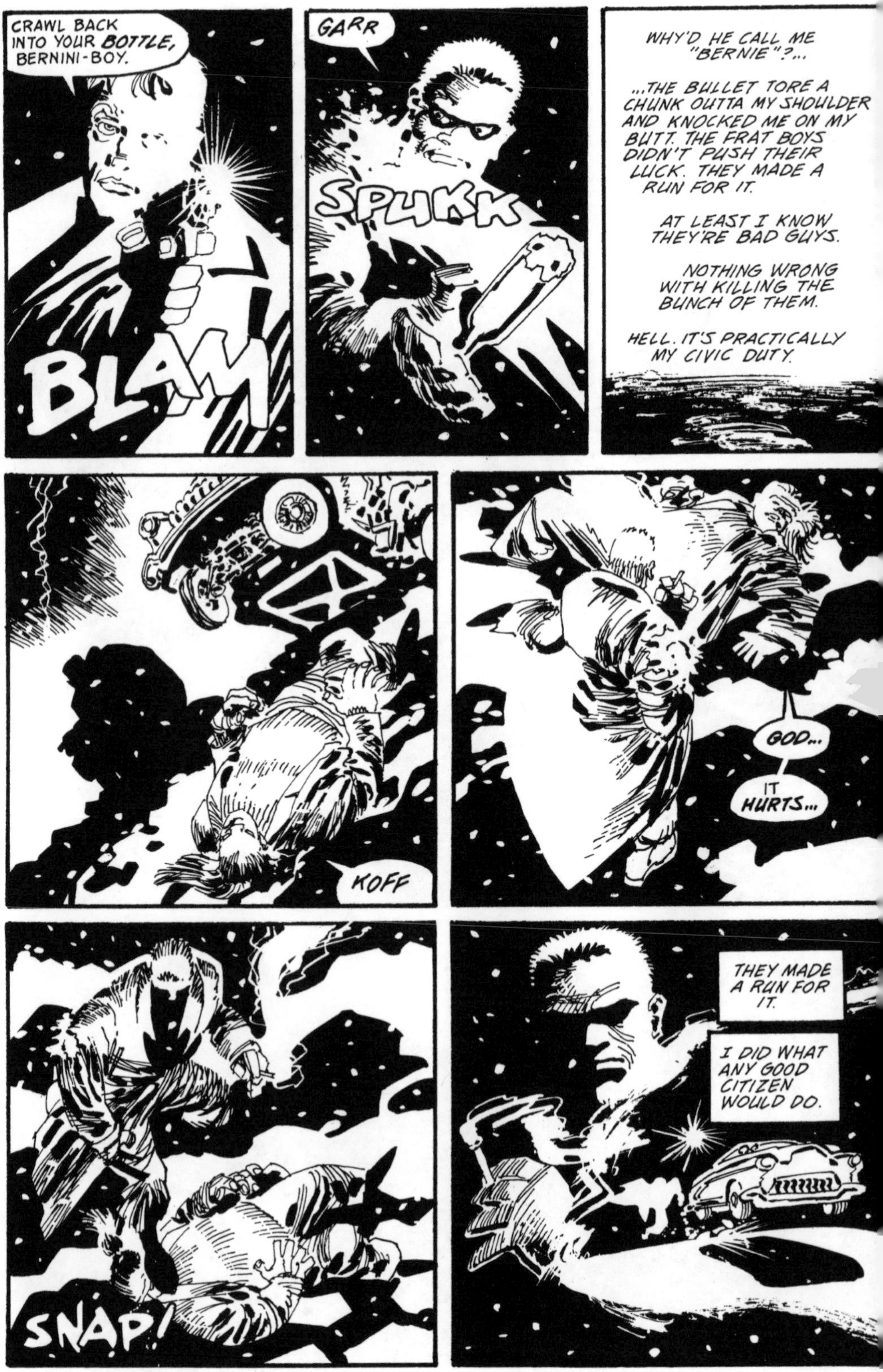

CRAWL BACK INTO YOUR BOTTLE, BERNINI-BOY.
BLAM
GARR
SPUKK
WHY'D HE CALL ME "BERNIE"?...
...THE BULLET TORE A CHUNK OUTTA MY SHOULDER AND KNOCKED ME ON MY BUTT. THE FRAT BOYS DIDN'T PUSH THEIR LUCK. THEY MADE A RUN FOR IT.
AT LEAST I KNOW THEY'RE BAD GUYS.
NOTHING WRONG WITH KILLING THE BUNCH OF THEM.
HELL. IT'S PRACTICALLY MY CIVIC DUTY.
KOFF
GOD...
IT HURTS...
SNAP!
THEY MADE A RUN FOR IT.
I DID WHAT ANY GOOD CITIZEN WOULD DO.

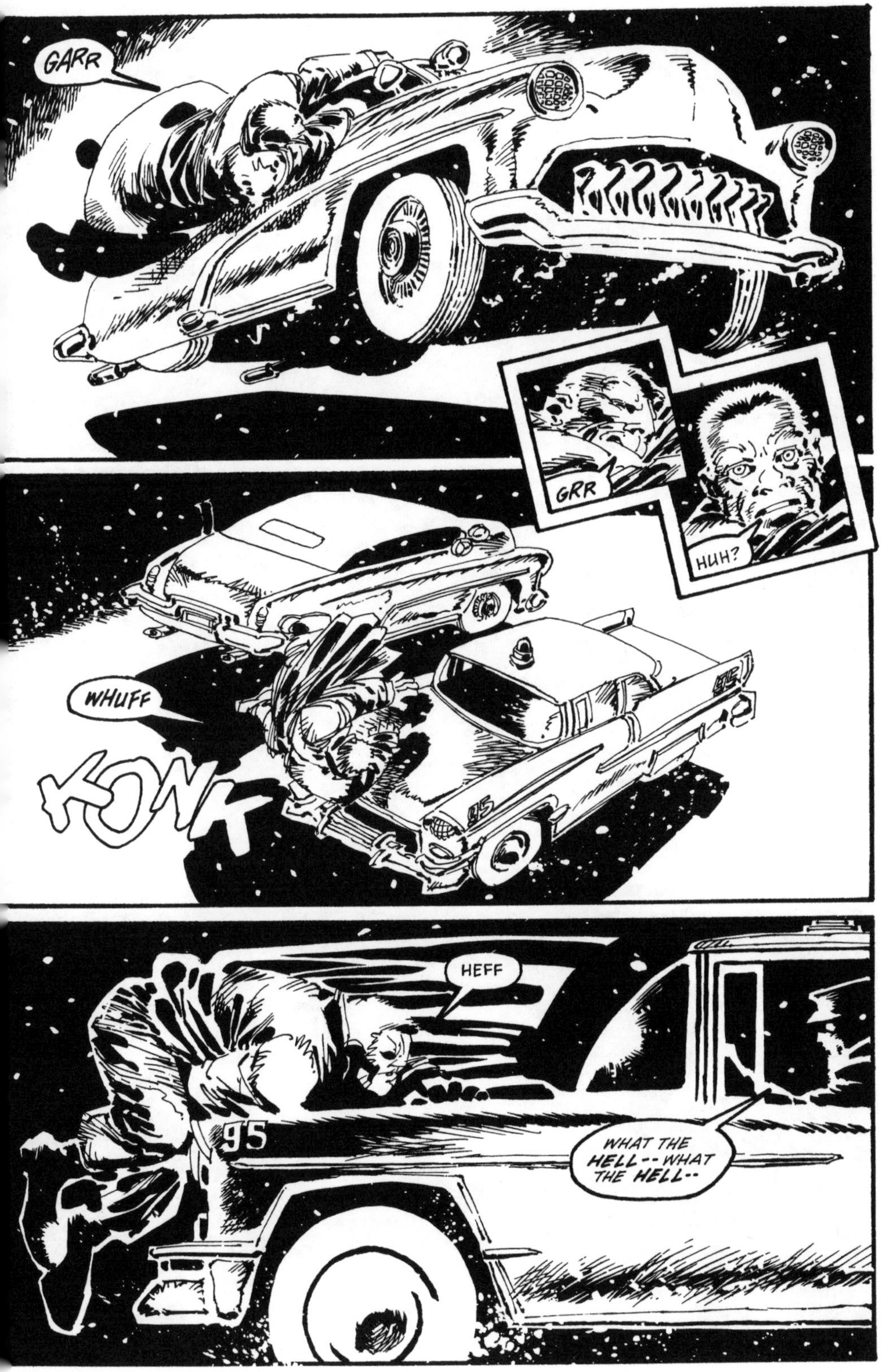
GARR
GRR
HUH?
WHUFF
KONK
HEFF
WHAT THE HELL -- WHAT THE HELL --

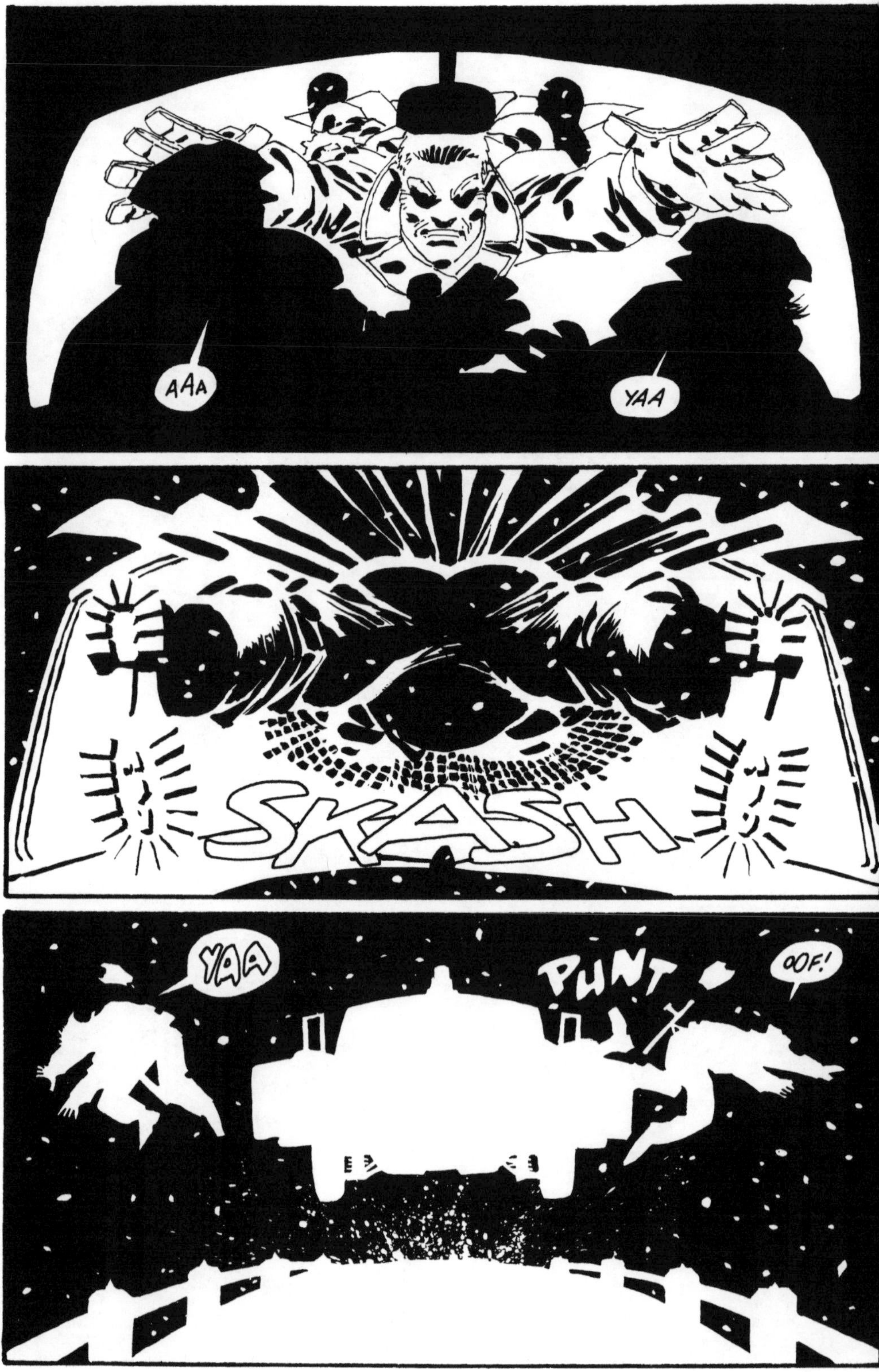
AAA
YAA
SKASH
YAA
PUNT
OOF!

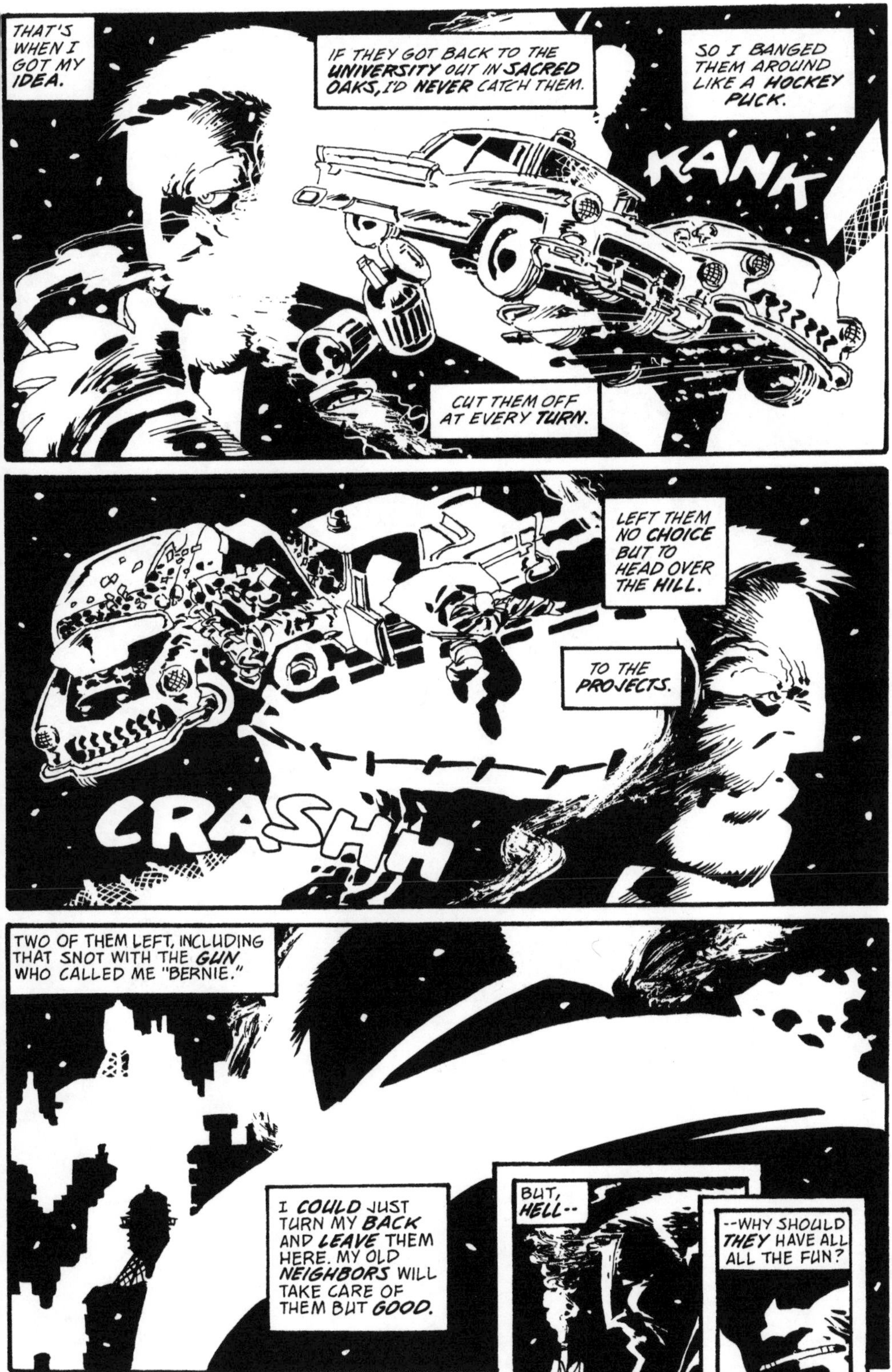
THAT'S WHEN I GOT MY IDEA.
IF THEY GOT BACK TO THE UNIVERSITY OUT IN SACRED OAKS, I'D NEVER CATCH THEM.
SO I BANGED THEM AROUND LIKE A HOCKEY PUCK.
KANK
CUT THEM OFF AT EVERY TURN.
LEFT THEM NO CHOICE BUT TO HEAD OVER THE HILL.
TO THE PROJECTS.
CRASHH
TWO OF THEM LEFT, INCLUDING THAT SNOT WITH THE GUN WHO CALLED ME "BERNIE."
I COULD JUST TURN MY BACK AND LEAVE THEM HERE. MY OLD NEIGHBORS WILL TAKE CARE OF THEM BUT GOOD.
BUT, HELL--
--WHY SHOULD THEY HAVE ALL ALL THE FUN?

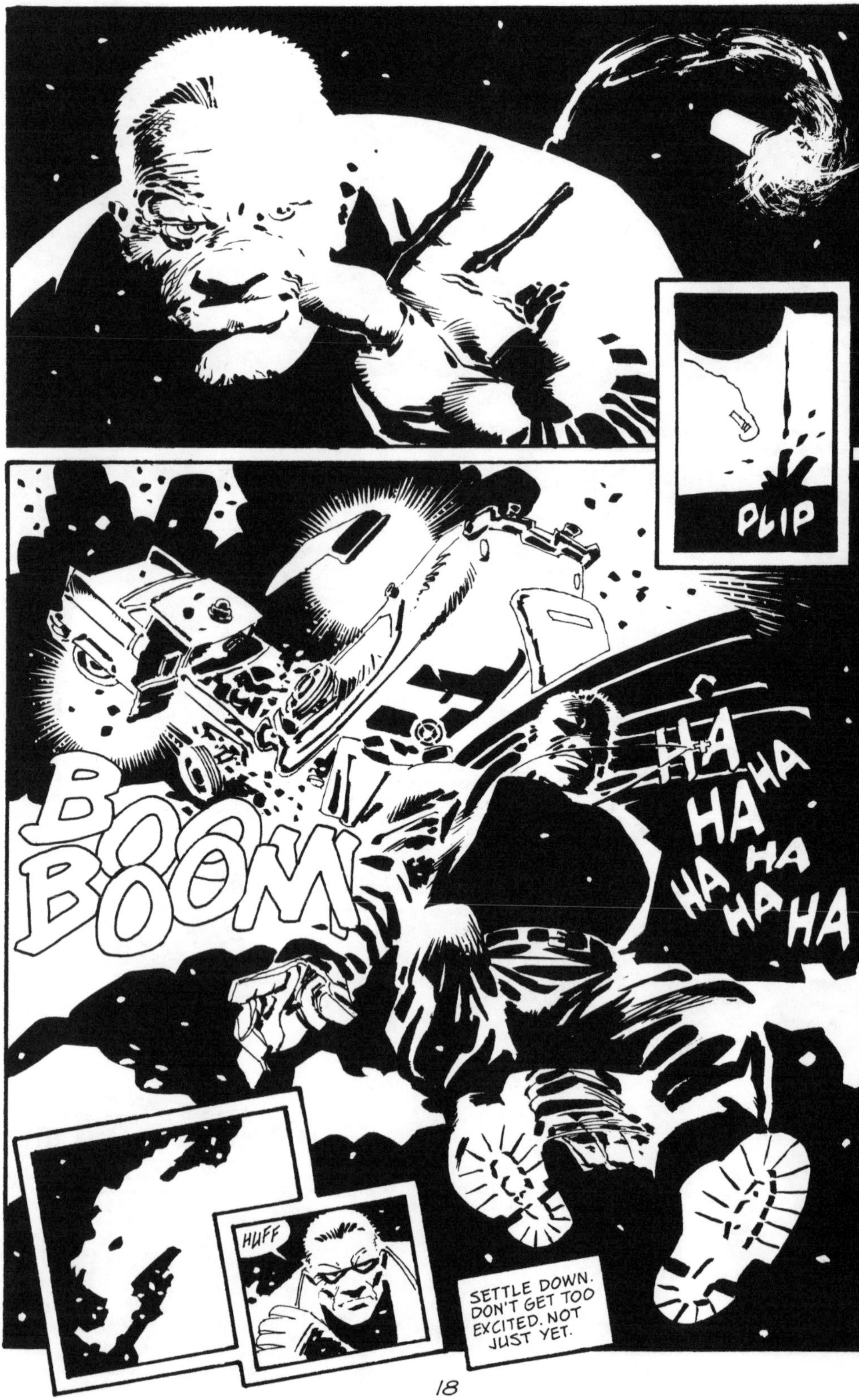
PLIP
BOOOM
BOOOM
HA HA HA HA HA HA HA HA HA
HUFF
SETTLE DOWN. DON'T GET TOO EXCITED. NOT JUST YET.

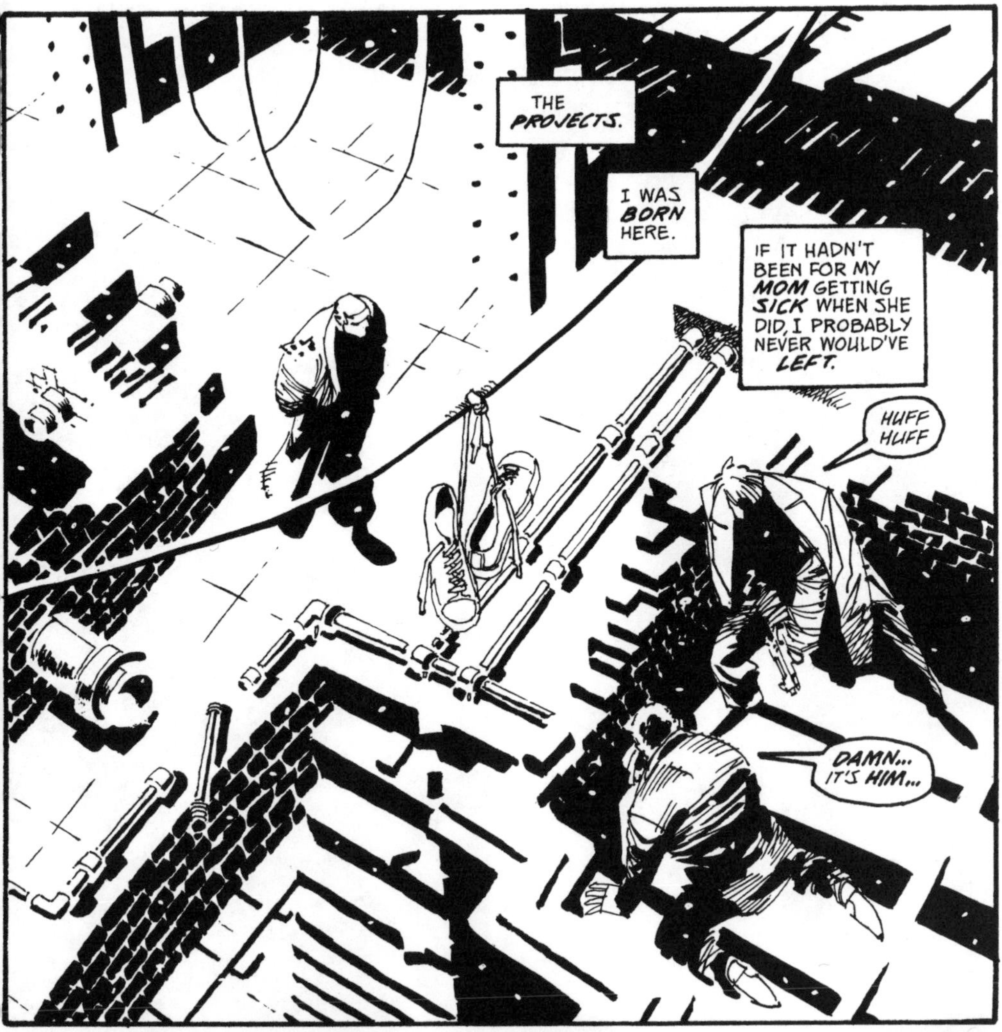
THE PROJECTS.
I WAS BORN HERE.
IF IT HADN'T BEEN FOR MY MOM GETTING SICK WHEN SHE DID, I PROBABLY NEVER WOULD'VE LEFT.
HUFF HUFF
DAMN... IT'S HIM...

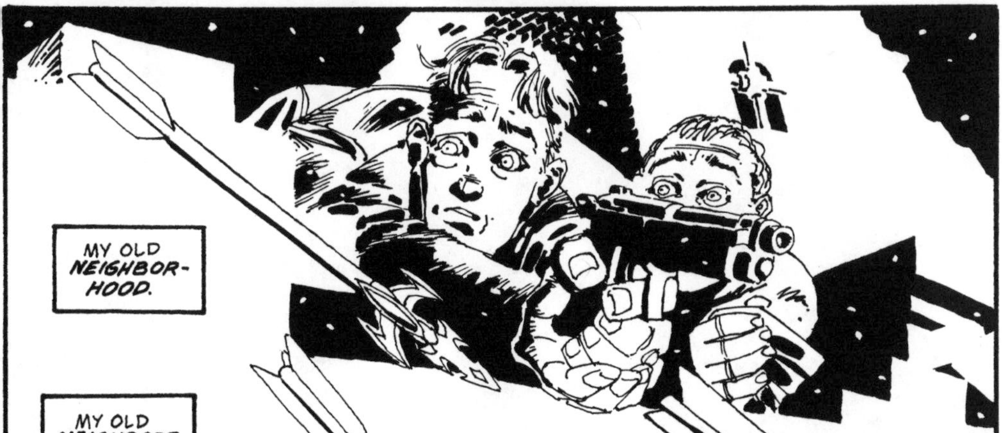
MY OLD NEIGHBOR-HOOD.
MY OLD NEIGHBORS.

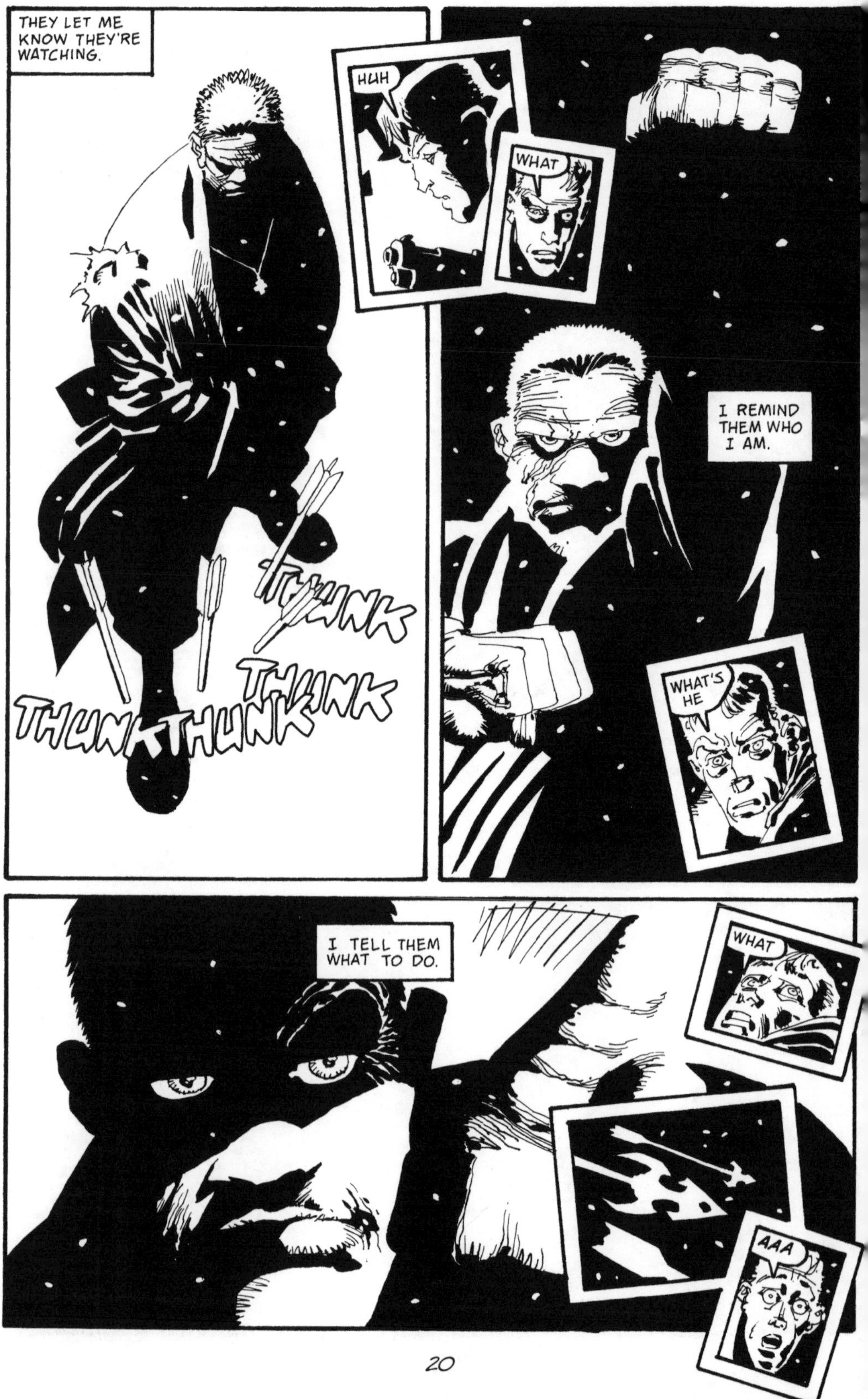
THEY LET ME KNOW THEY'RE WATCHING.
THUNK
THINK
THUNKTHUNK
HUH
WHAT
I REMIND THEM WHO I AM.
WHAT'S HE
I TELL THEM WHAT TO DO.
WHAT
AAA

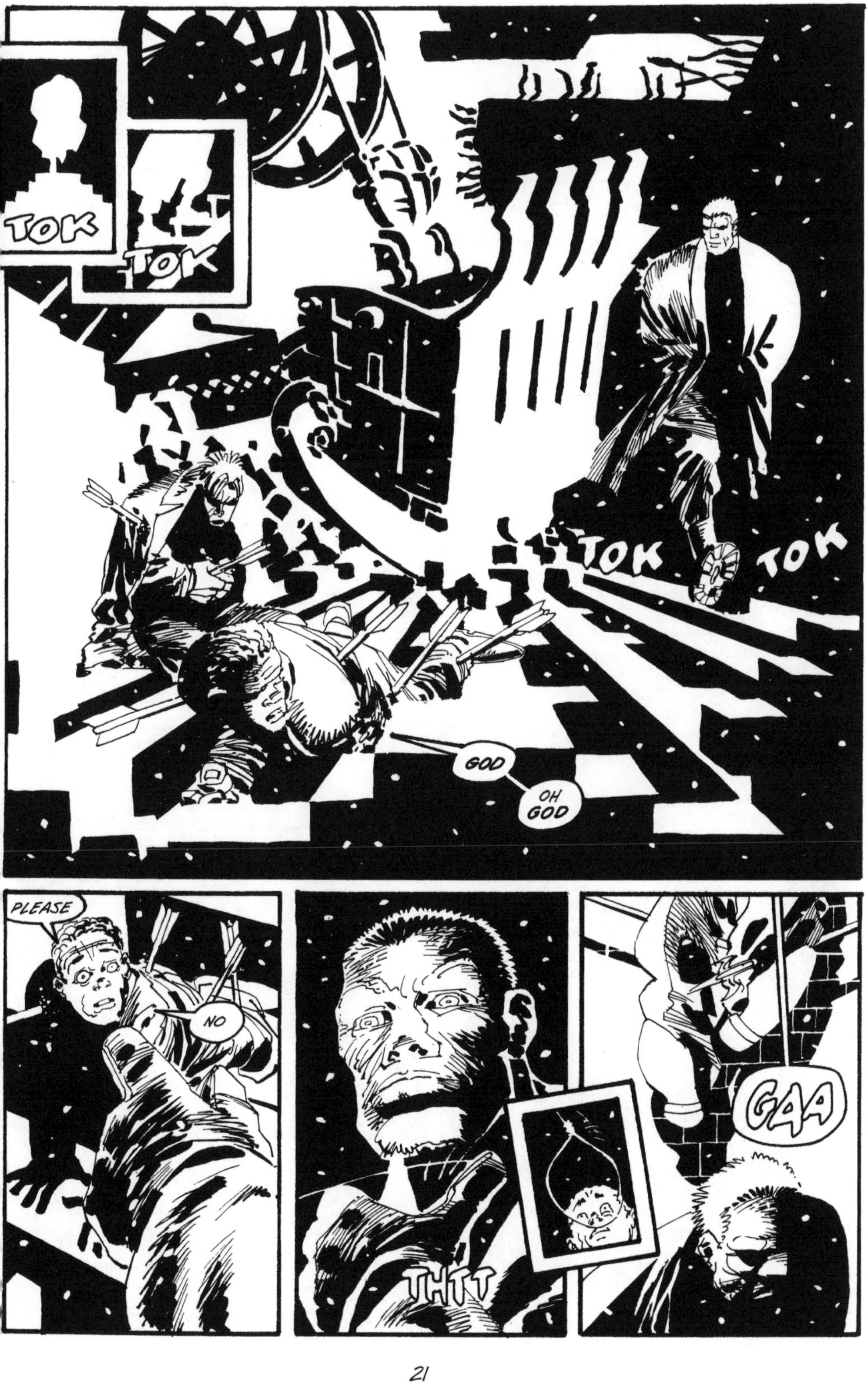
TOK
TOK
TOK
TOK
GOD
OH GOD
PLEASE
NO
THTT
GAA

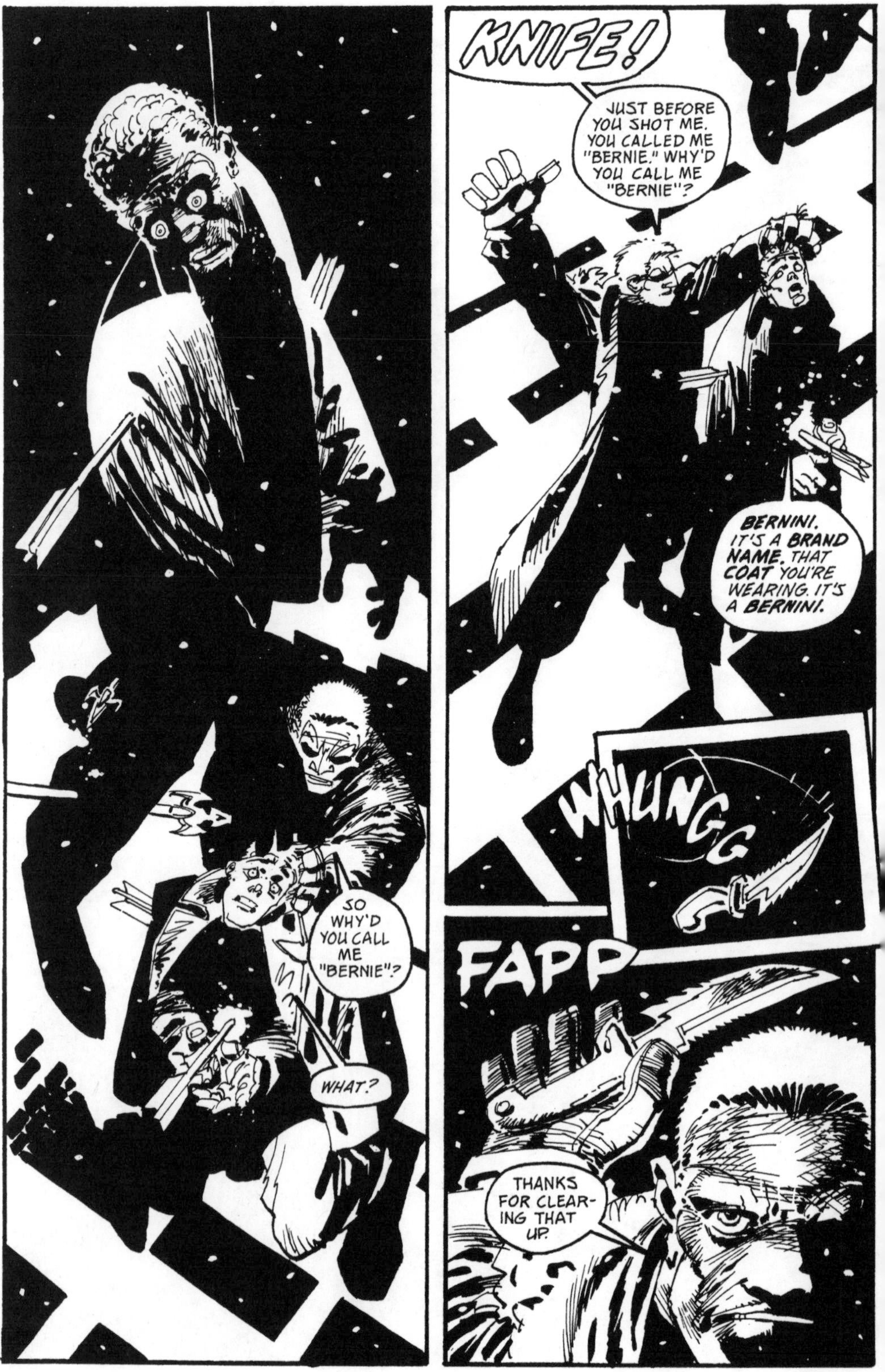
SO WHY'D YOU CALL ME "BERNIE"?
WHAT?
KNIFE!
JUST BEFORE YOU SHOT ME. YOU CALLED ME "BERNIE." WHY'D YOU CALL ME "BERNIE"?
BERNINI. IT'S A BRAND NAME. THAT COAT YOU'RE WEARING. IT'S A BERNINI.
WHUNGG
FAPP
THANKS FOR CLEARING THAT UP.

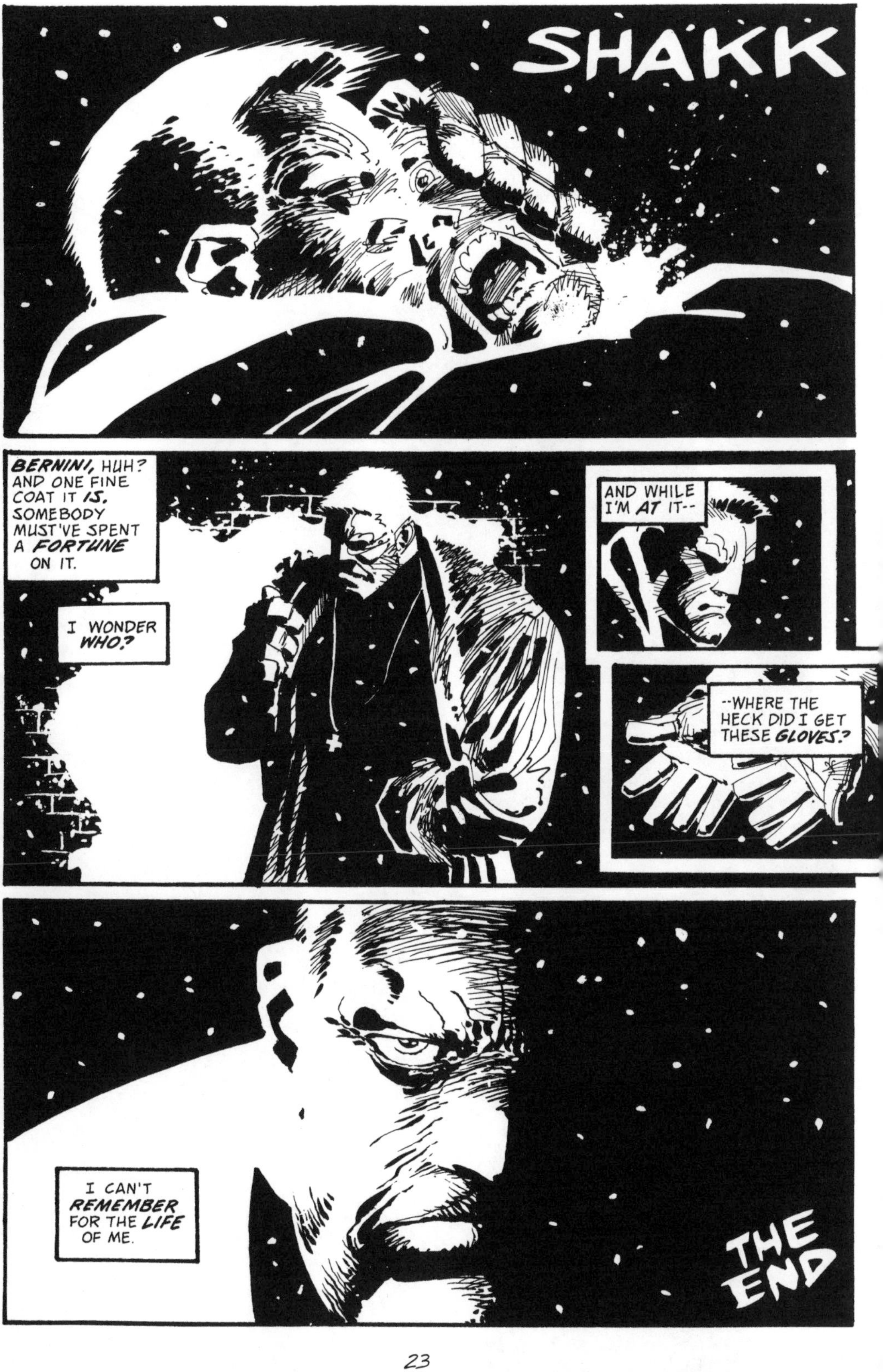
SHAKK
BERNINI, HUH? AND ONE FINE COAT IT IS. SOMEBODY MUST'VE SPENT A FORTUNE ON IT.
I WONDER WHO?
AND WHILE I'M AT IT--
--WHERE THE HECK DID I GET THESE GLOVES?
I CAN'T REMEMBER FOR THE LIFE OF ME.
THE END

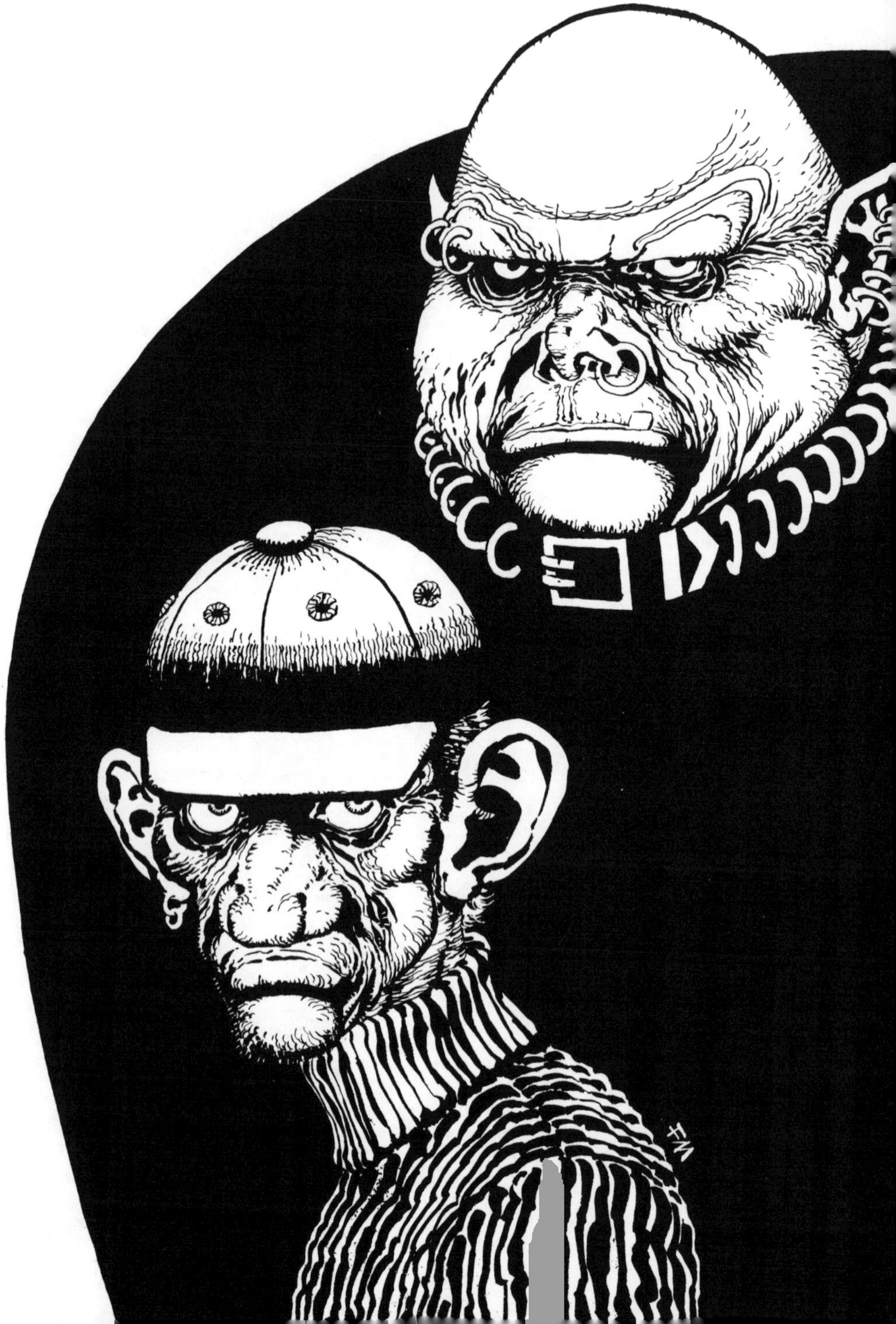

THE *PERIMETERS* OF OUR ASSIGNMENT WERE DESCRIBED TO US WITH *SPECIFICITY,* MR. SHLUBB. WE ARE TO *DE-POSIT OUR CARGO* INTO THE BODY OF WATER WHICH WE NOW OVERLOOK.

IT WAS LIKEWAYS MADE *CLEAR* TO US THAT ANY *EMBELLISH-MENT* OF SAID *PERI-METERS* WOULD NOT BE *ADVISORY.*

I CANNOT *PRESCRIBE* TO SUCH A NARROW INTERPRETATION OF THE PERIMETERS WHICH YOU NOW INVOKE, MR. KLUMP.

DOUGLAS *KLUMP* AND BURT *SHLUBB,* LOW-RENT *HIT MEN* WHO GO BY THE NAMES OF...

"FAT MAN AND LITTLE BOY"

BE THIS AS IT *MIGHT* AND WITH ALL DUE *RESPECT,* MR. SHLUBB, I MUST NONETHELESS *SUGGEST* THAT SIMPLE *FOOTWEAR* IS OF LITTLE VALUE WHEN COMPARED TO THE *RISK* OF INCURRING *ILL WILL* ON THE PART OF OUR ALREADY DISPLEASED *EMPLOYERS.*

THE BEFOREMENTIONED *FOOTWEAR* BEING A PAIR OF FINELY CRAFTED *BOOTS,* THE VALUE OF WHICH I ESTIMATE TO BE NO LESS THAN *TWO HUN-DRED DOLLARS*--AND WHICH HAPPEN TO BE *EXACTLY* THE CORRECT SIZE FOR MY *OWN* POORLY CLAD *FEET,* MR. KLUMP.

YOUR DISCOMFITURE *NOTWITH-STANDING*, SURELY YOU *REMEMBER* THAT WE ARE ON *NOTICE*, PURSUANT TO OUR LESS-THAN-ADEQUATE PERFORMANCE AT RENDERING *SILENT* IN A *PERMANENT* MANNER A CERTAIN *WITNESS TO MURDER?*

HENCE OUR *REGULATION* TO DUTIES OF SUCH A COMMON AND JANITORIAL NATURE AS THESE WE NOW *PERFORM*, MR. *SHLUBB*.

HEREWITH IT IS *INCONTINENT* UPON ME TO MOST STRENUOUSLY *CHALLENGE* YOUR ASSESSMENT OF THE *CONSEQUENCES* OF THE SIMPLE ACT OF *ACQUIREMENT* I AM AT THIS MOMENT CONTEMPLATING, MR. *KLUMP.* SURELY THE *BEARER* OF THE EXQUISITE FOOTWEAR IN QUESTION IS *UNLIKELY* TO INFORM OUR EMPLOYERS OF THIS MINOR TRANS-GRESSION.

SAID *BEARER* BEING, ONE CAN READILY PRESUME, A *STIFF.*

GIVEN OUR CURRENT *STATUS* IN THE EXTRALEGAL COMMUNITY, EVEN A *MINOR* TRANSGRESSION COULD BE CAUSE FOR *DISCIPLINE* MOST *SEVERE*, MR. *SHLUBB.*

STILL I MUST *INSIST*, MR. *KLUMP.* OUR EXTENDED PERIOD OF LIMITED INCOME HAS REMANDED ME *BEREFT* OF ANY BUT THE MOST *EMBARRASSING* AND *BLISTER-INDUCING* OF PEDAL GARMENTS!

I *REGISTRATE* MY *PROTEST,* MR. *SHLUBB!*

YOUR *PROTEST* IS DULY *NOTED*, MR. *KLUMP*... AND HERE I MUST CONFESS TO STUNNED *SURPRISE!* FOR WITHIN THE MUCH DESIRED *BOOTS* THERE ARE NO *FEET!*

WHICH CAN ONLY RAISE THE *QUESTION* AS TO WHY THE *CARPET* WE DID CARRY WAS OF SUCH *WEIGHT*, IF THERE IS WRAPPED INSIDE IT NO *CORPSE?* AND WHY NOW THIS *SOUND*, NOT UNLIKE THE *TICKING* OF A *CLOCK?*

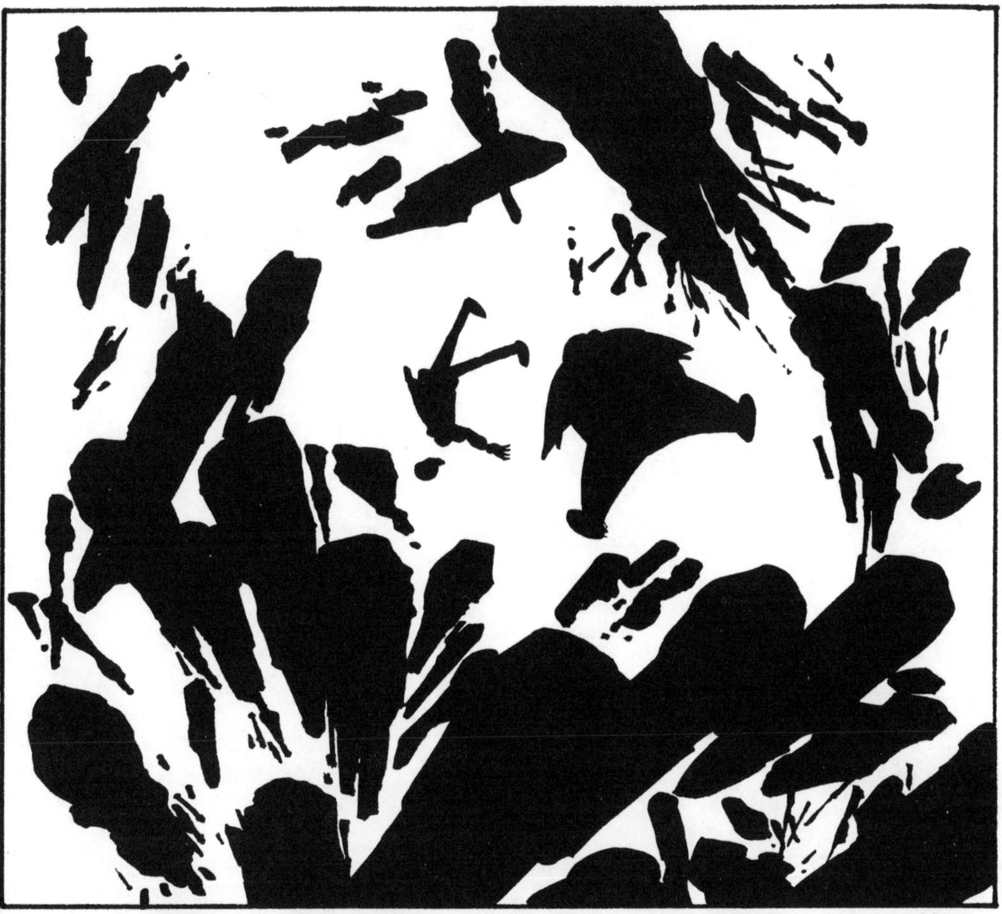

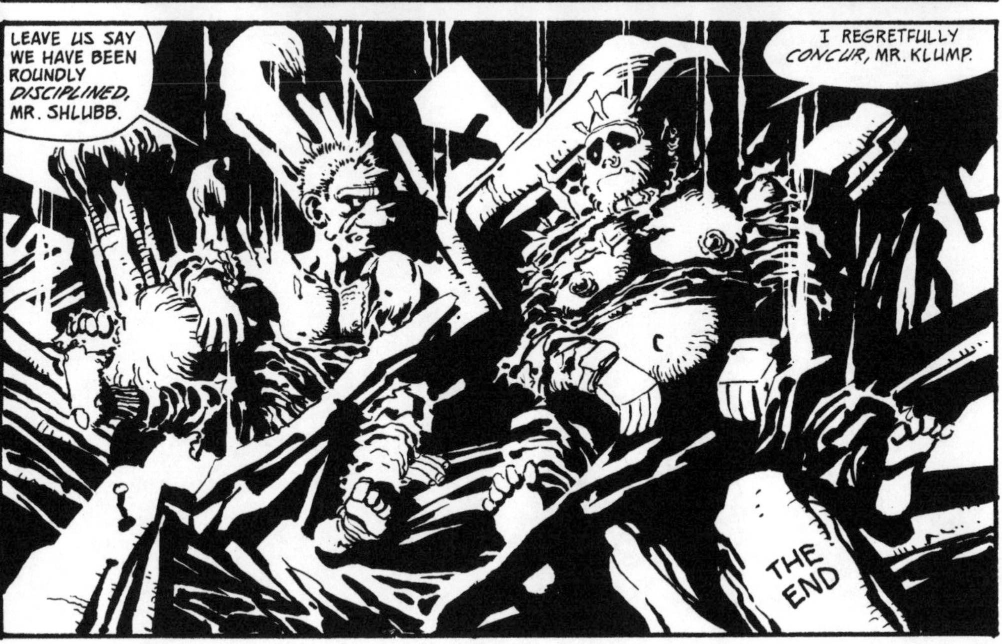
LEAVE US SAY WE HAVE BEEN ROUNDLY *DISCIPLINED,* MR. SHLUBB.
I REGRETFULLY *CONCUR,* MR. KLUMP.
THE END

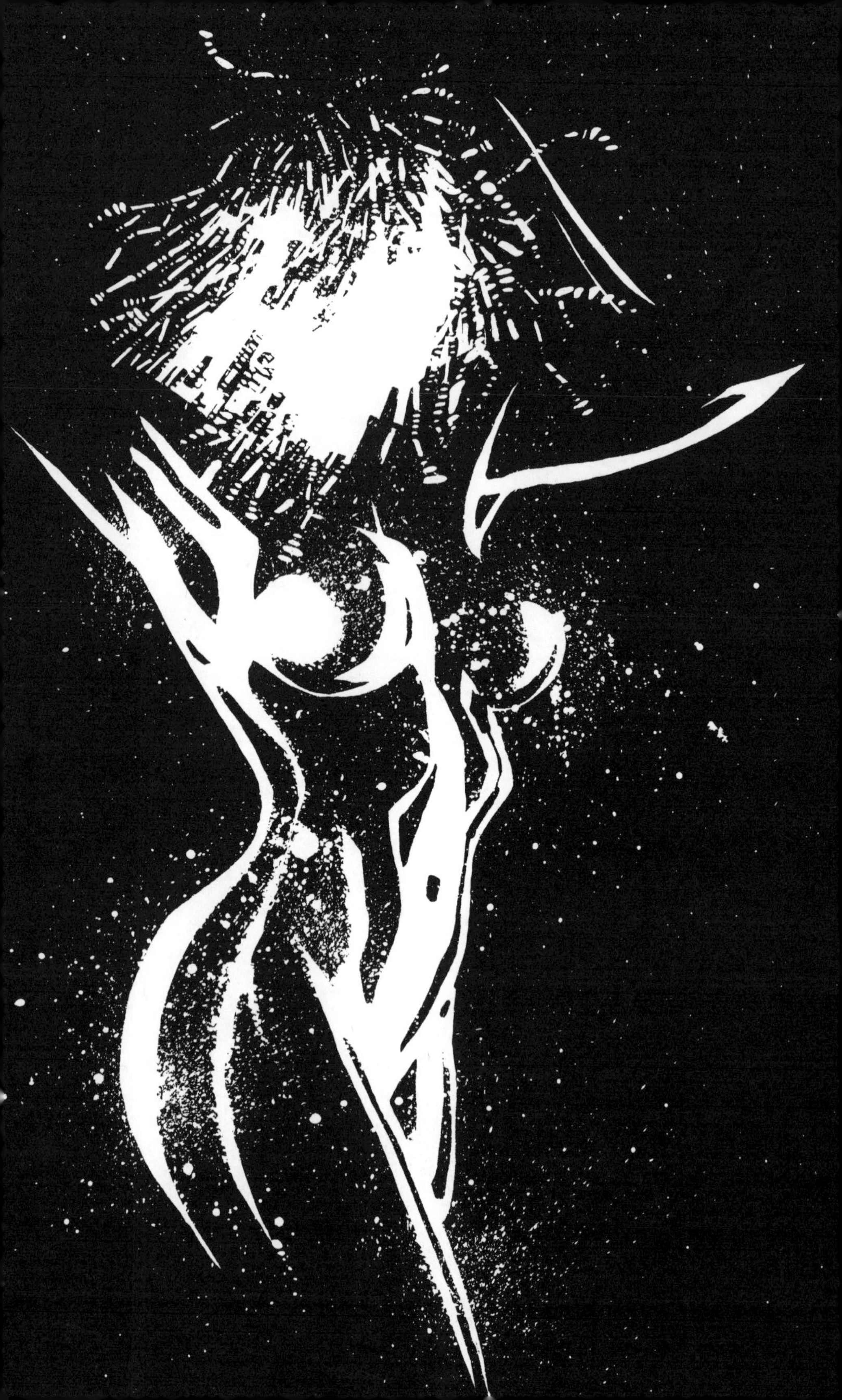

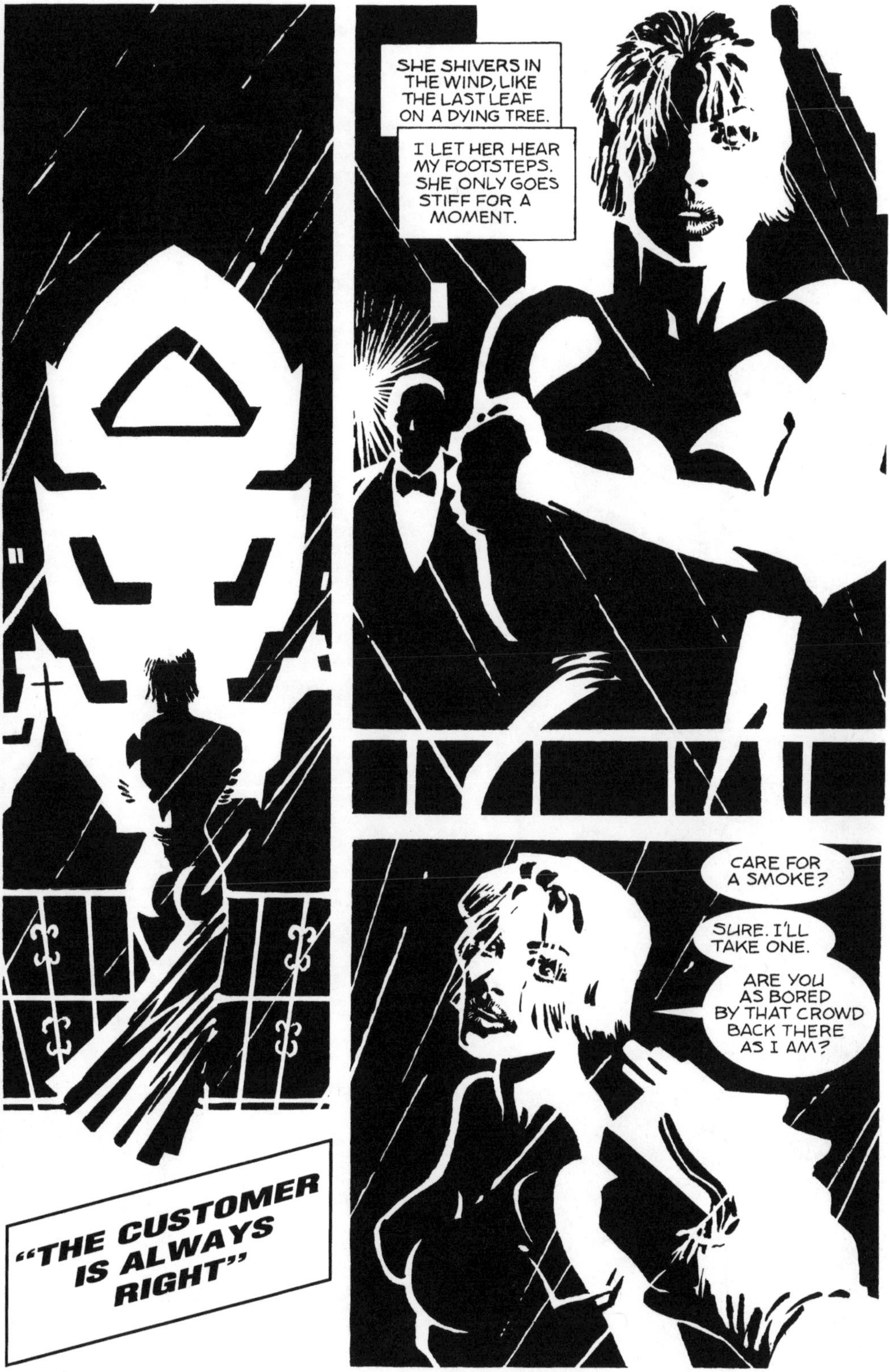

SHE SHIVERS IN THE WIND, LIKE THE LAST LEAF ON A DYING TREE.
I LET HER HEAR MY FOOTSTEPS. SHE ONLY GOES STIFF FOR A MOMENT.
"THE CUSTOMER IS ALWAYS RIGHT"
CARE FOR A SMOKE?
SURE. I'LL TAKE ONE.
ARE YOU AS BORED BY THAT CROWD BACK THERE AS I AM?

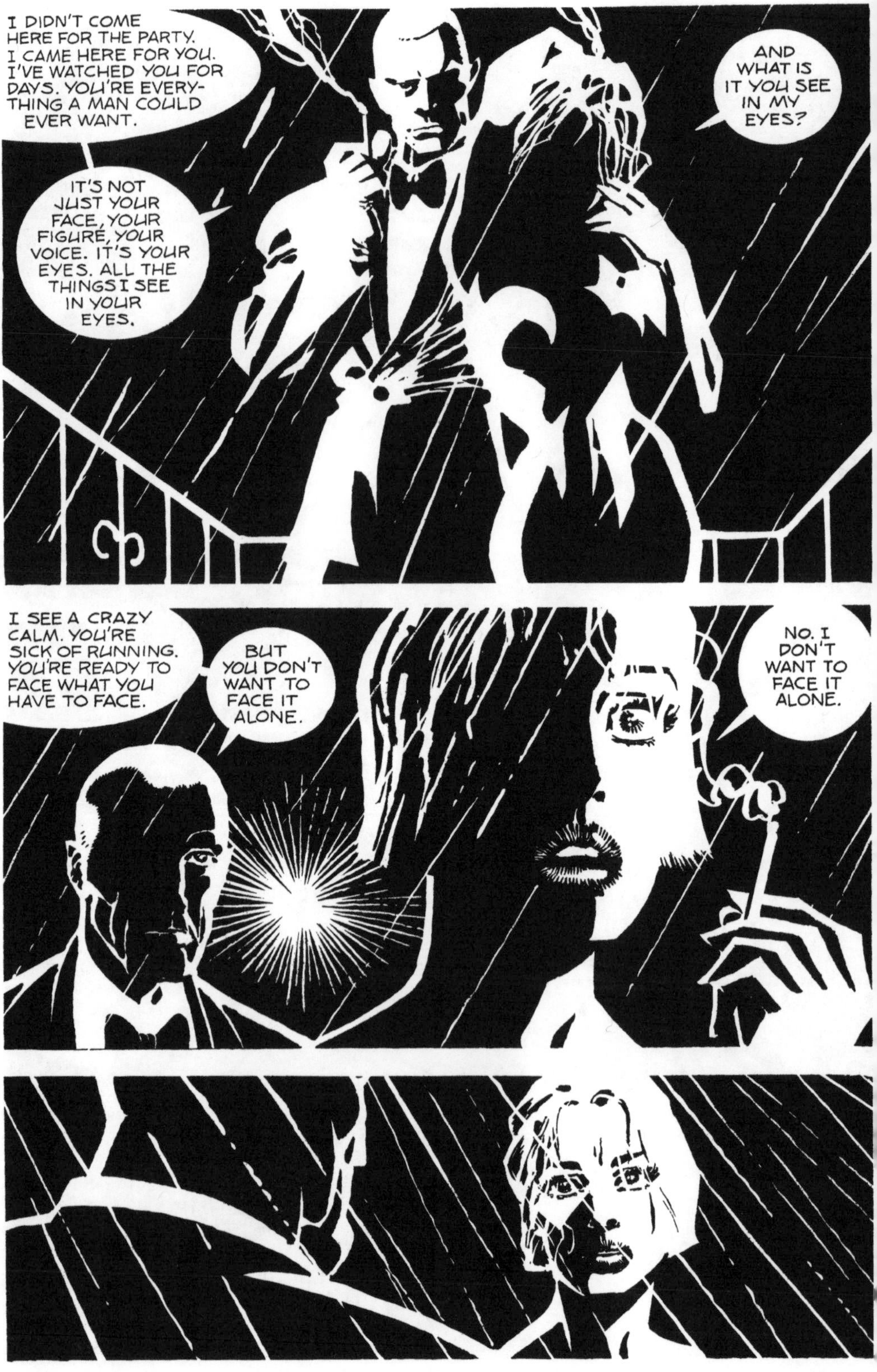
I DIDN'T COME HERE FOR THE PARTY. I CAME HERE FOR YOU. I'VE WATCHED YOU FOR DAYS. YOU'RE EVERY-THING A MAN COULD EVER WANT.
IT'S NOT JUST YOUR FACE, YOUR FIGURE, YOUR VOICE. IT'S YOUR EYES. ALL THE THINGS I SEE IN YOUR EYES.
AND WHAT IS IT YOU SEE IN MY EYES?
I SEE A CRAZY CALM. YOU'RE SICK OF RUNNING. YOU'RE READY TO FACE WHAT YOU HAVE TO FACE.
BUT YOU DON'T WANT TO FACE IT ALONE.
NO. I DON'T WANT TO FACE IT ALONE.

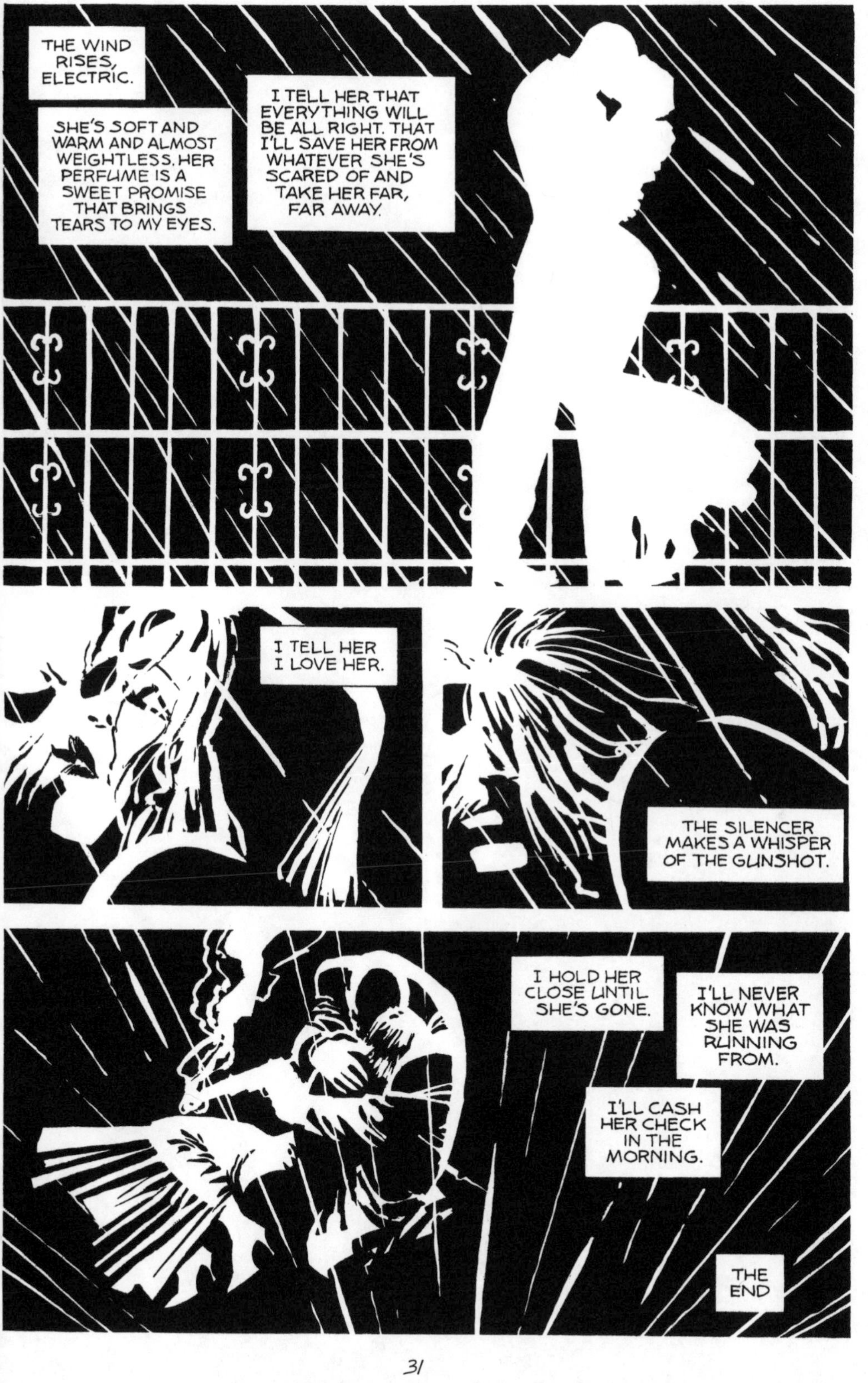
THE WIND RISES, ELECTRIC.
SHE'S SOFT AND WARM AND ALMOST WEIGHTLESS. HER PERFUME IS A SWEET PROMISE THAT BRINGS TEARS TO MY EYES.
I TELL HER THAT EVERYTHING WILL BE ALL RIGHT. THAT I'LL SAVE HER FROM WHATEVER SHE'S SCARED OF AND TAKE HER FAR, FAR AWAY.
I TELL HER I LOVE HER.
THE SILENCER MAKES A WHISPER OF THE GUNSHOT.
I HOLD HER CLOSE UNTIL SHE'S GONE.
I'LL NEVER KNOW WHAT SHE WAS RUNNING FROM.
I'LL CASH HER CHECK IN THE MORNING.
THE END

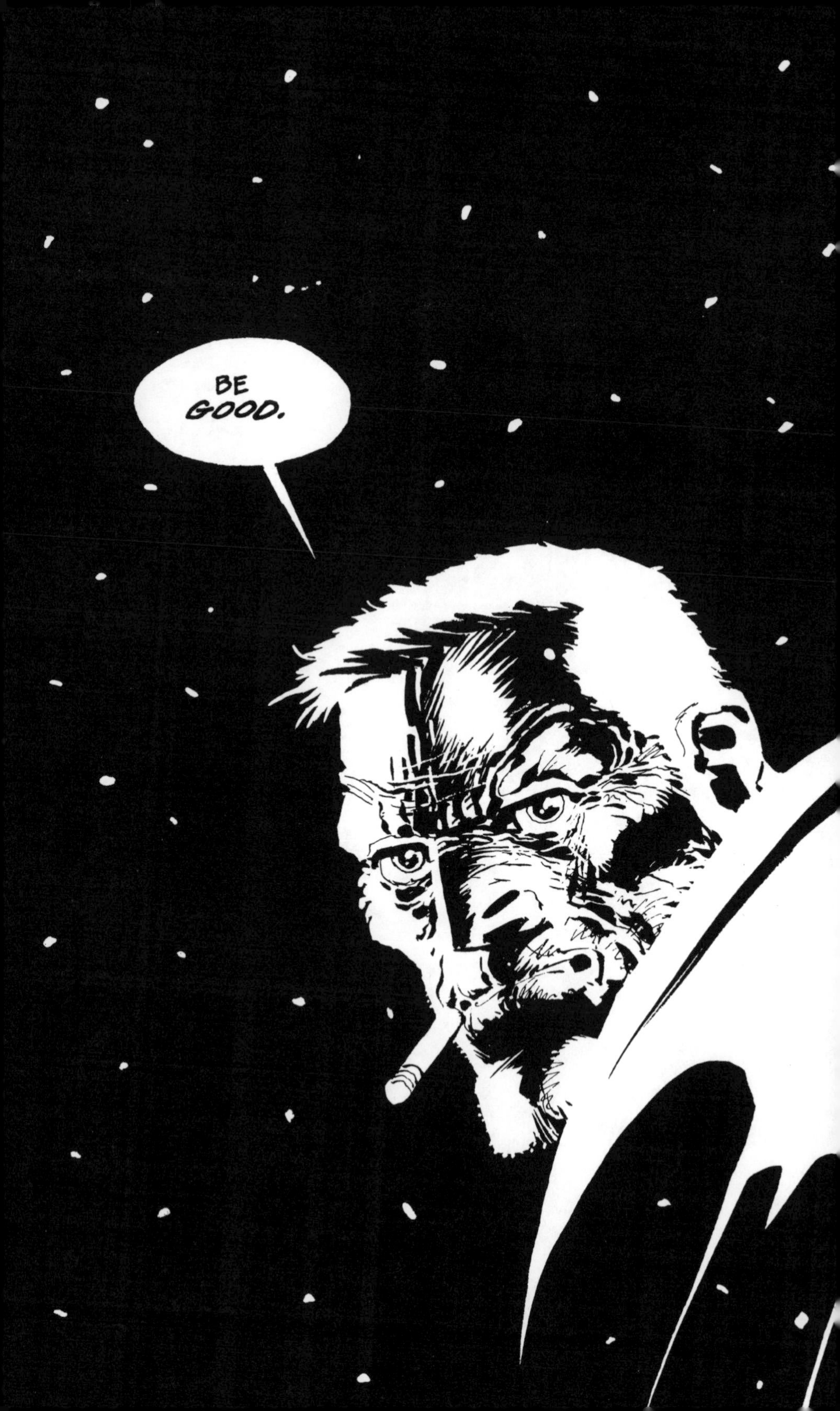
BE GOOD.

silent night

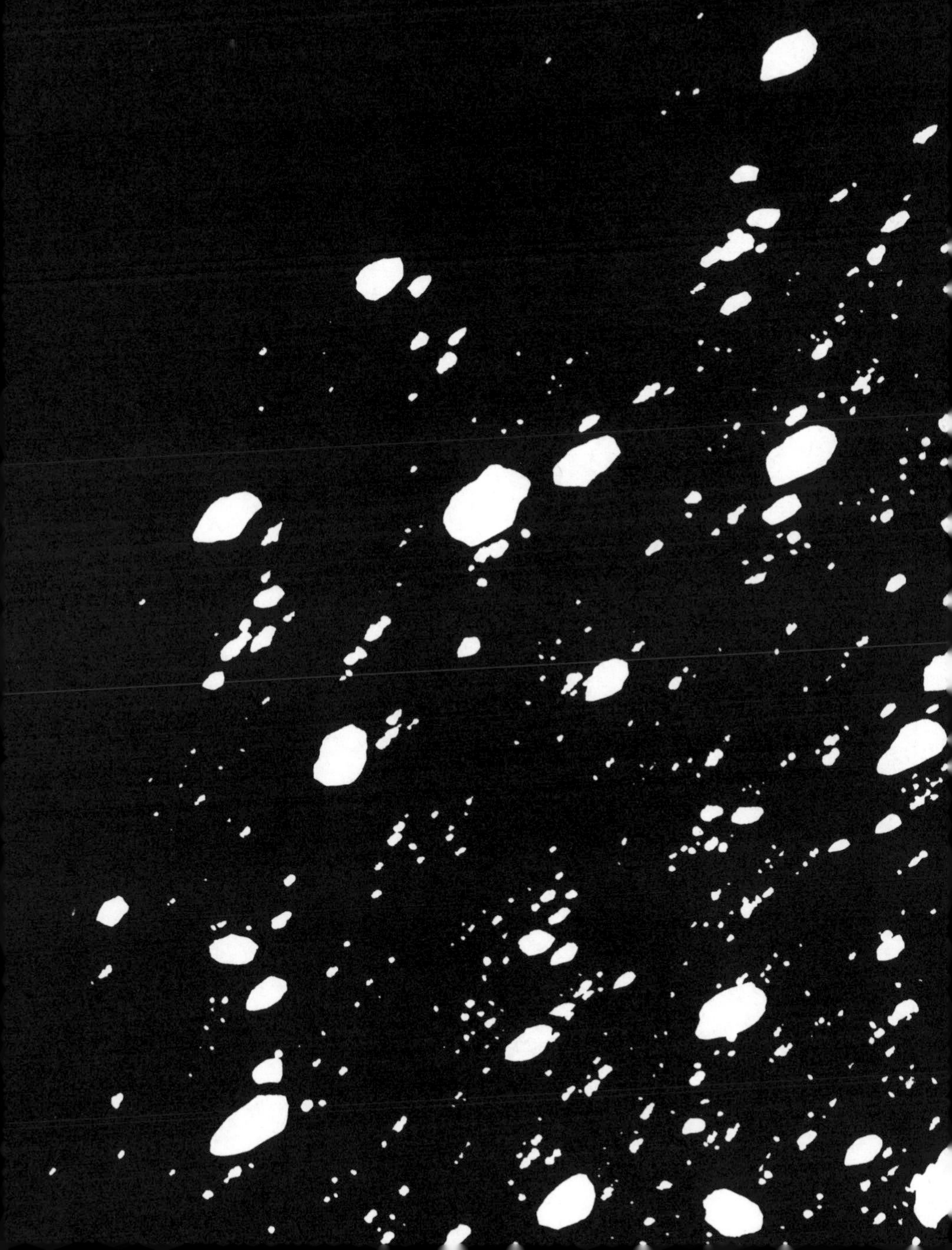

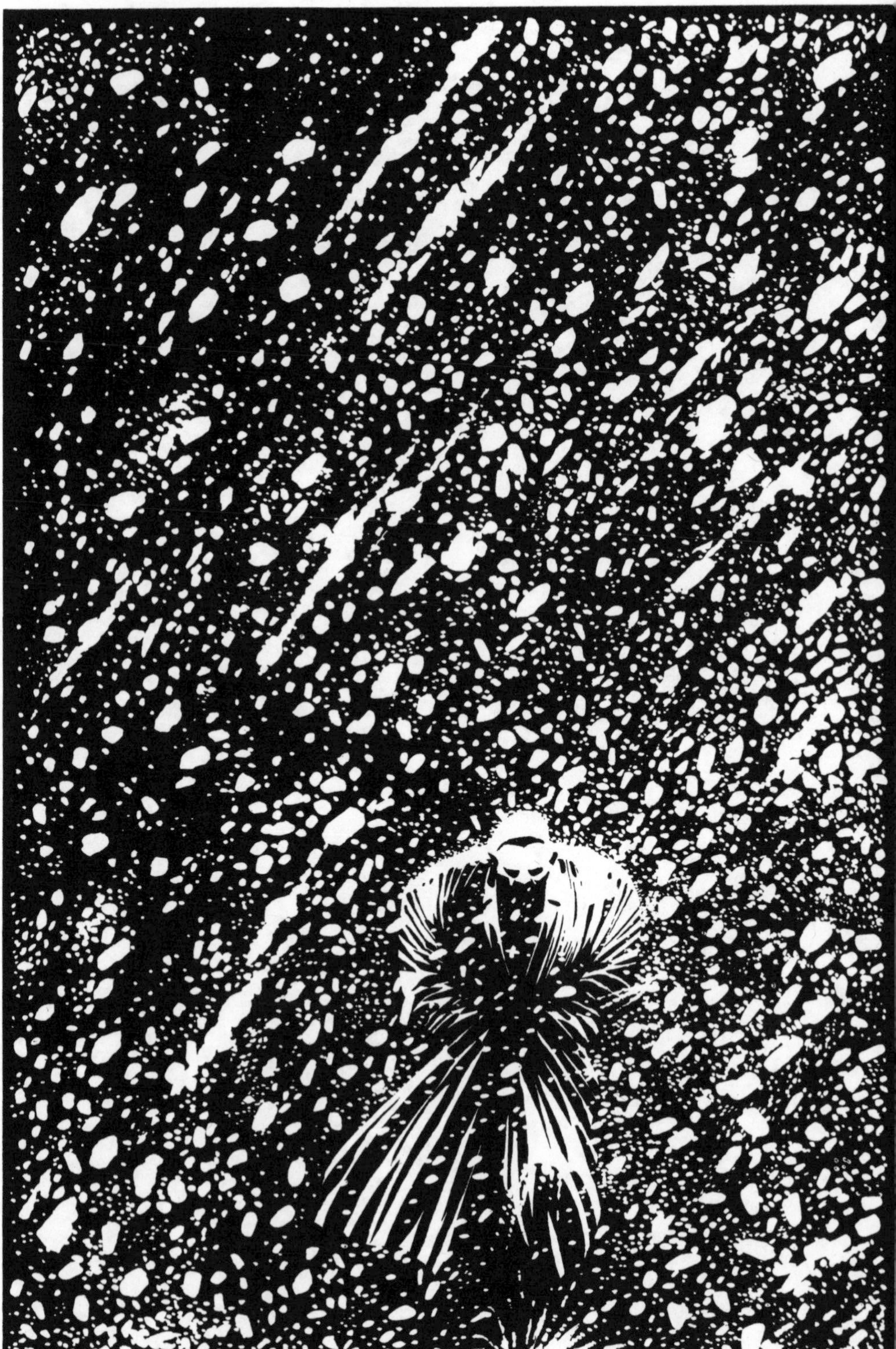

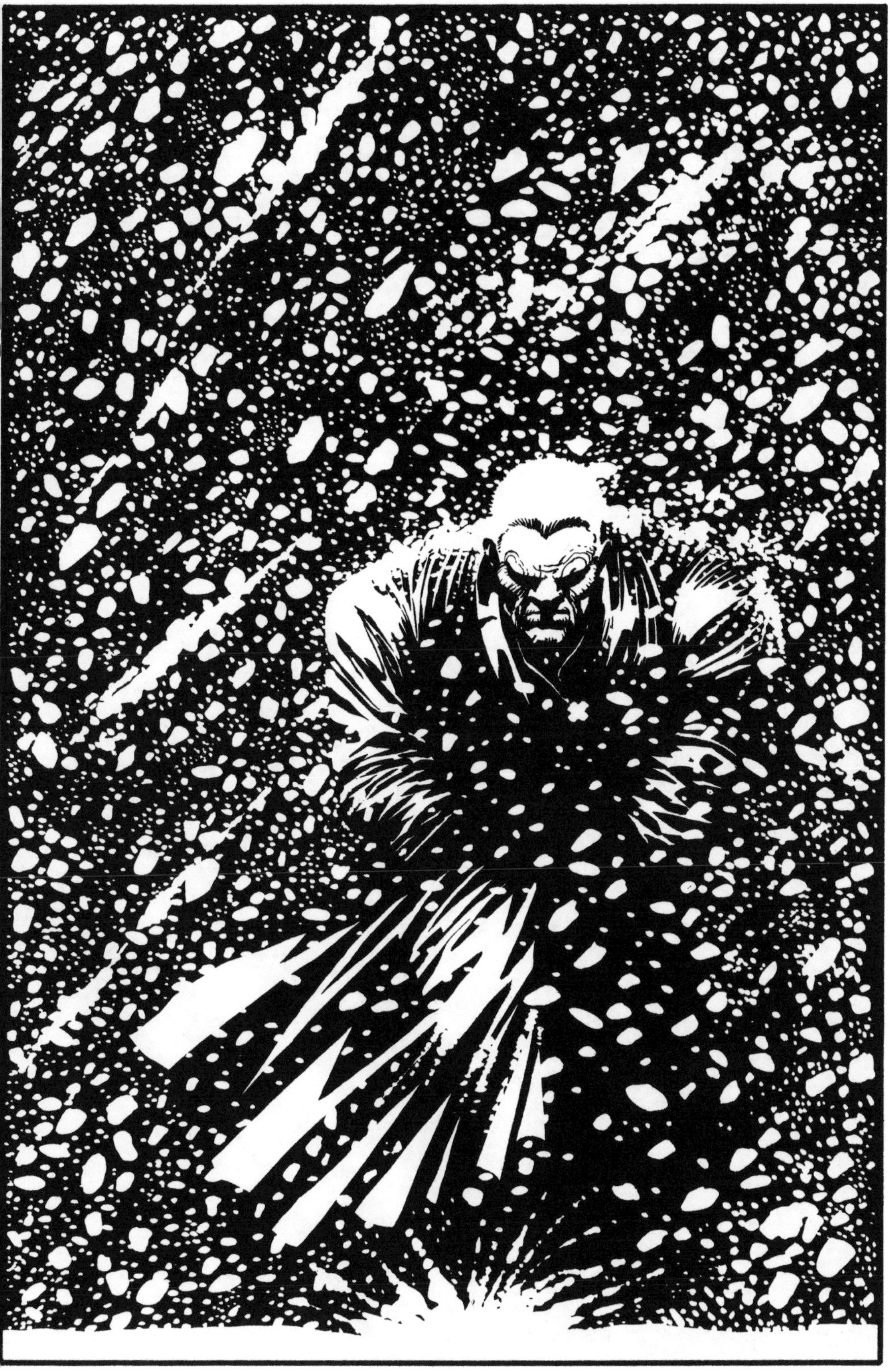

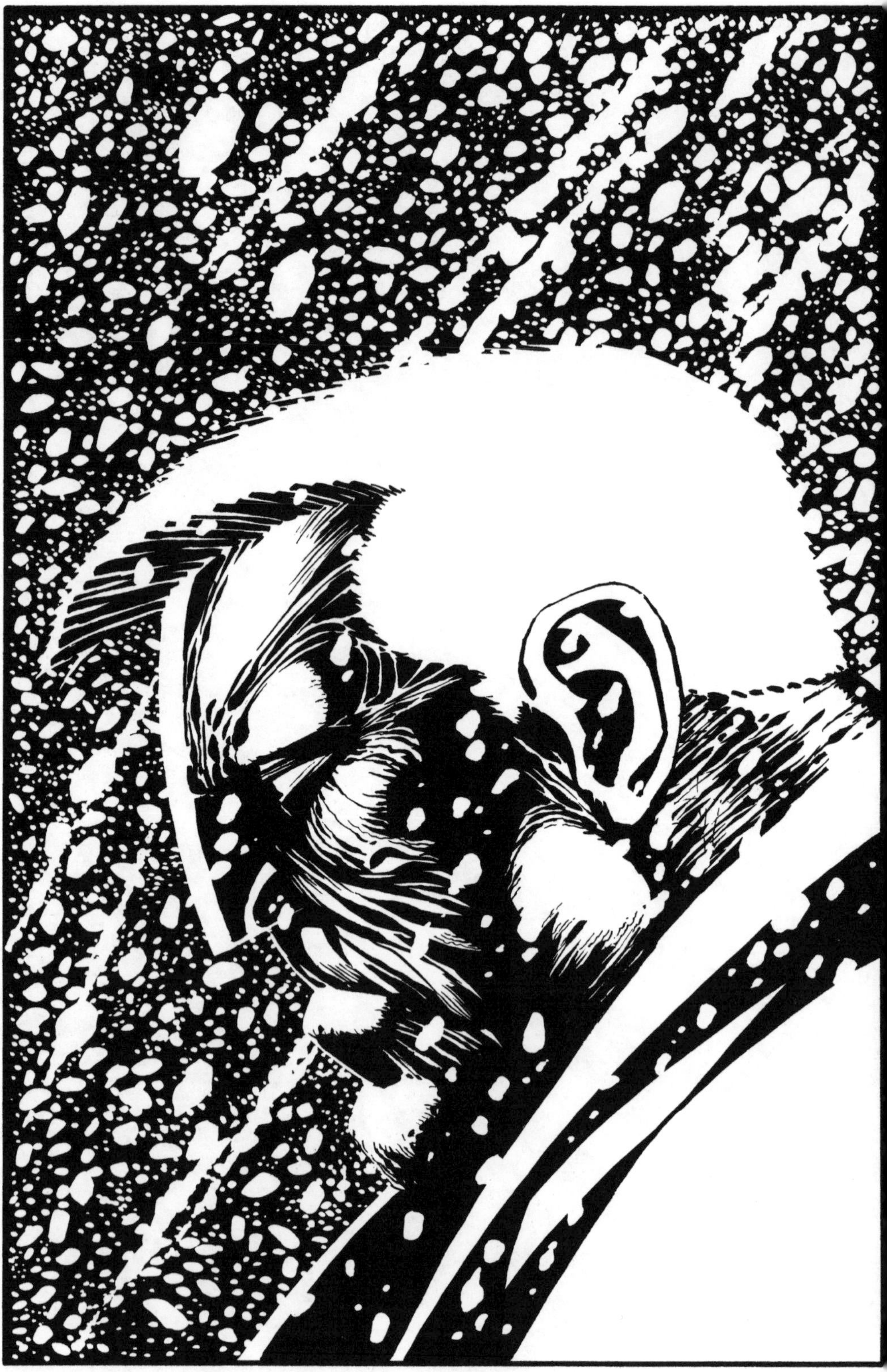

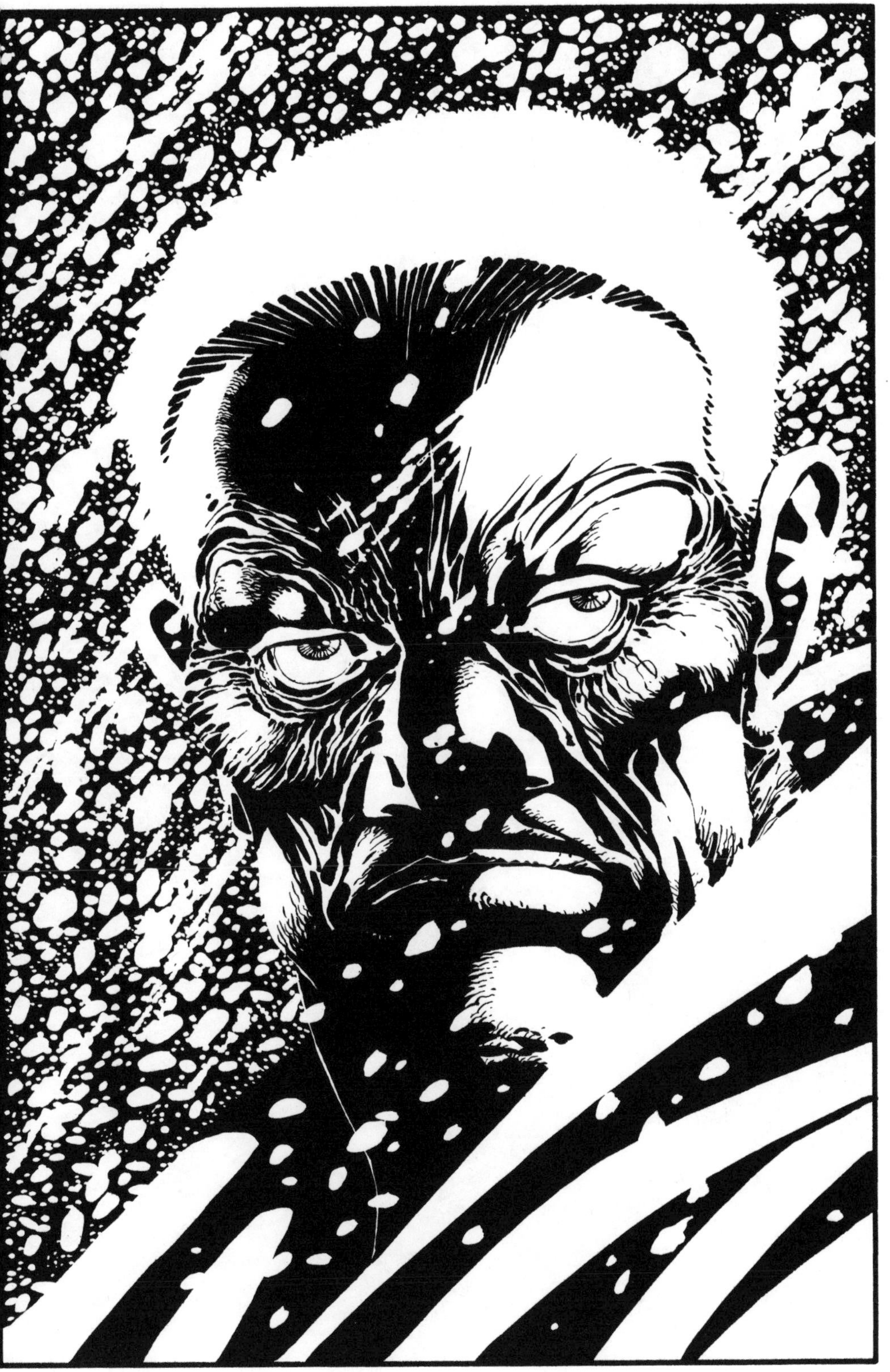

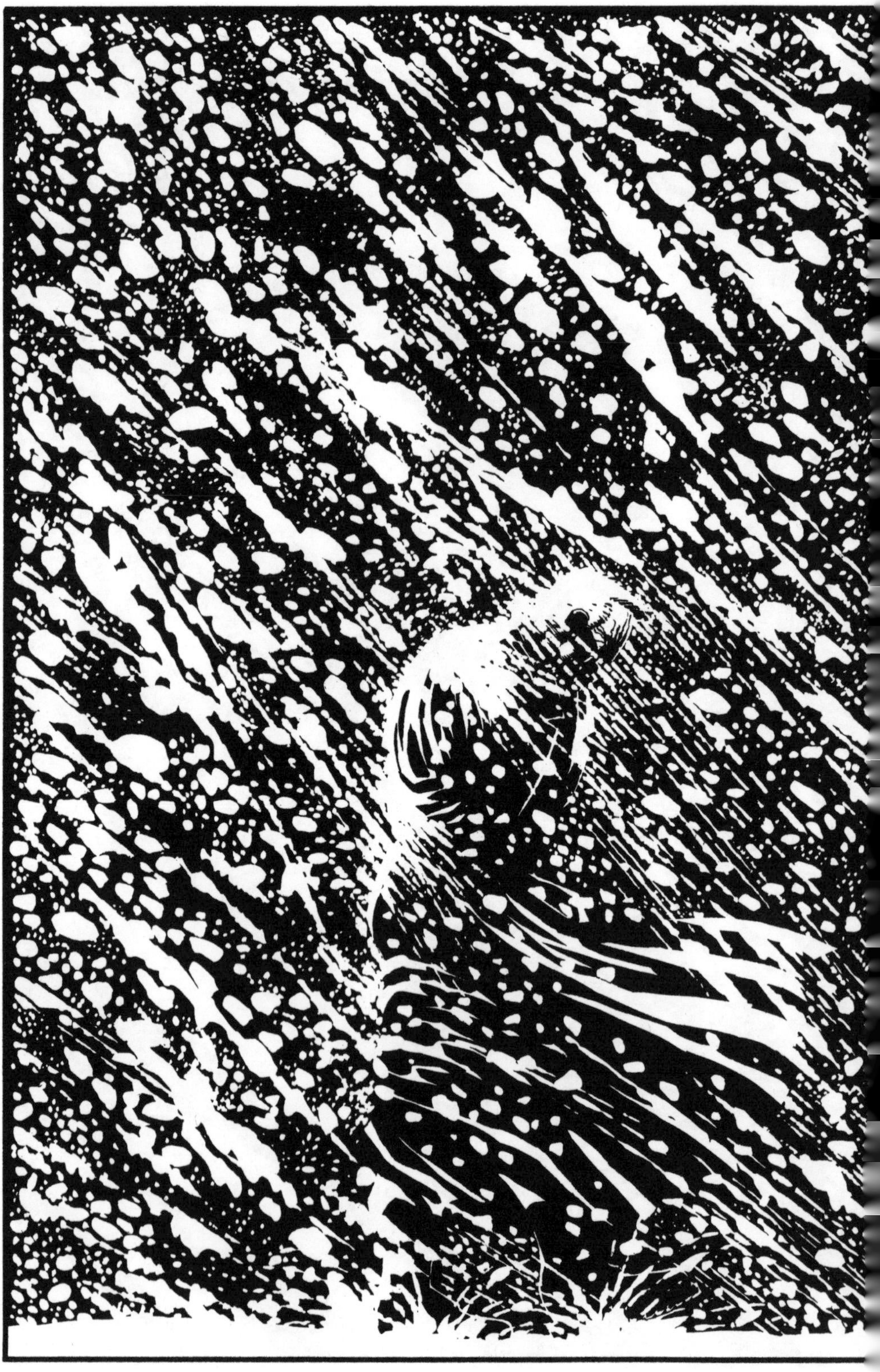

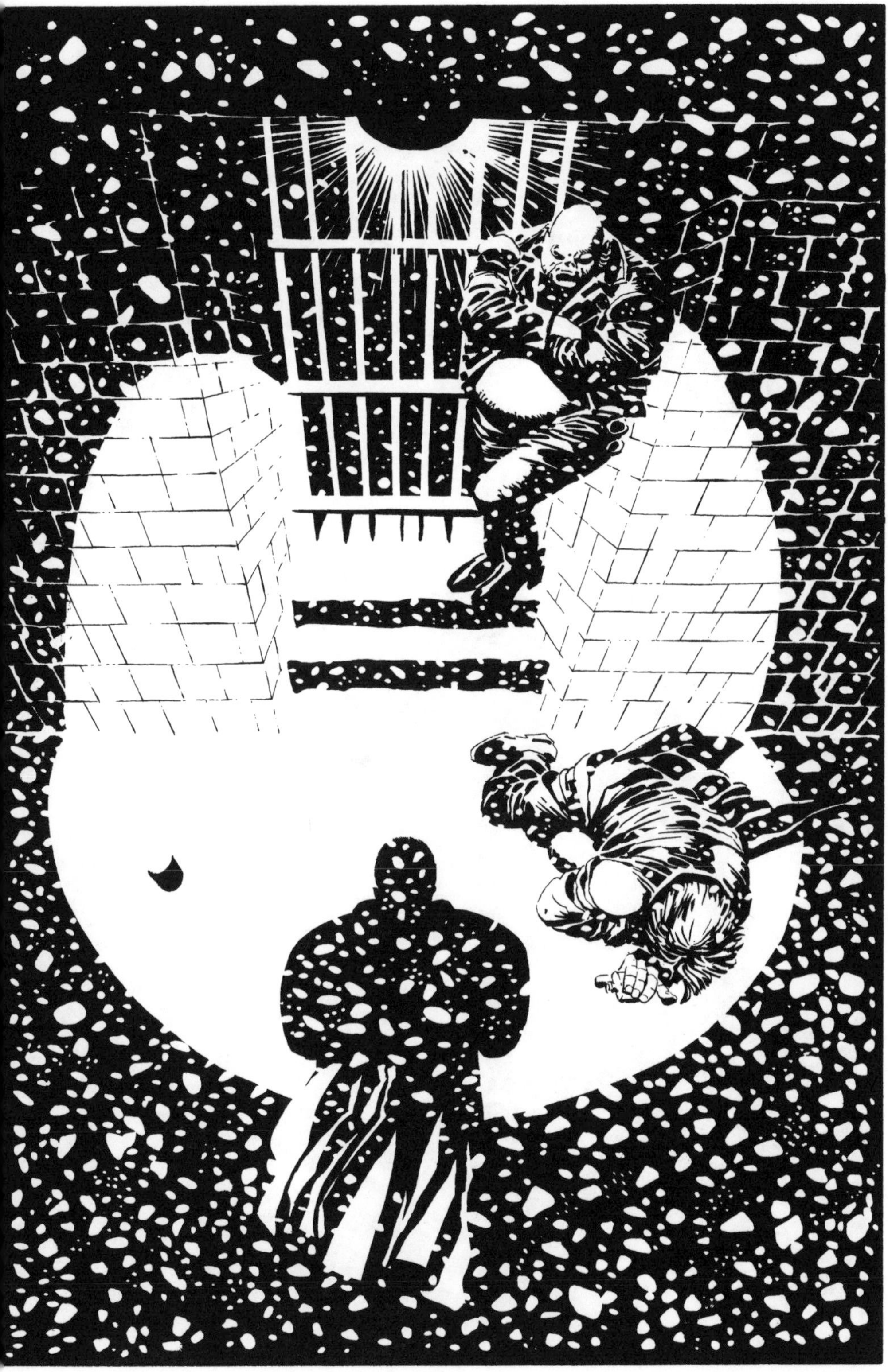

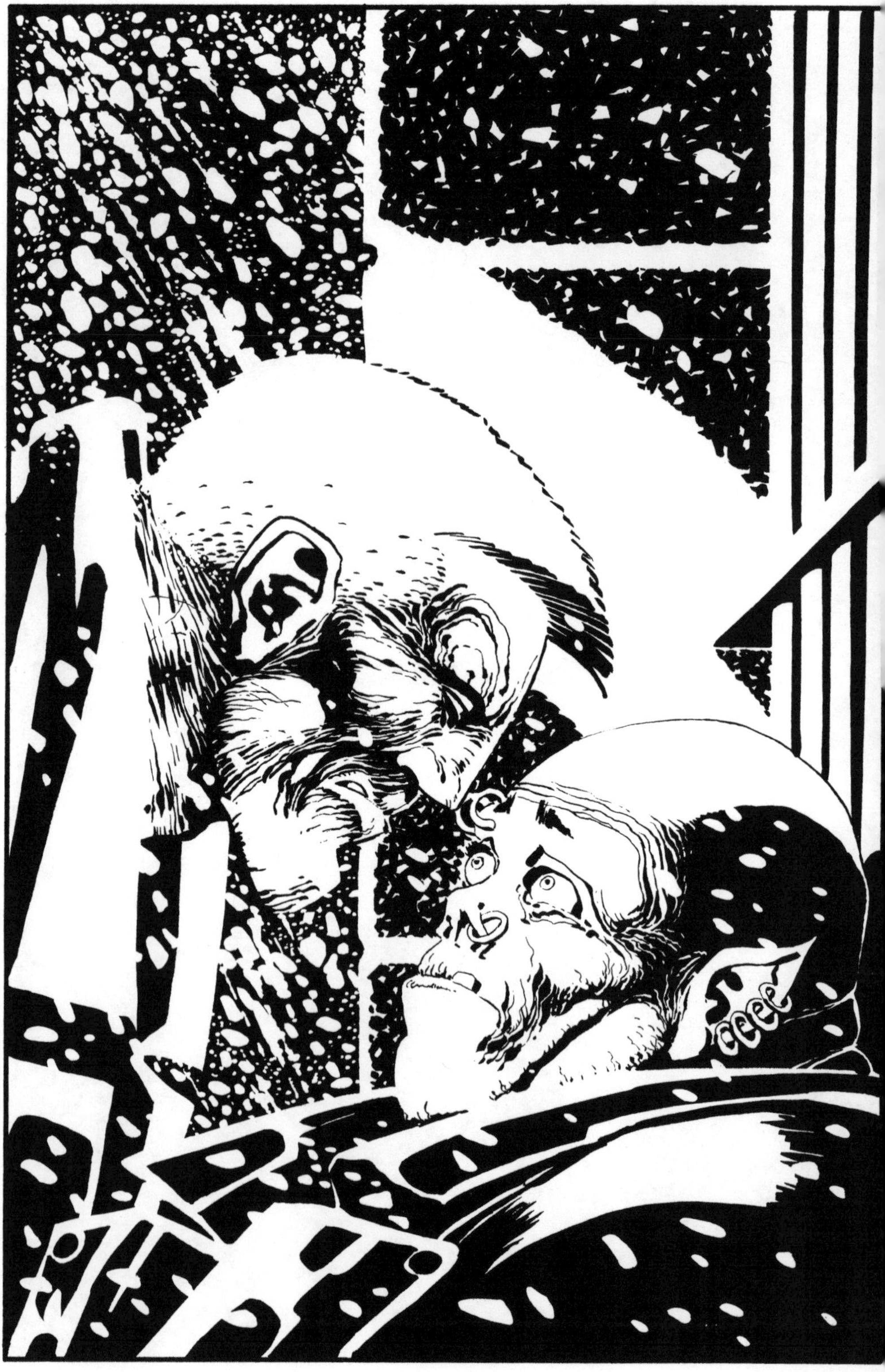

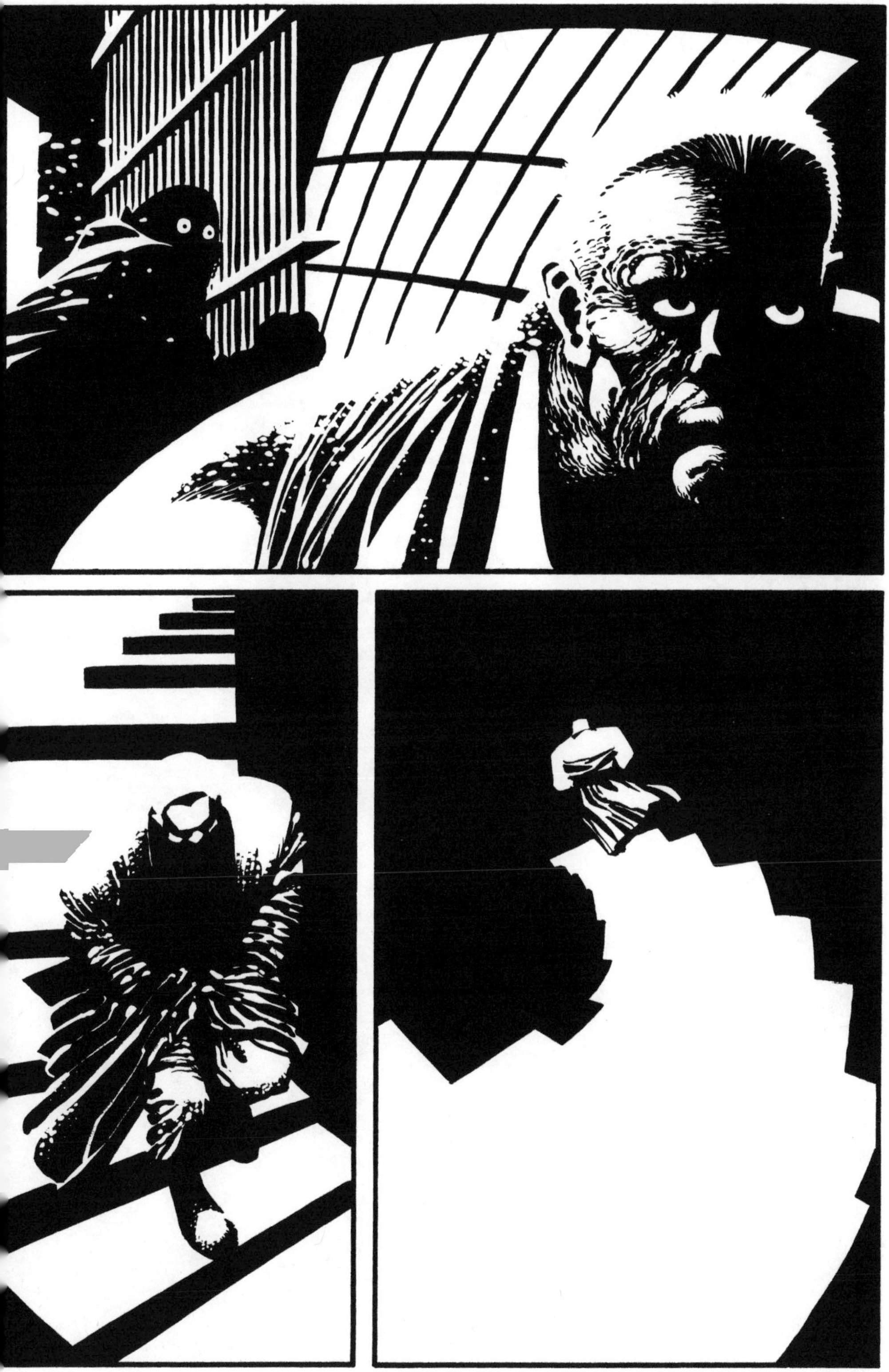

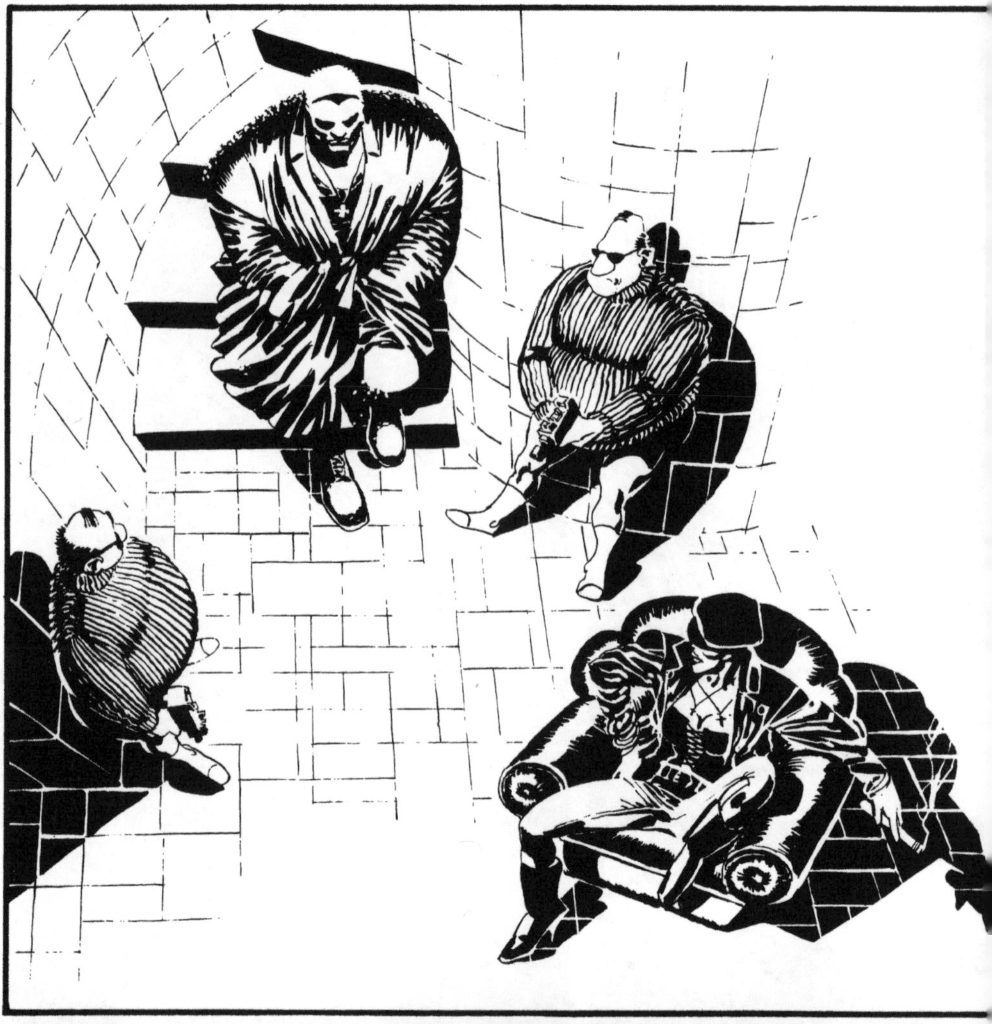

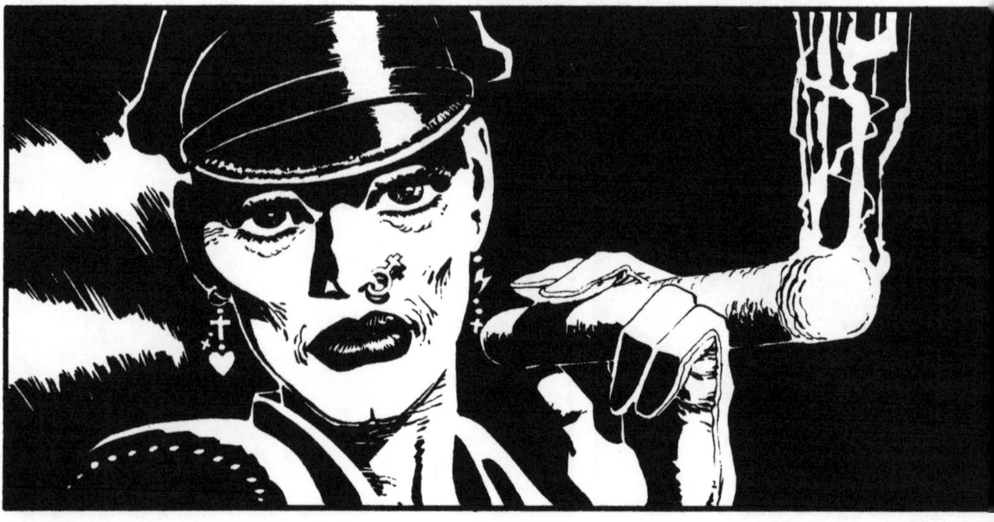

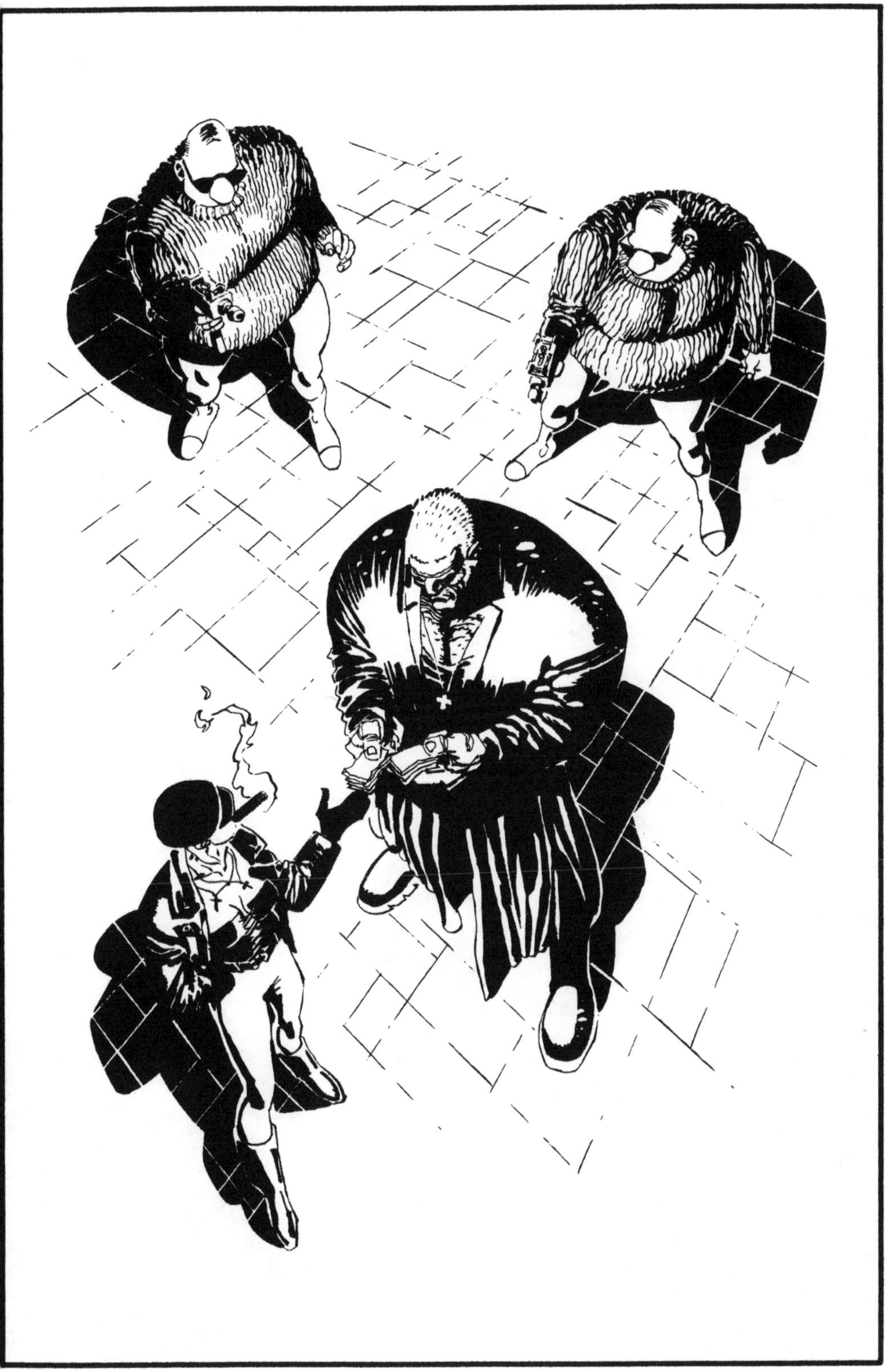

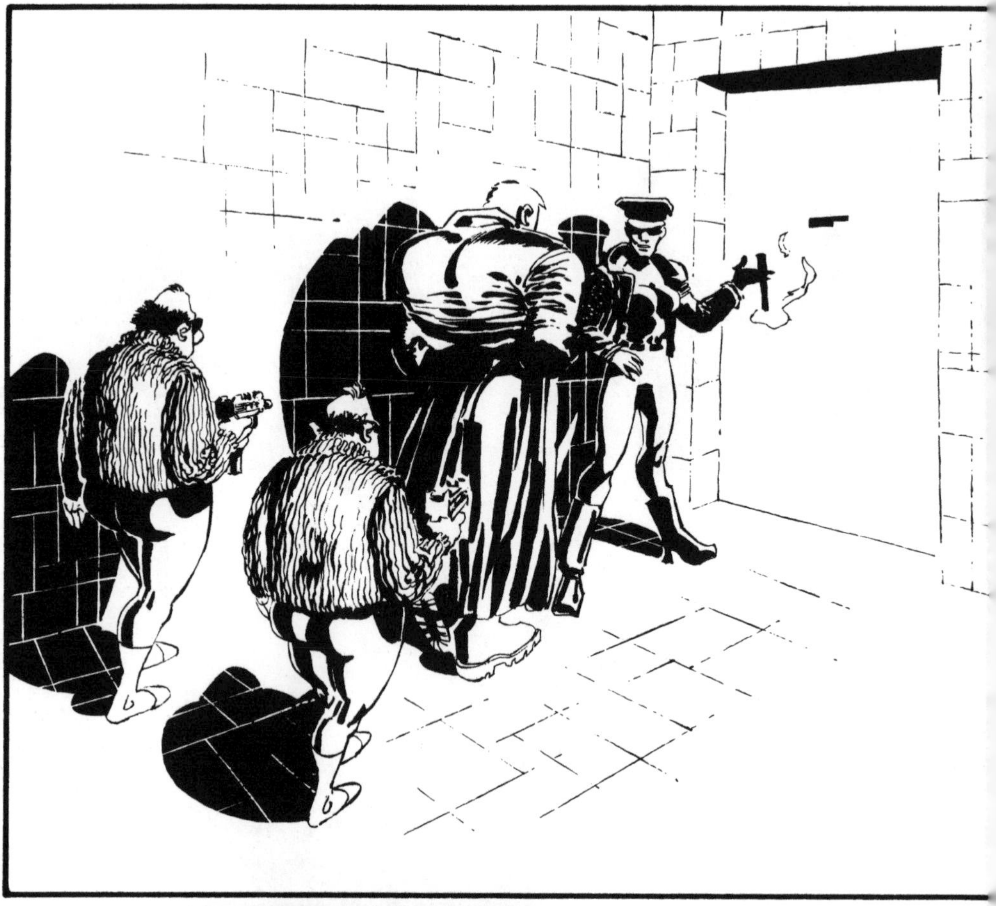

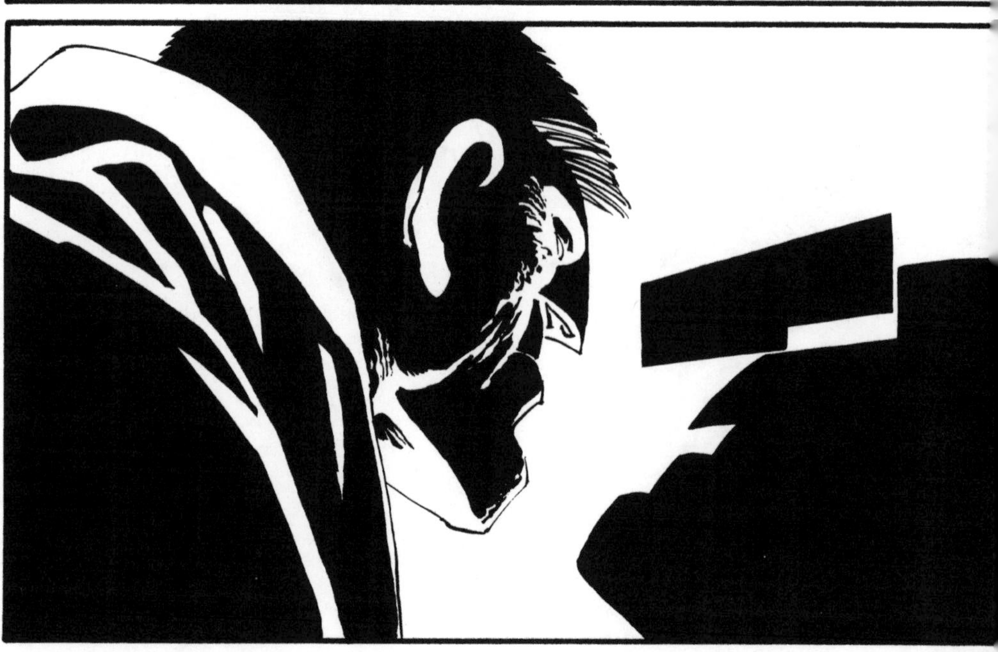

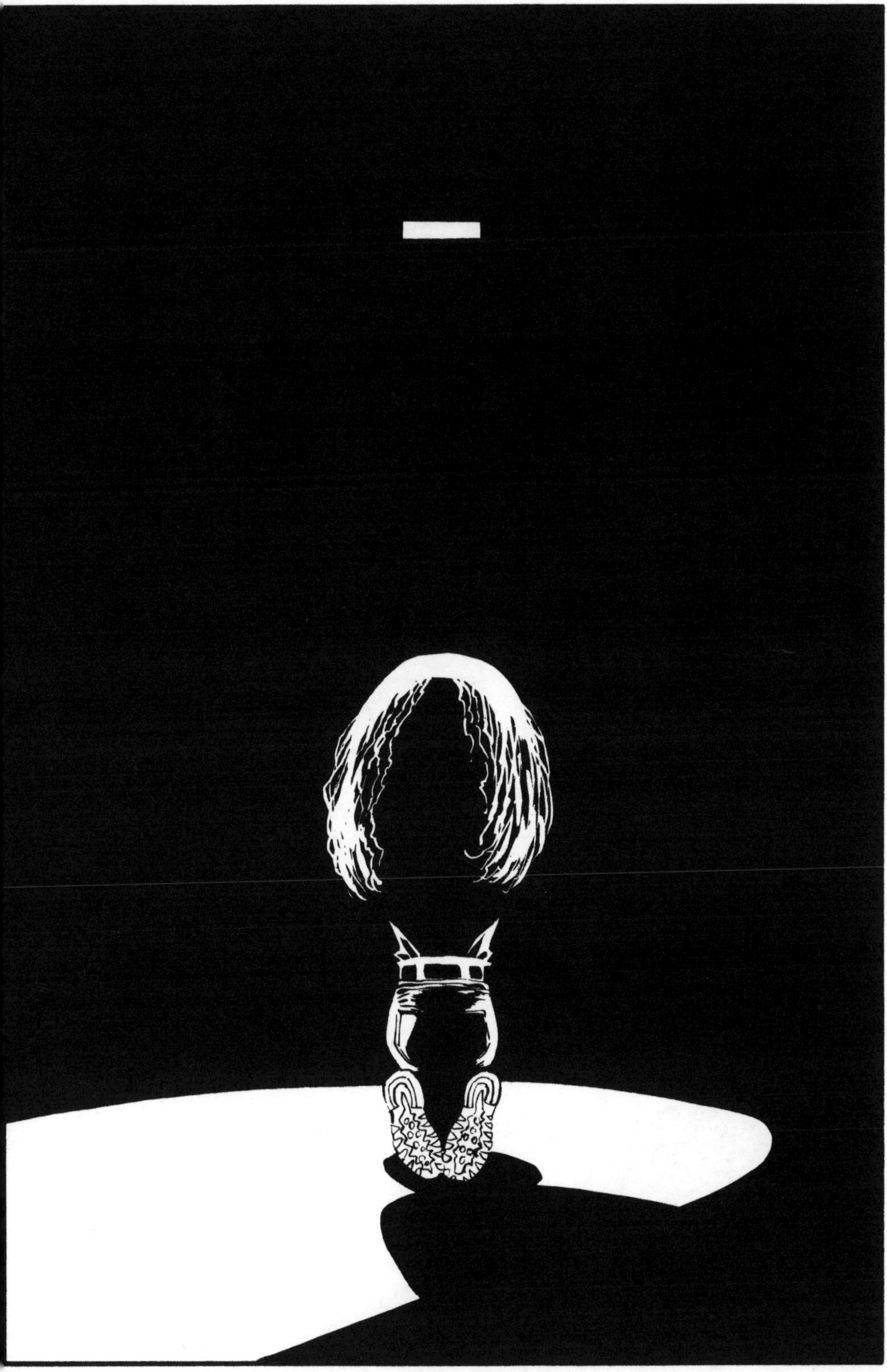

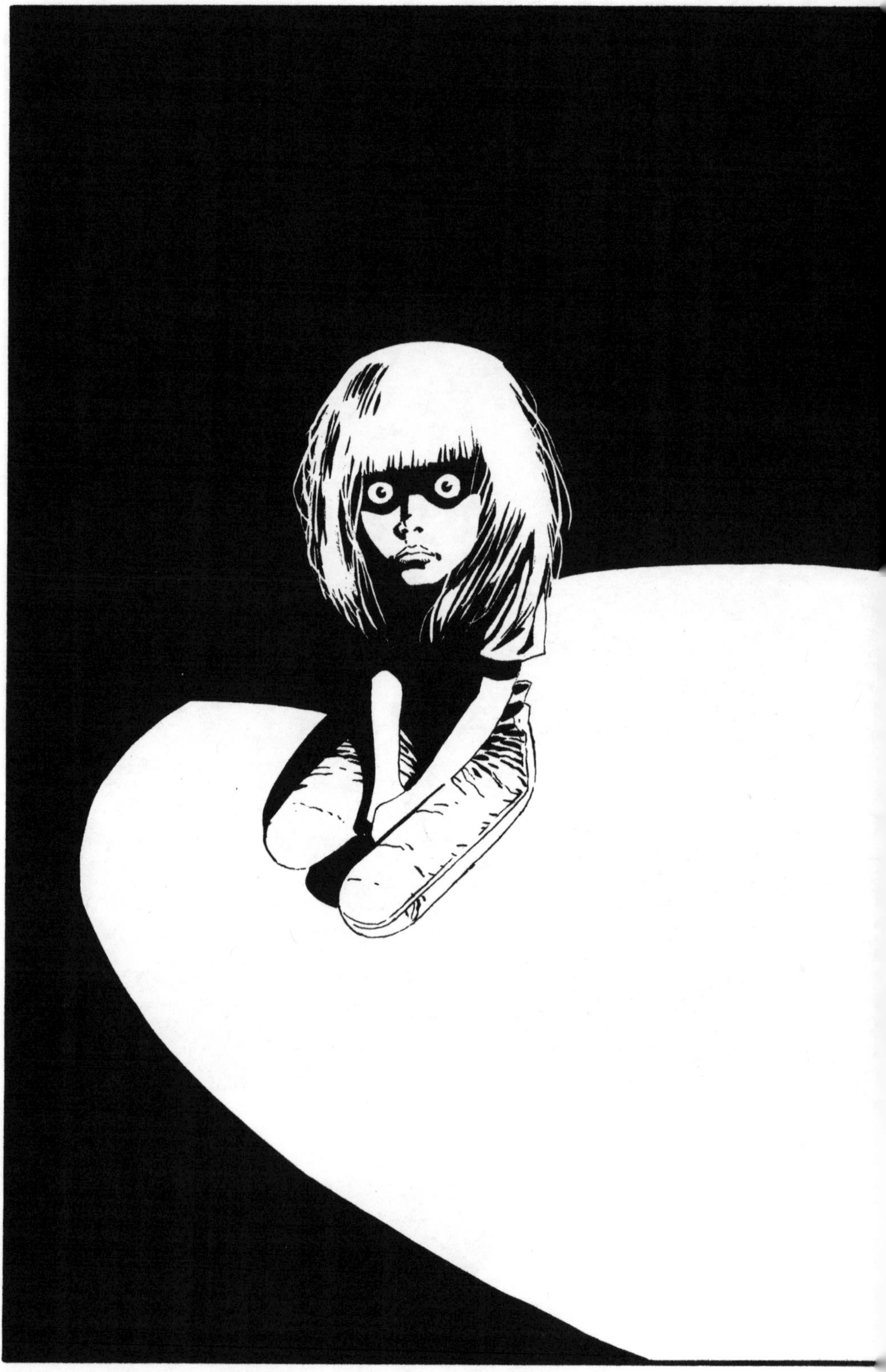

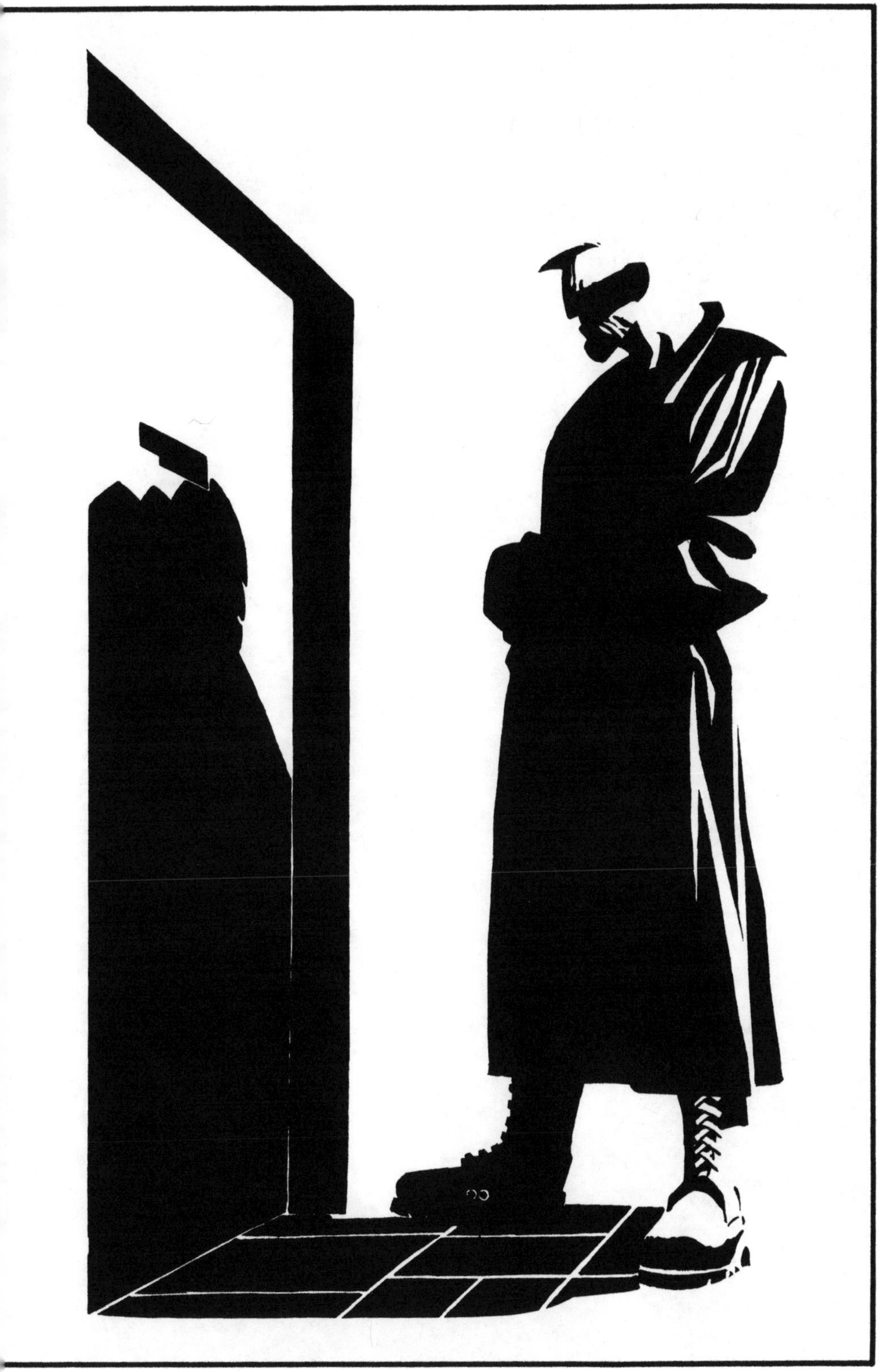

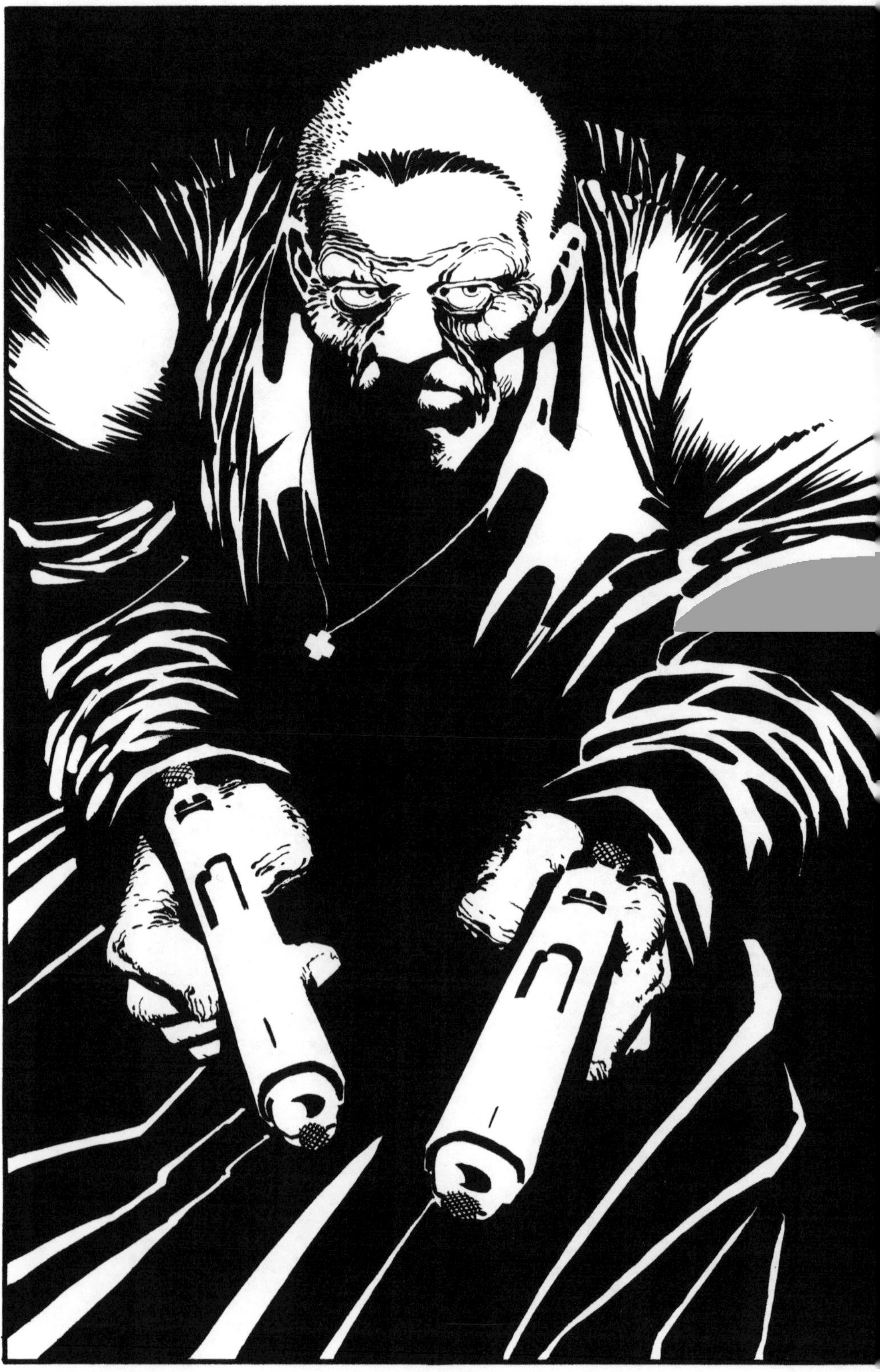

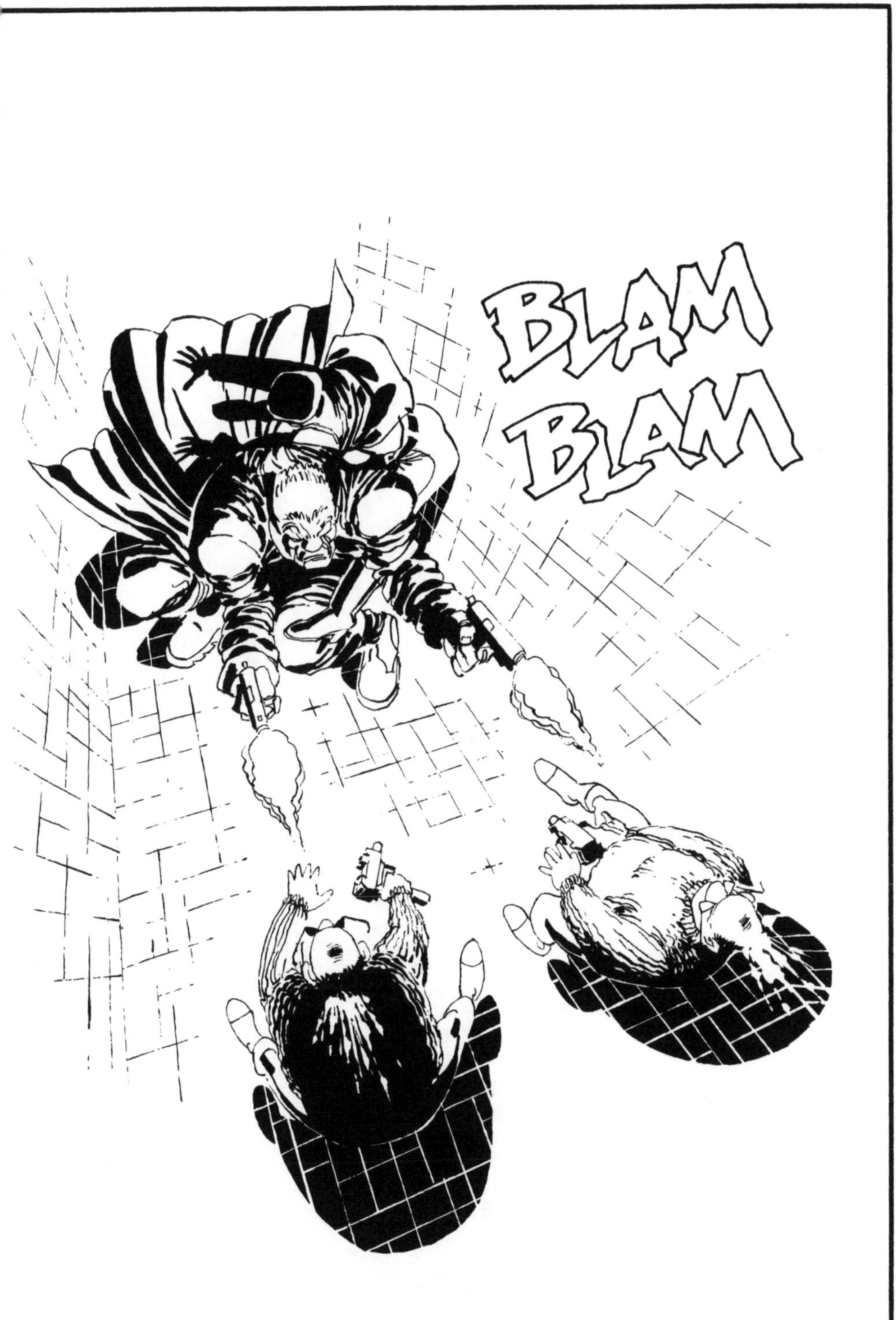
BLAM
BLAM

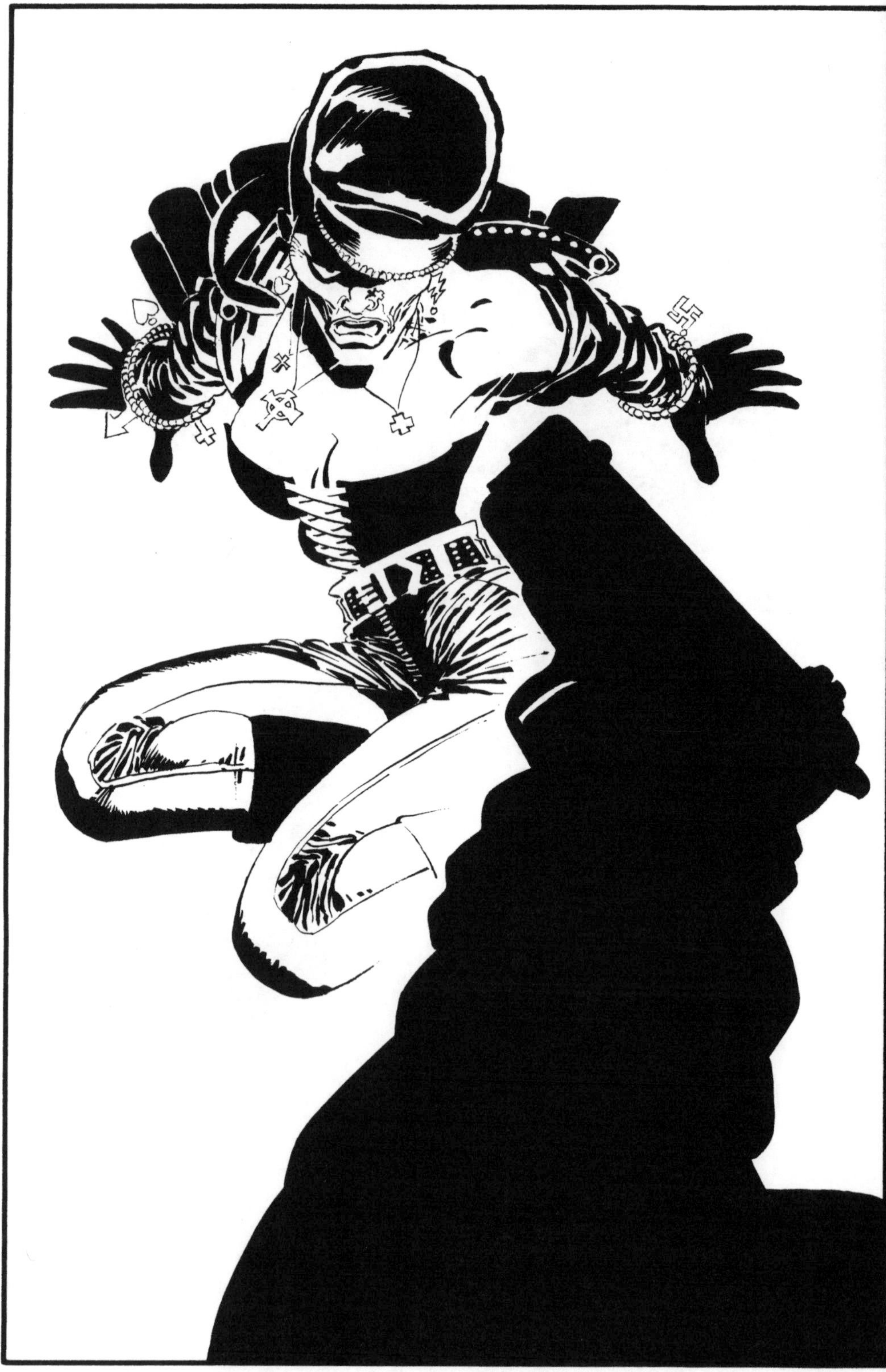

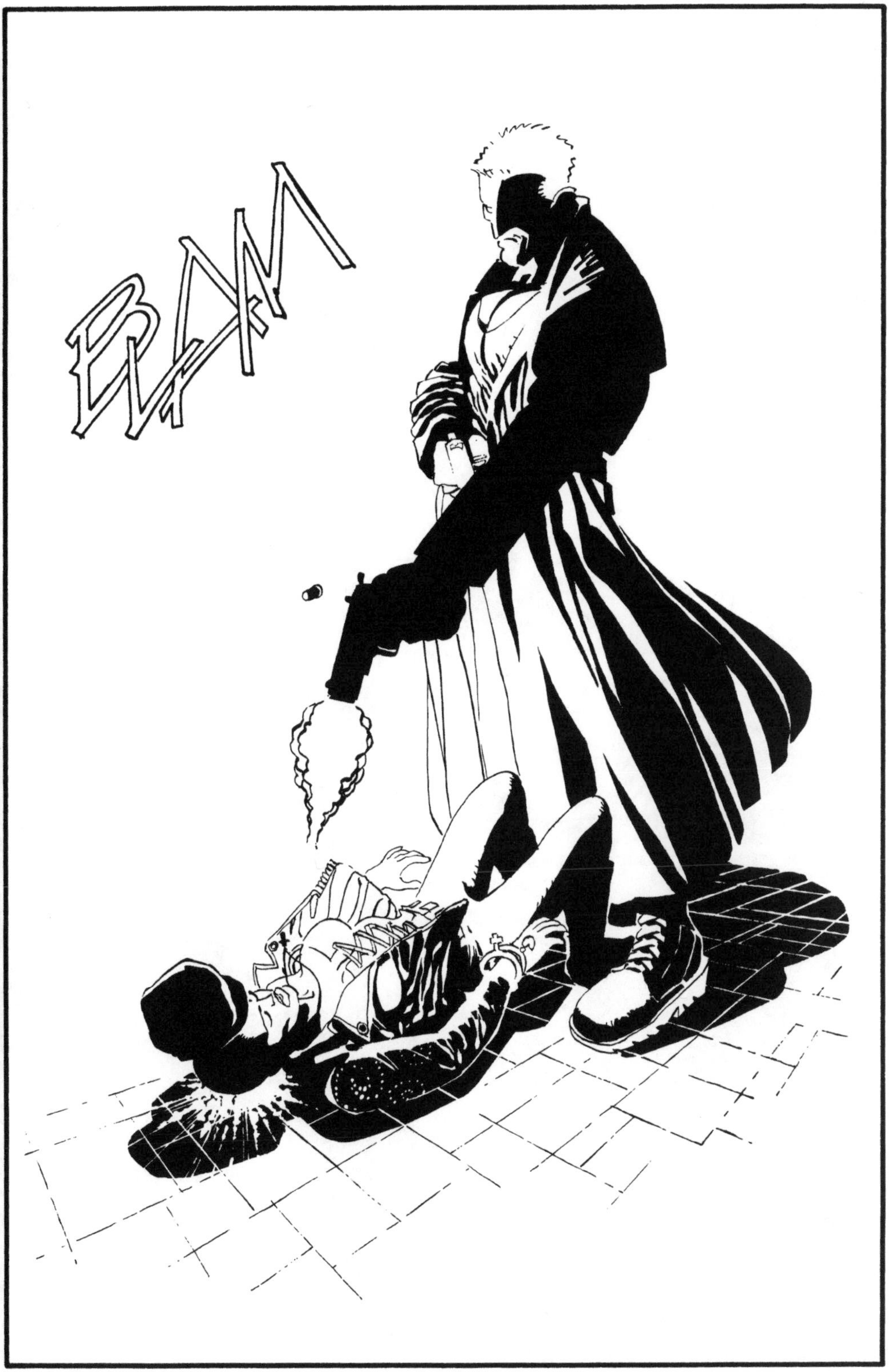
BLAM

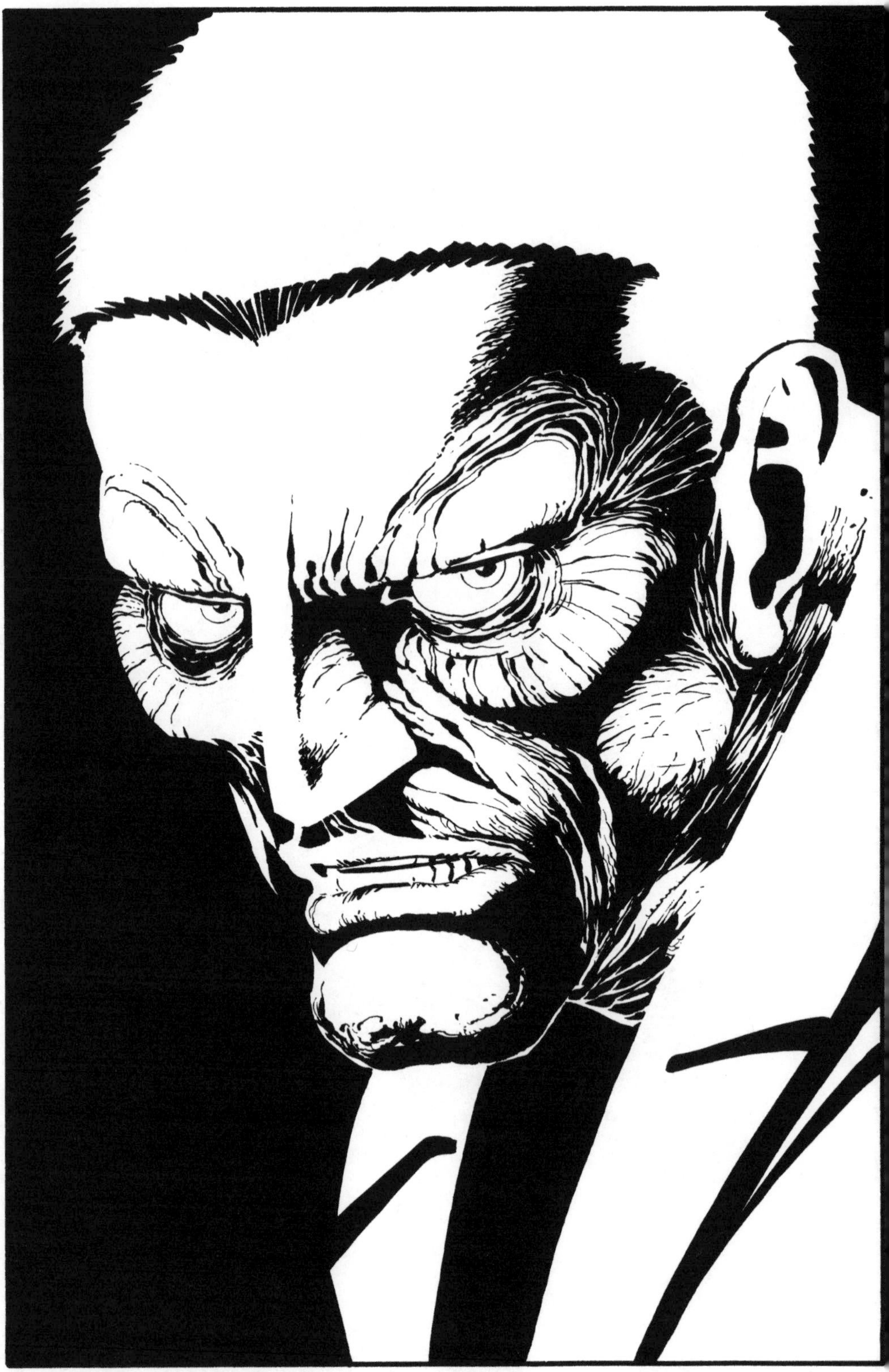

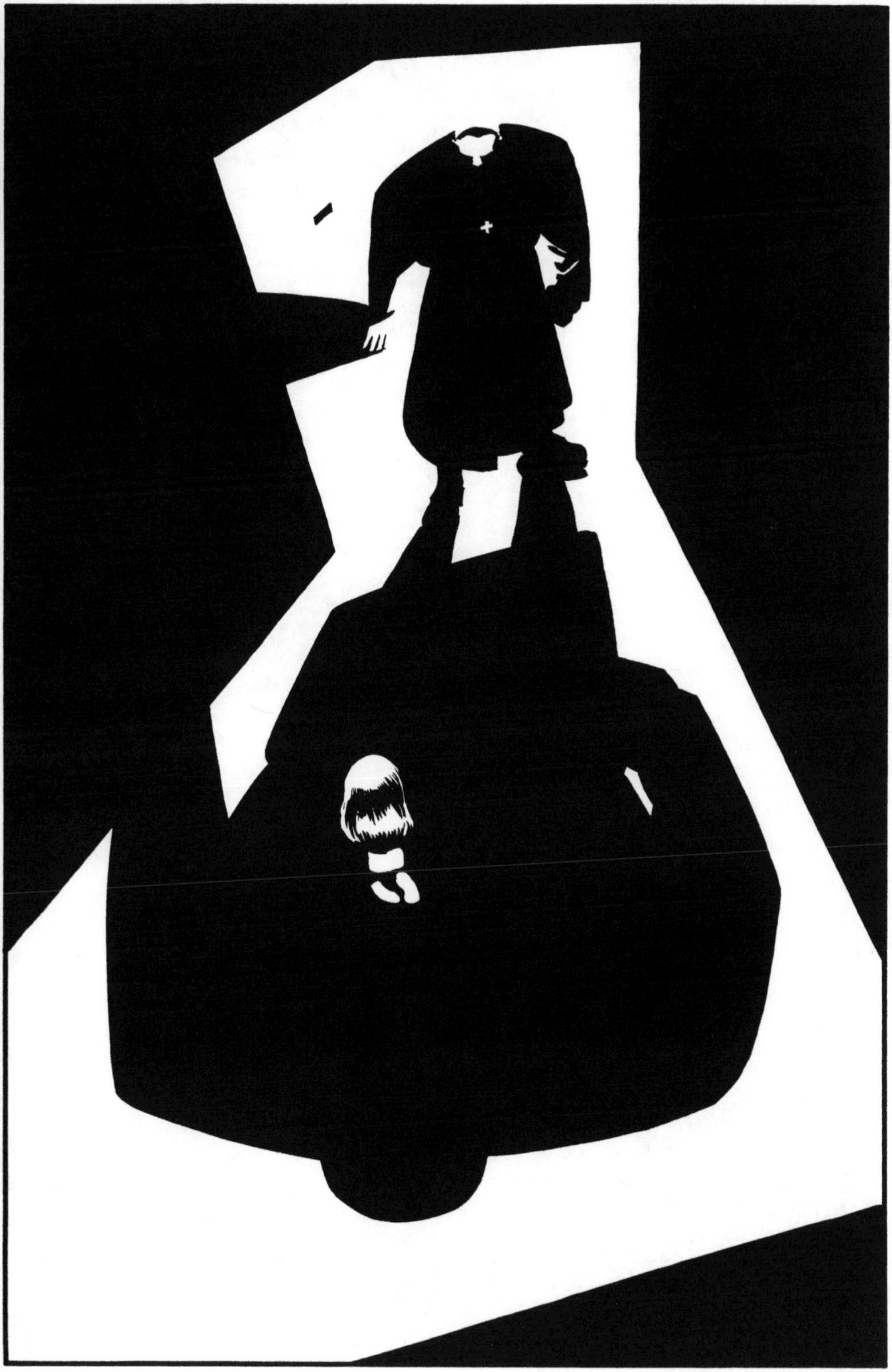

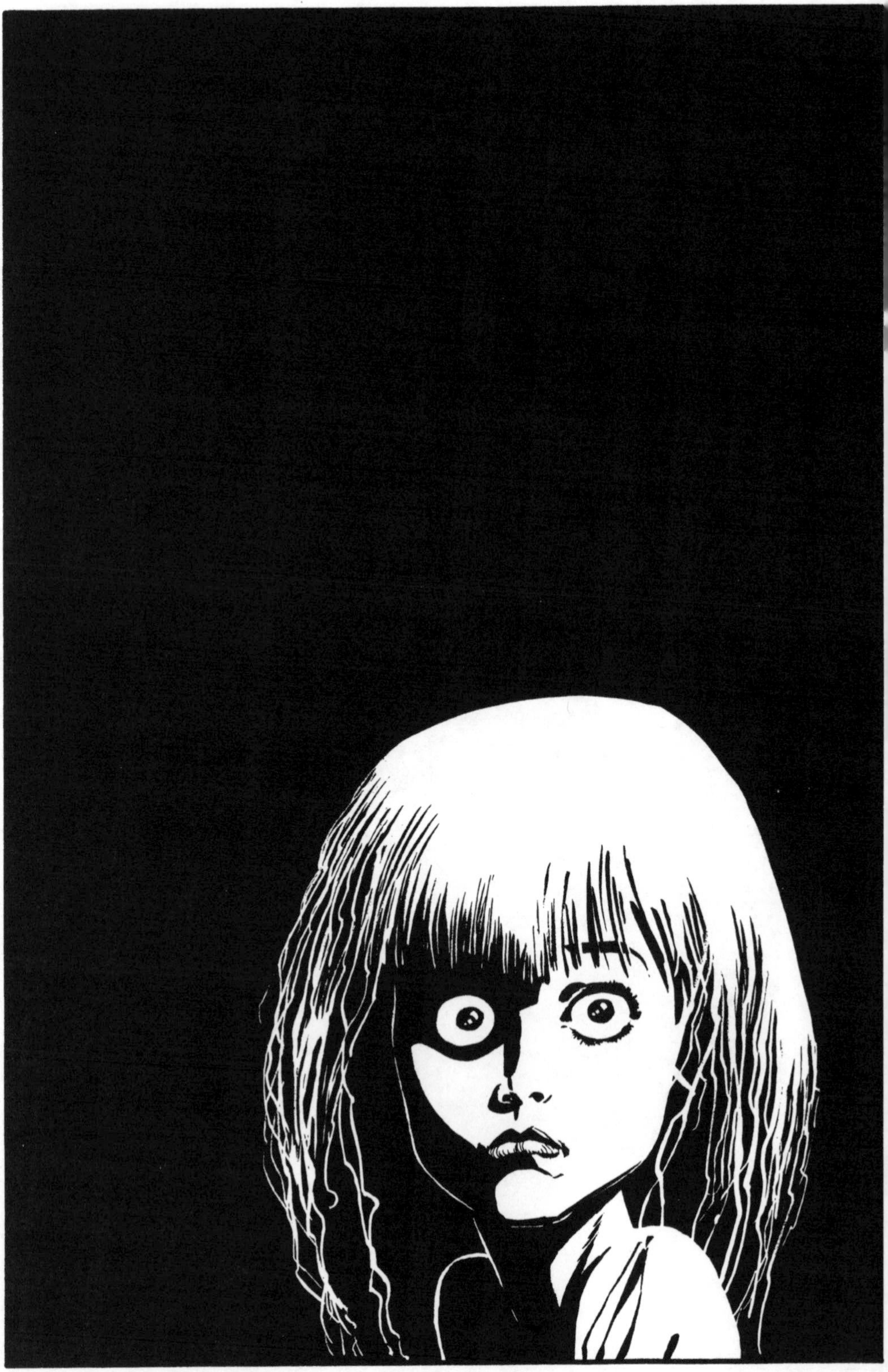

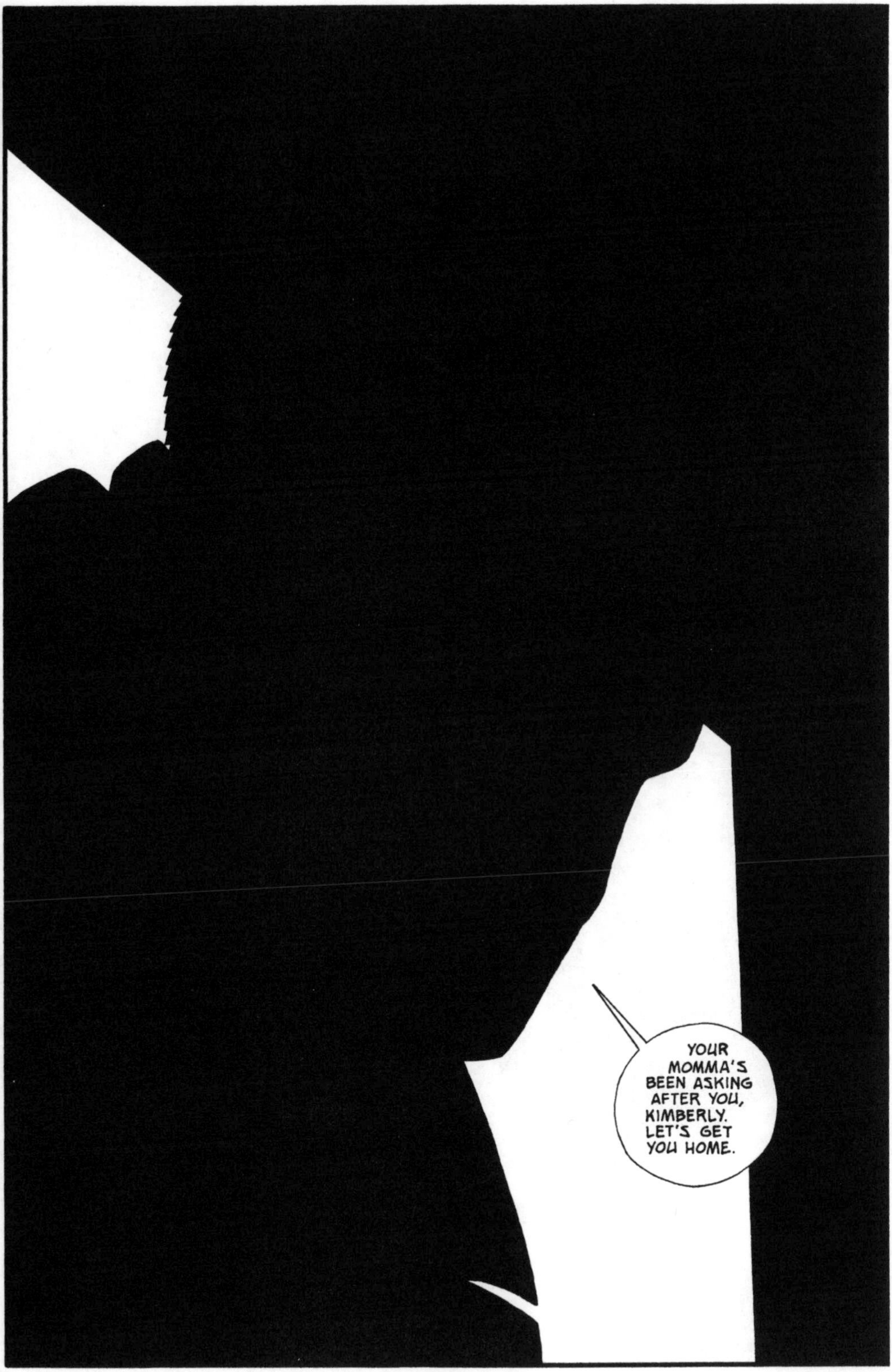
YOUR MOMMA'S BEEN ASKING AFTER YOU, KIMBERLY. LET'S GET YOU HOME.

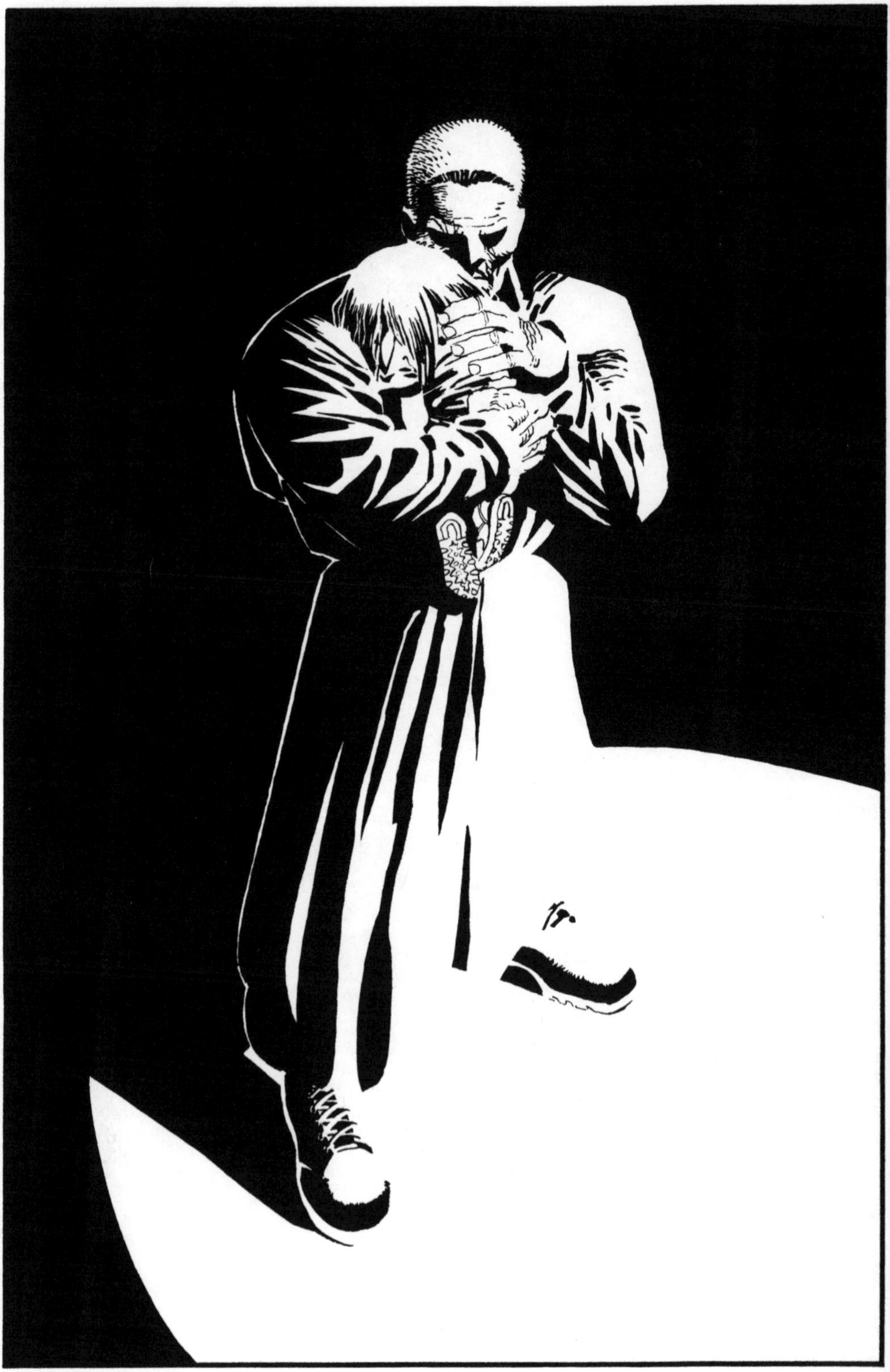

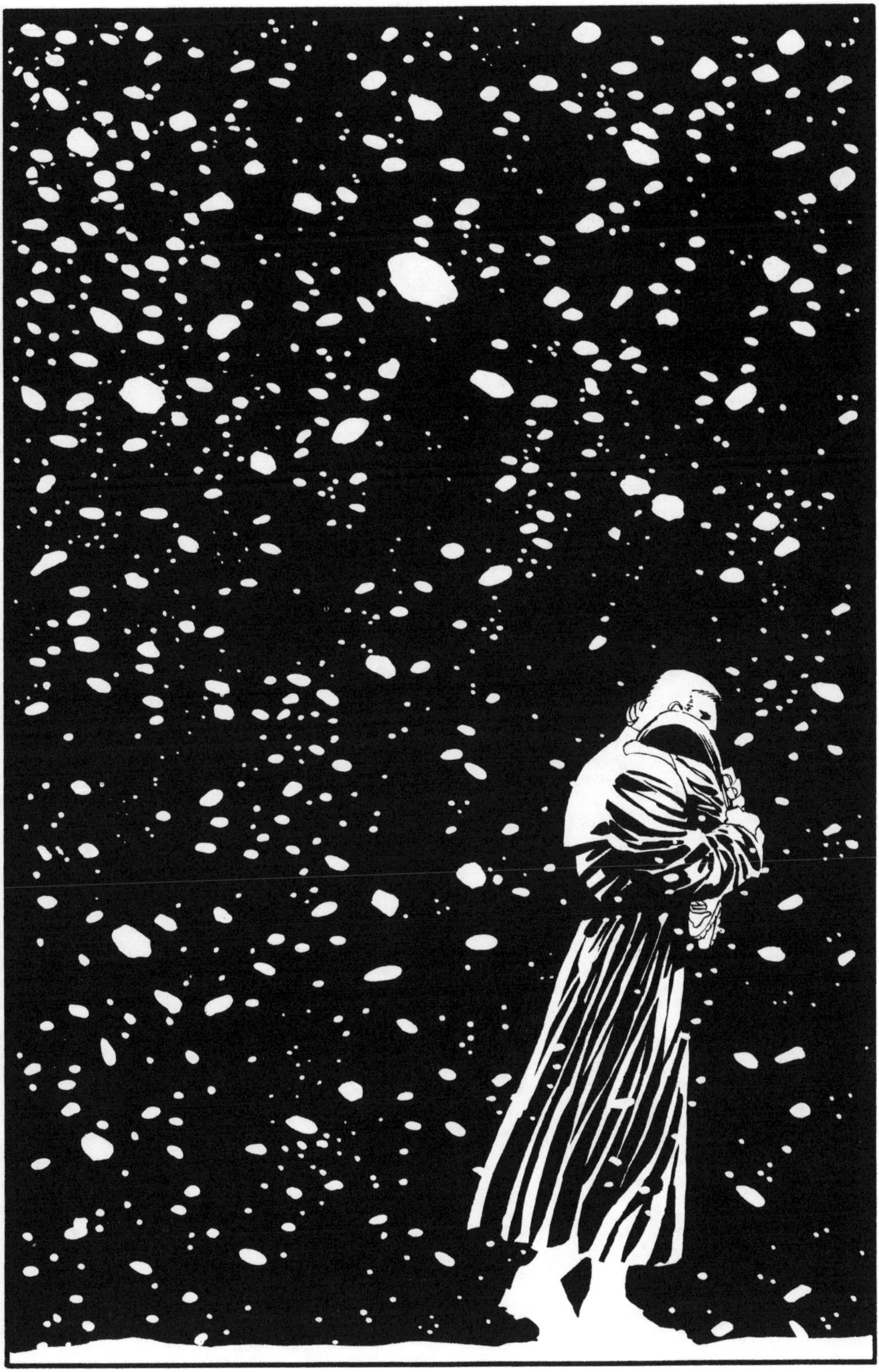

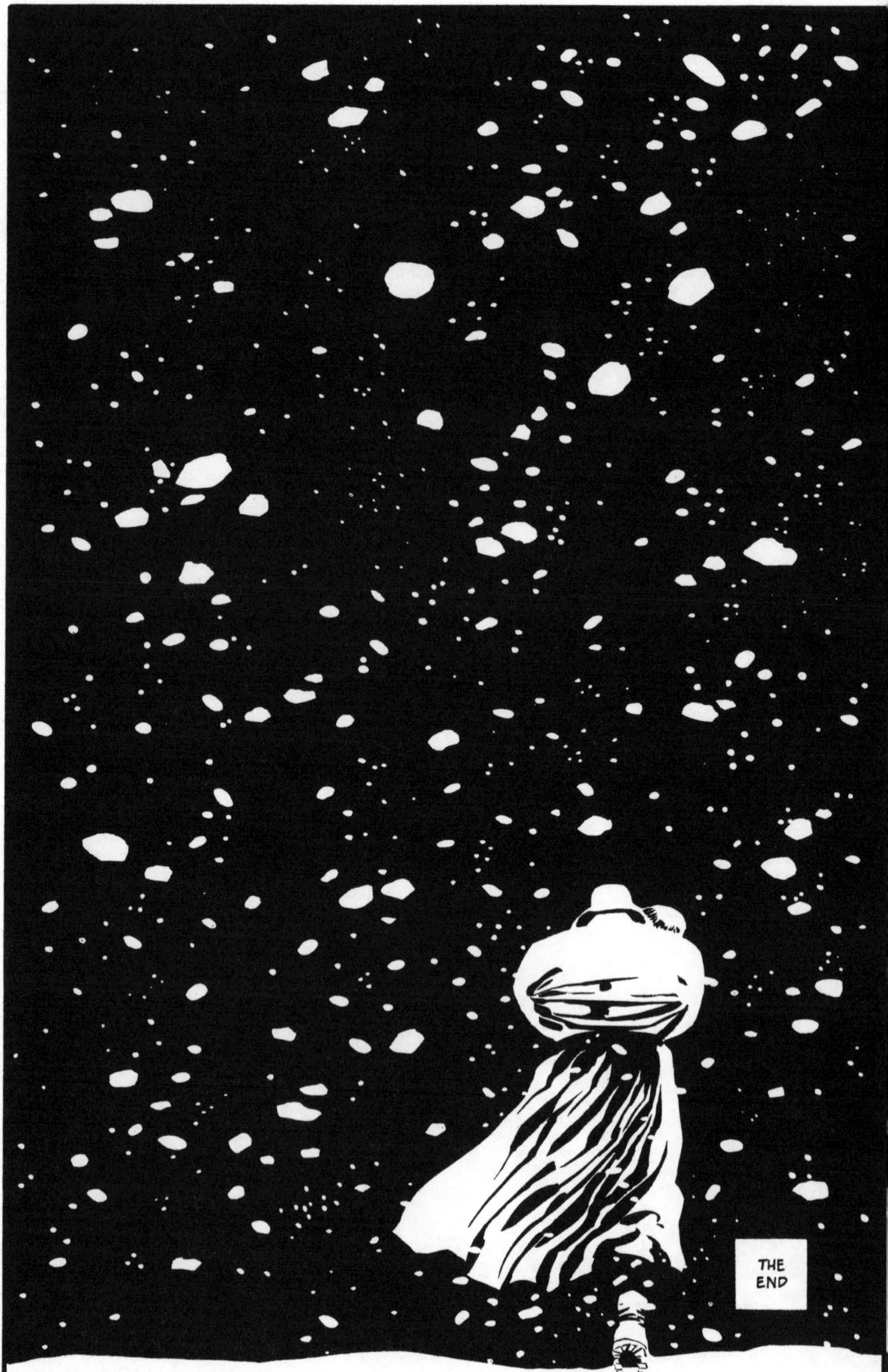
THE END

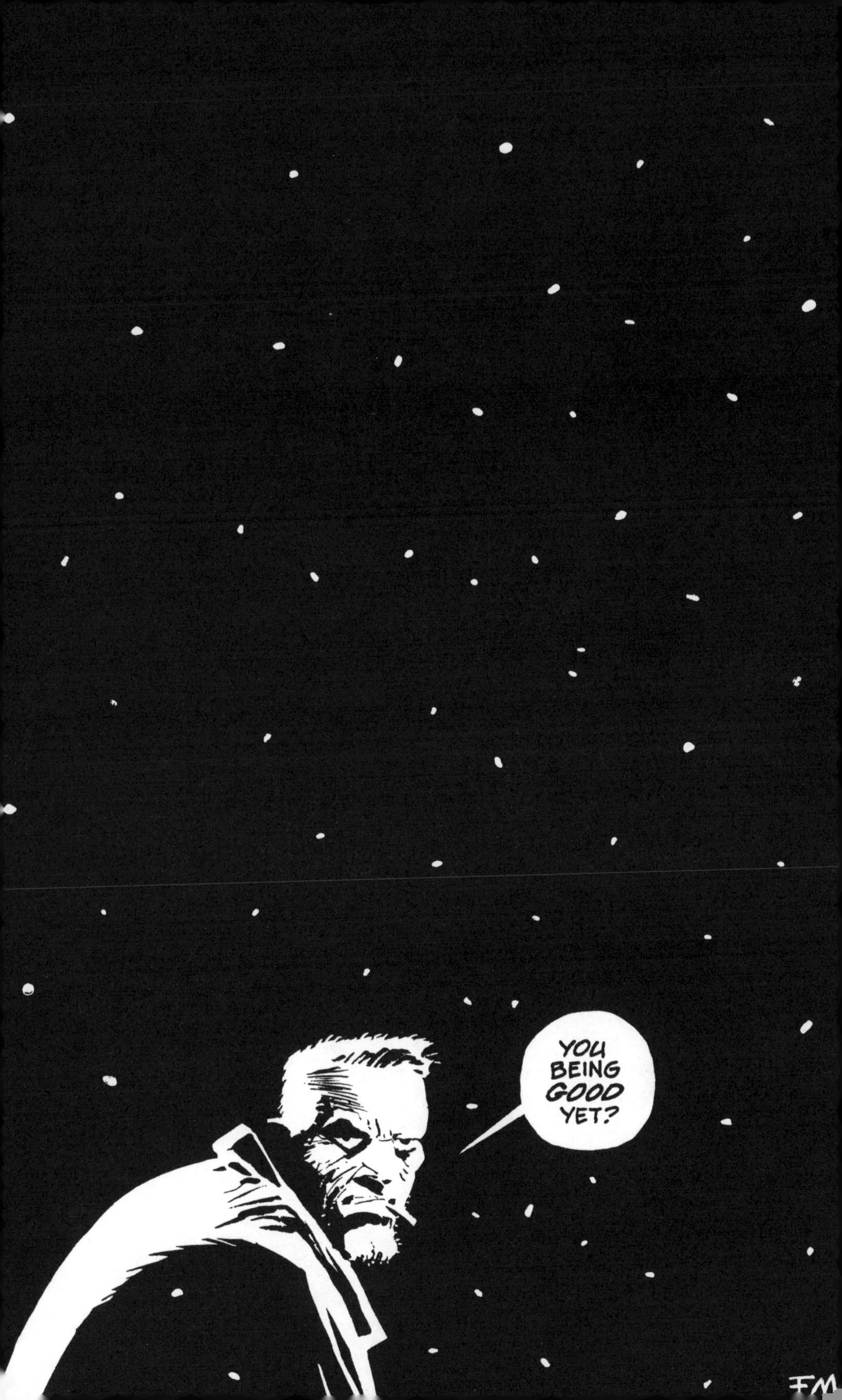
YOU BEING GOOD YET?
FM

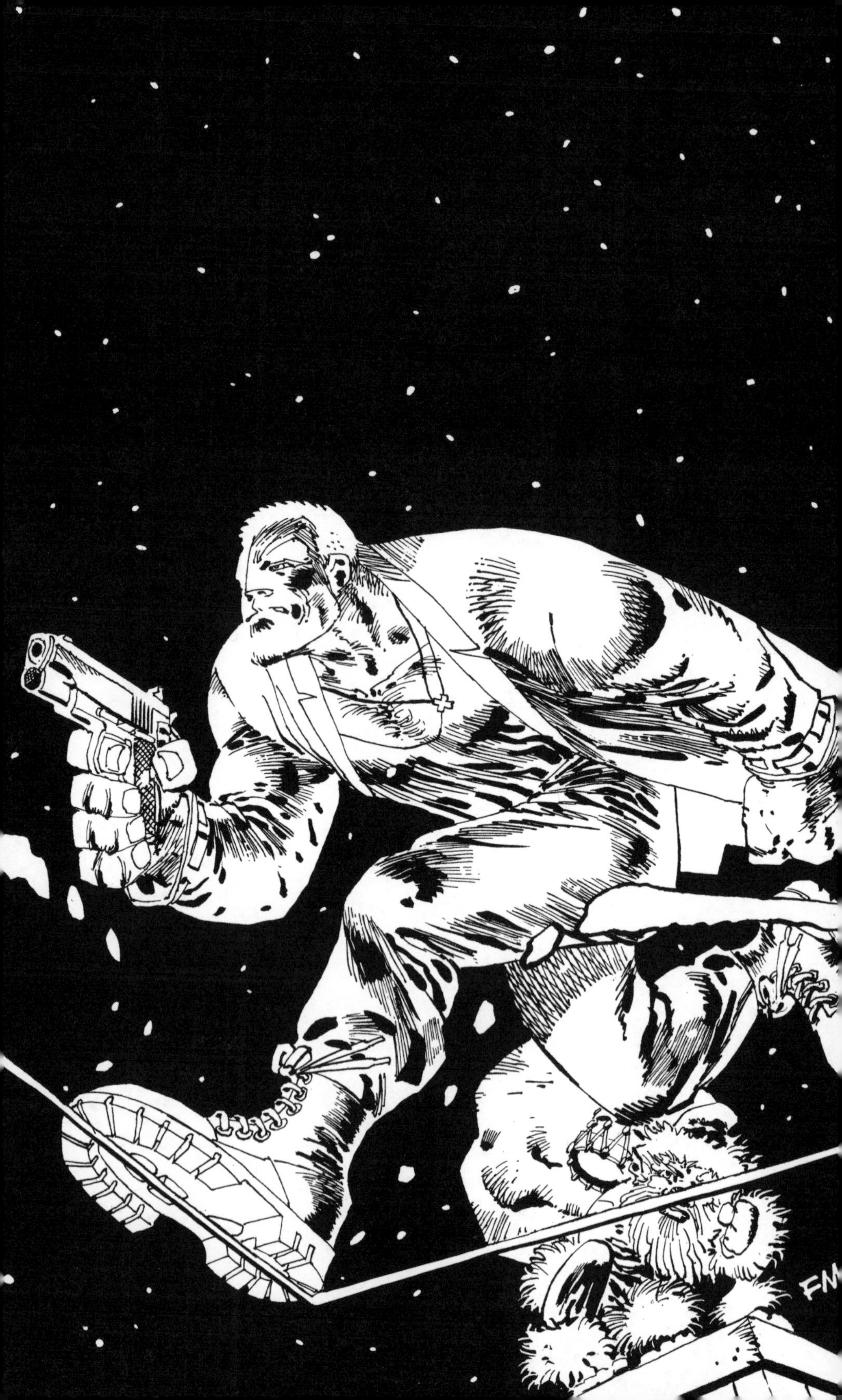

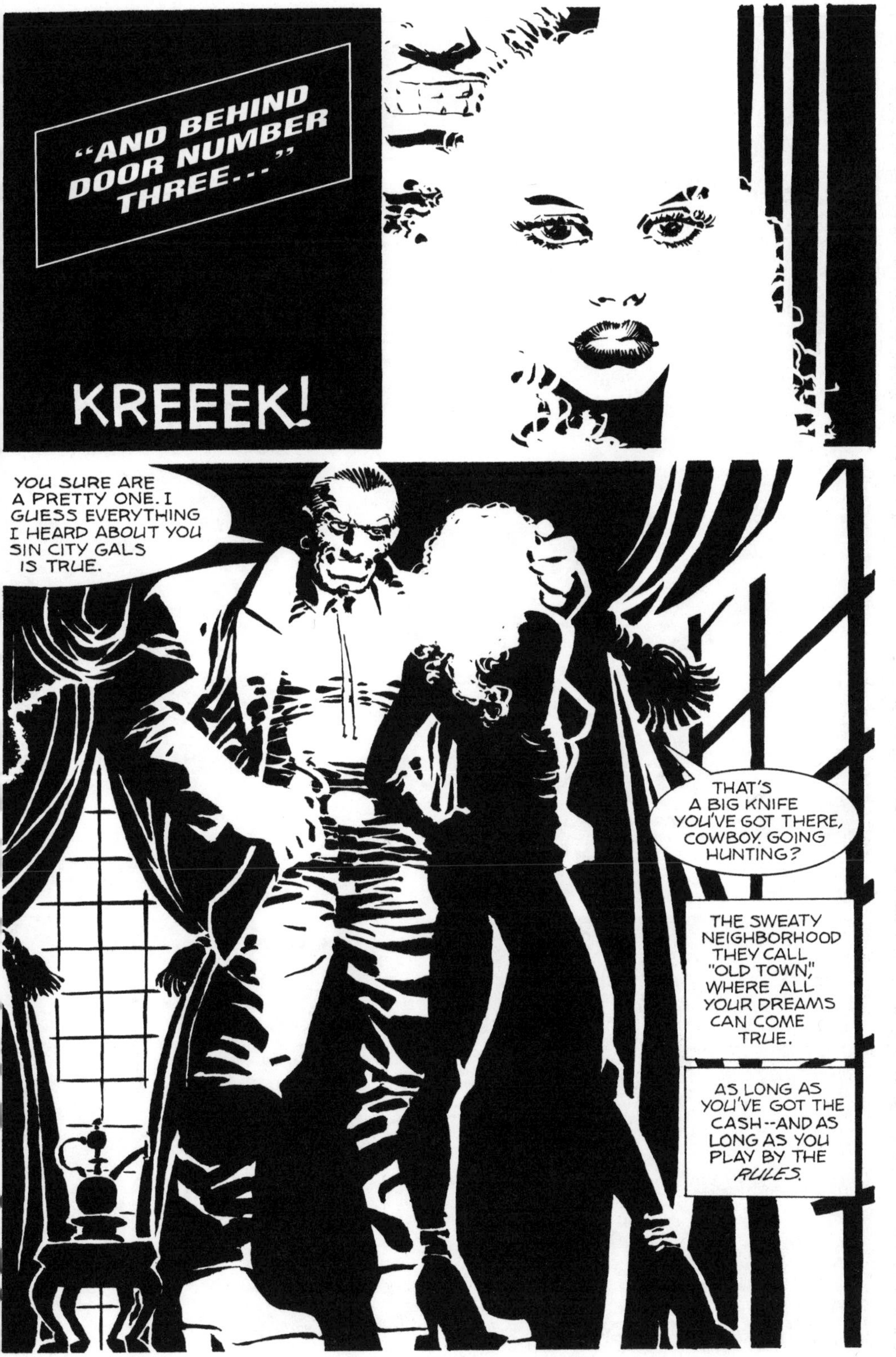
"AND BEHIND DOOR NUMBER THREE..."
KREEEK!
YOU SURE ARE A PRETTY ONE. I GUESS EVERYTHING I HEARD ABOUT YOU SIN CITY GALS IS TRUE.
THAT'S A BIG KNIFE YOU'VE GOT THERE, COWBOY. GOING HUNTING?
THE SWEATY NEIGHBORHOOD THEY CALL "OLD TOWN," WHERE ALL YOUR DREAMS CAN COME TRUE.
AS LONG AS YOU'VE GOT THE CASH--AND AS LONG AS YOU PLAY BY THE RULES.

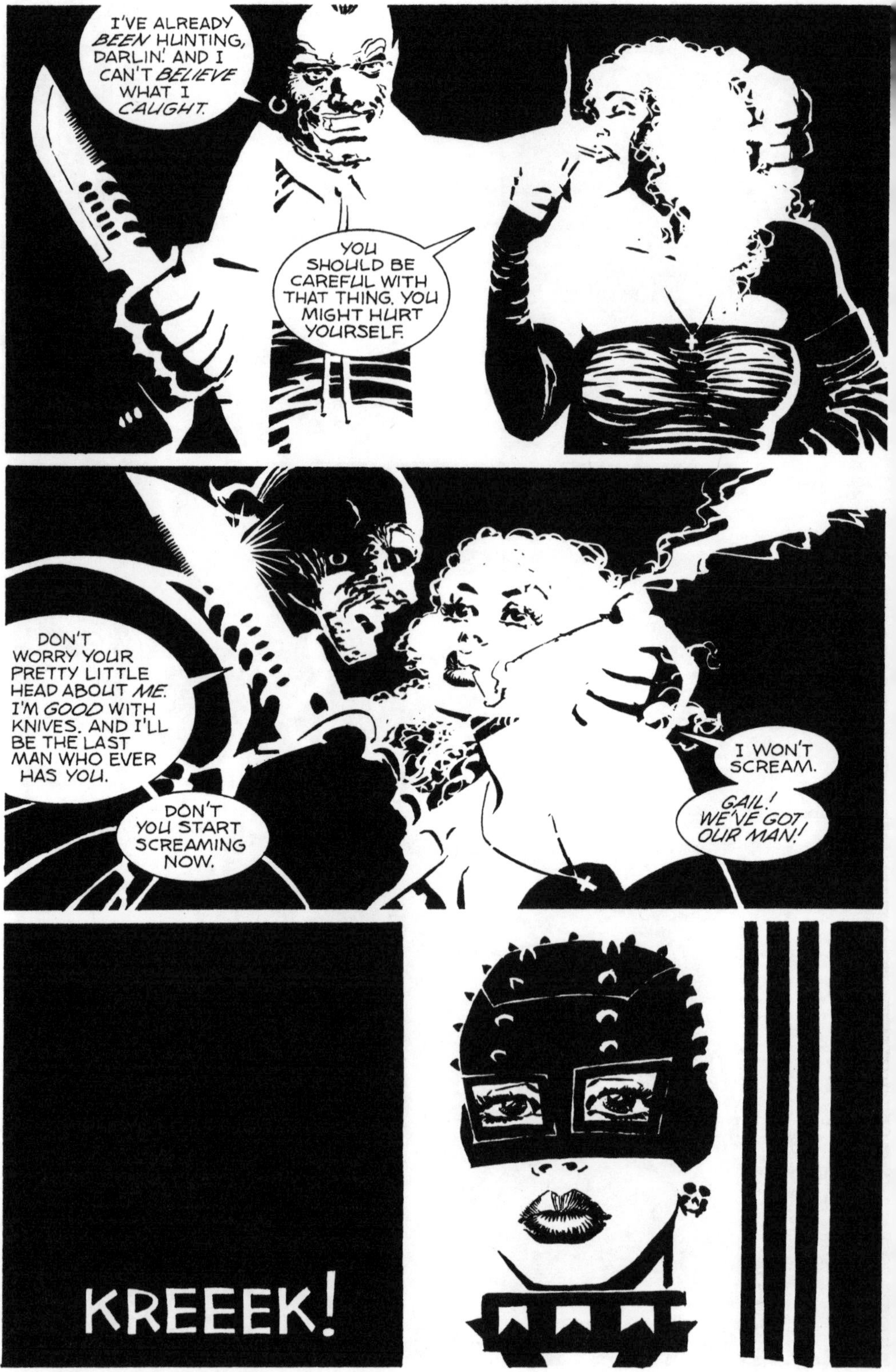

I'VE ALREADY *BEEN* HUNTING, DARLIN'. AND I CAN'T *BELIEVE* WHAT I *CAUGHT*.
YOU SHOULD BE CAREFUL WITH THAT THING. YOU MIGHT HURT YOURSELF.
DON'T WORRY YOUR PRETTY LITTLE HEAD ABOUT *ME*. I'M *GOOD* WITH KNIVES. AND I'LL BE THE LAST MAN WHO EVER HAS YOU.
DON'T YOU START SCREAMING NOW.
I WON'T SCREAM.
GAIL! WE'VE GOT OUR MAN!
KREEEK!

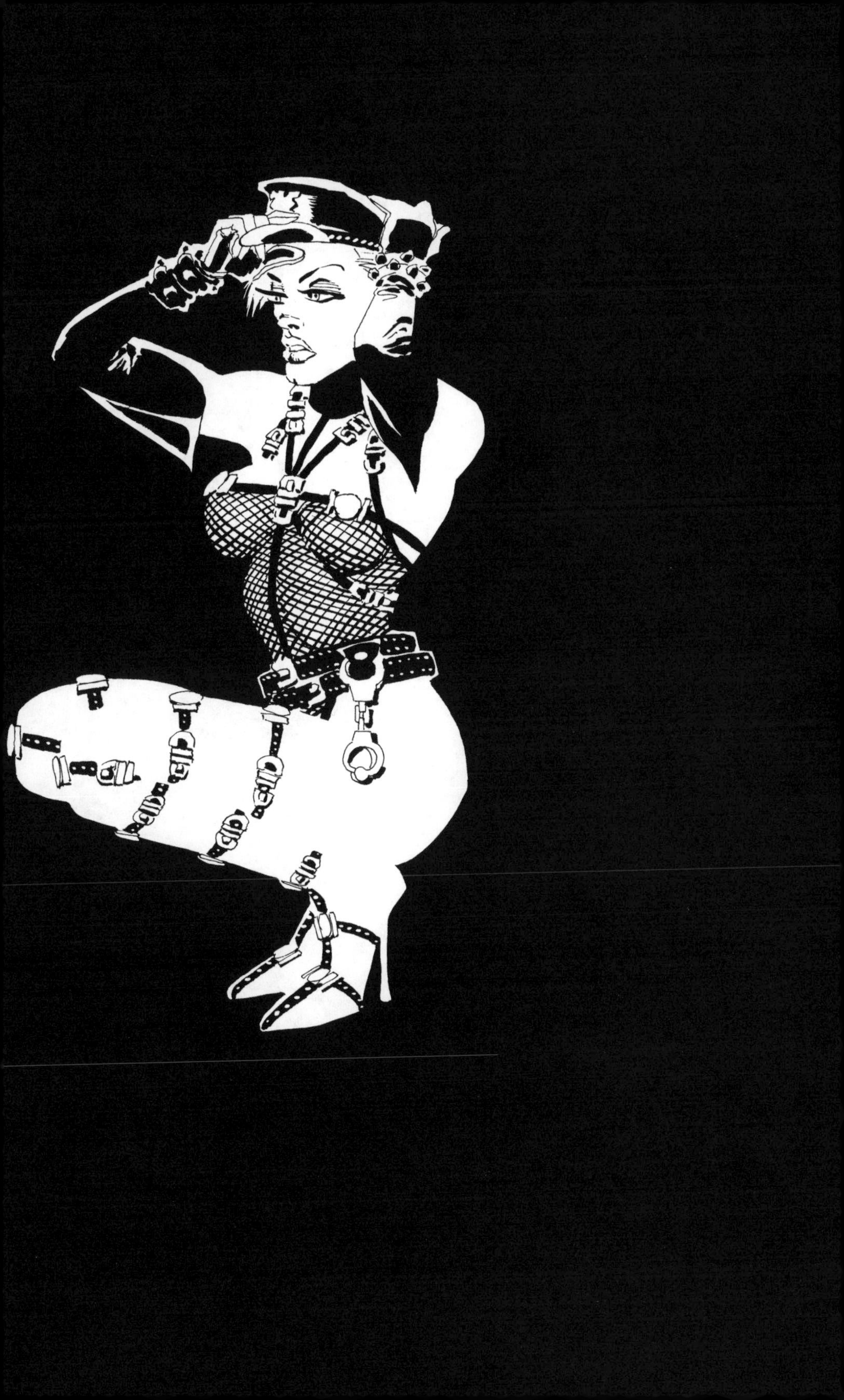

BLUE EYES

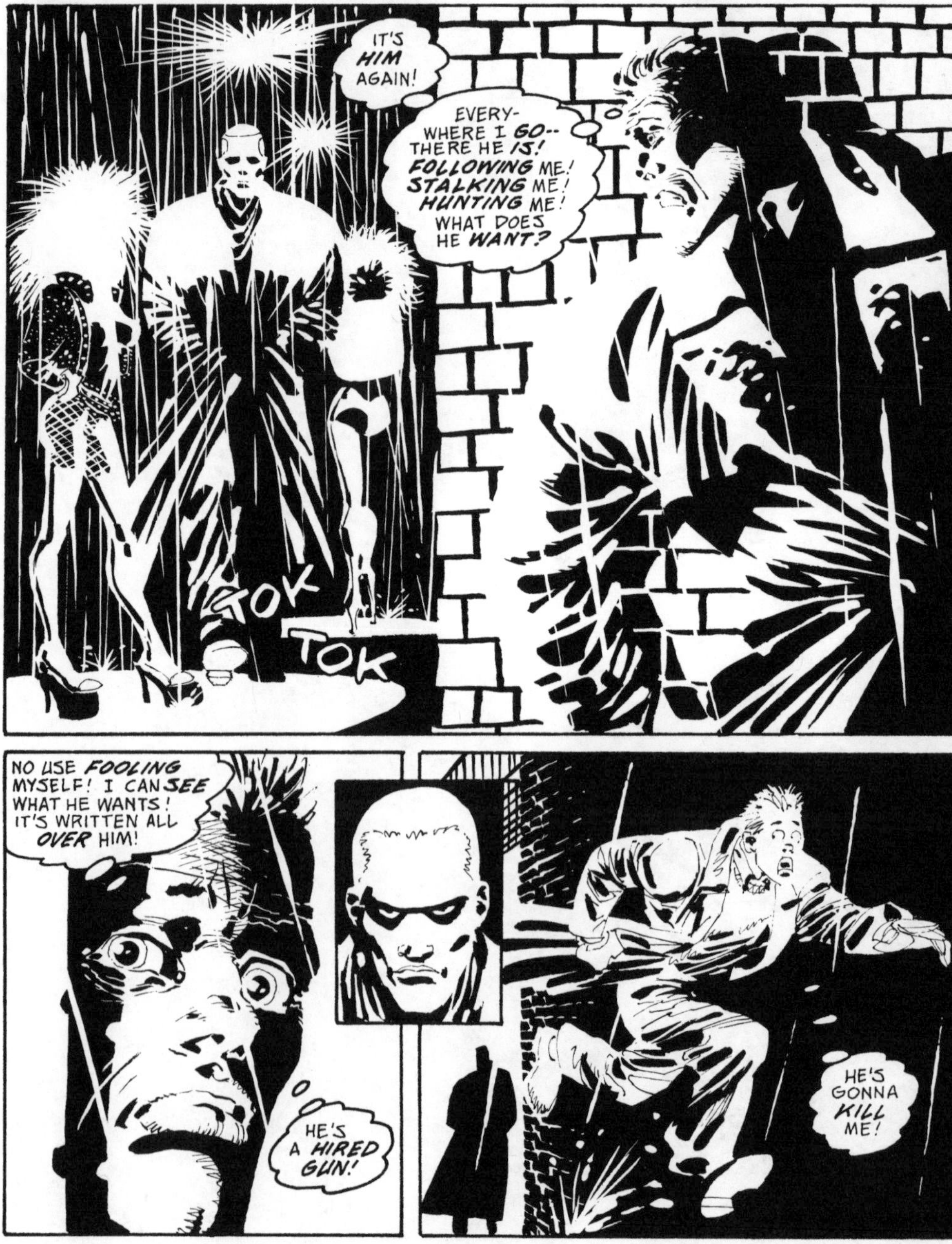
IT'S HIM AGAIN!
EVERY-WHERE I GO-- THERE HE IS! FOLLOWING ME! STALKING ME! HUNTING ME! WHAT DOES HE WANT?
TOK
NO USE FOOLING MYSELF! I CAN SEE WHAT HE WANTS! IT'S WRITTEN ALL OVER HIM!
HE'S A HIRED GUN!
HE'S GONNA KILL ME!

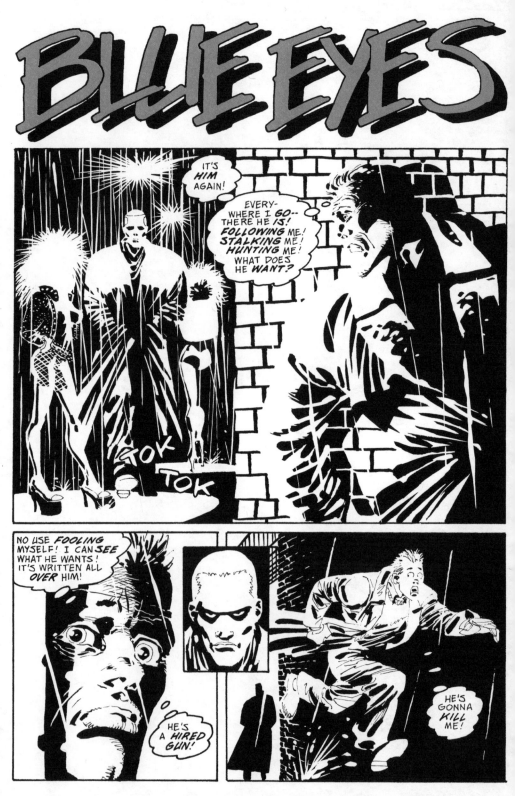

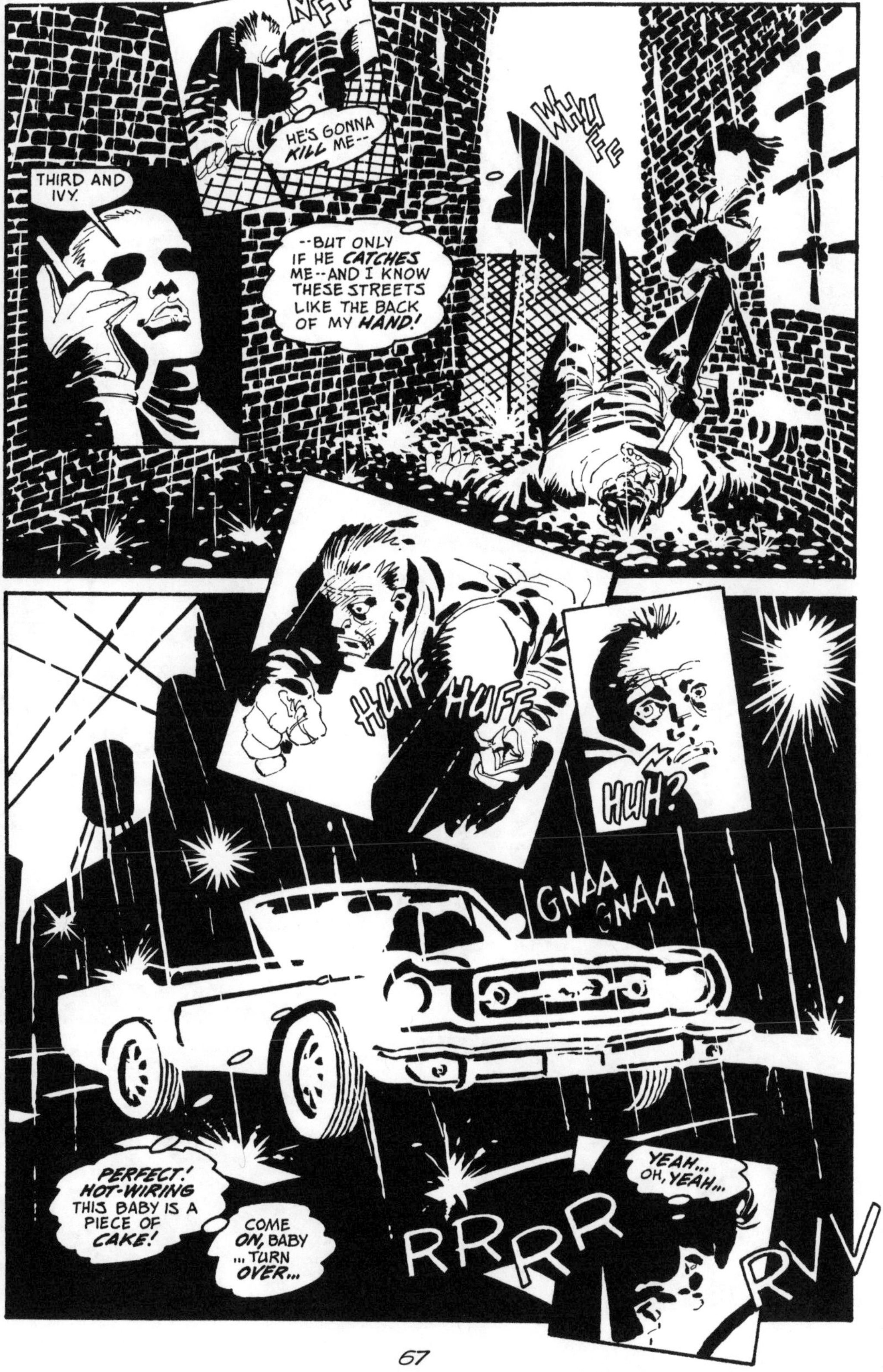
NFF
HE'S GONNA KILL ME--
THIRD AND IVY.
--BUT ONLY IF HE CATCHES ME--AND I KNOW THESE STREETS LIKE THE BACK OF MY HAND!
WHUFF
HUFF HUFF
HUH?
GNAA GNAA
PERFECT! HOT-WIRING THIS BABY IS A PIECE OF CAKE!
COME ON, BABY ...TURN OVER...
YEAH... OH, YEAH...
RRRRR
RVV

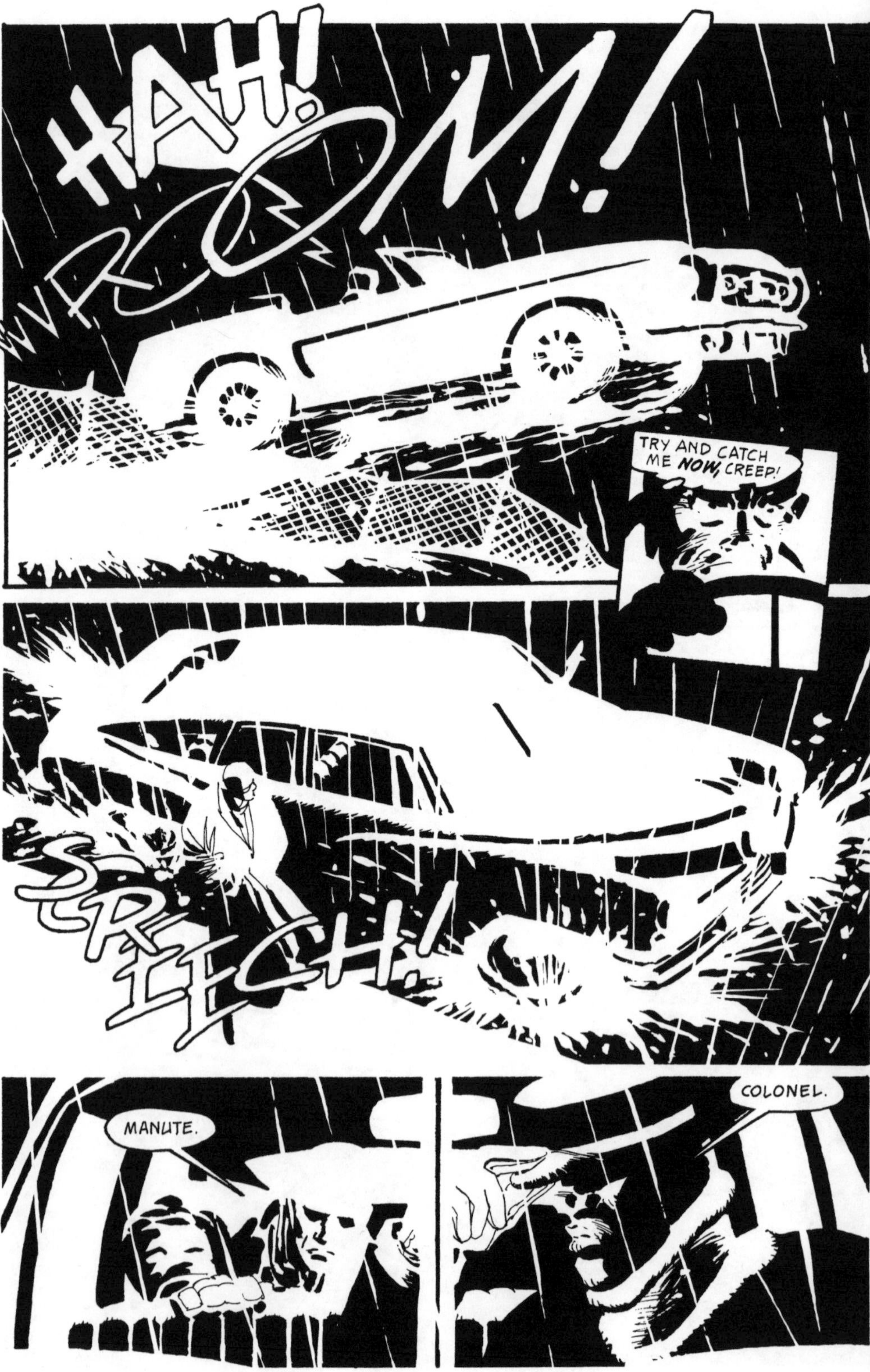
HAH!
WVROOM!
TRY AND CATCH ME **NOW,** CREEP!
SCREECH!
MANUTE.
COLONEL.

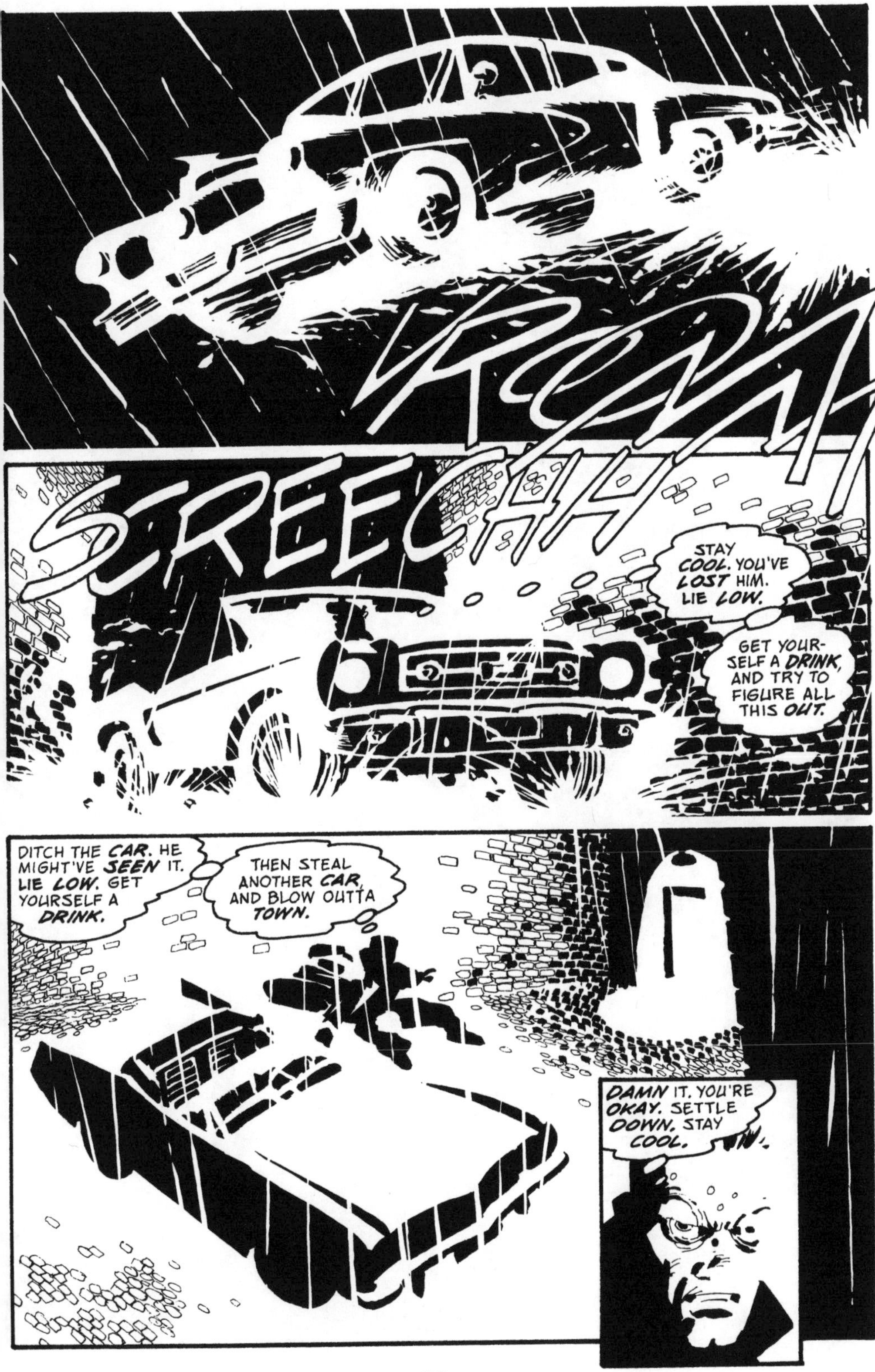
SCREECHHH
STAY COOL. YOU'VE LOST HIM. LIE LOW.
GET YOURSELF A DRINK, AND TRY TO FIGURE ALL THIS OUT.
DITCH THE CAR. HE MIGHT'VE SEEN IT. LIE LOW. GET YOURSELF A DRINK.
THEN STEAL ANOTHER CAR, AND BLOW OUTTA TOWN.
DAMN IT. YOU'RE OKAY. SETTLE DOWN. STAY COOL.

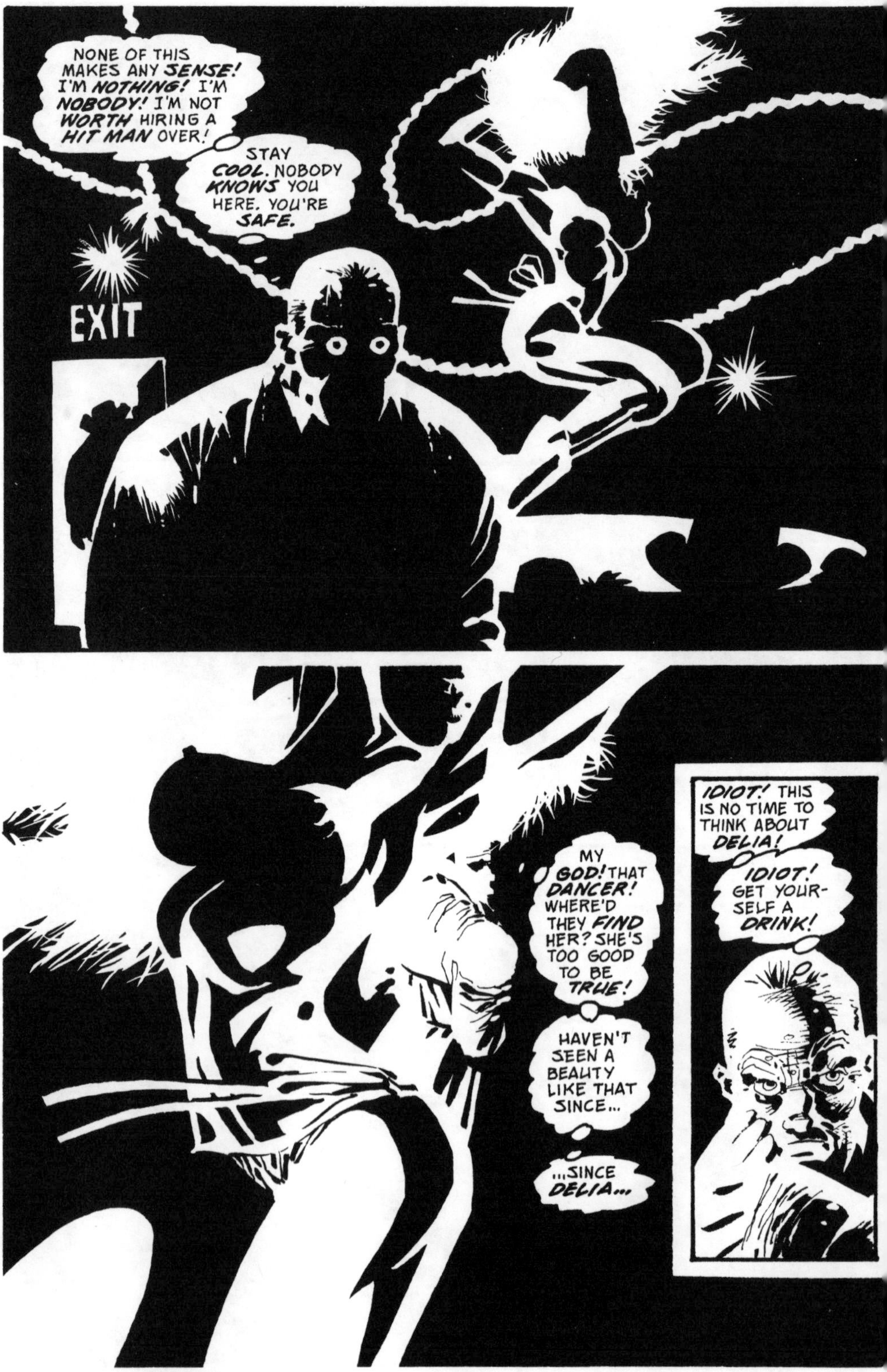
NONE OF THIS MAKES ANY SENSE! I'M NOTHING! I'M NOBODY! I'M NOT WORTH HIRING A HIT MAN OVER!
STAY COOL. NOBODY KNOWS YOU HERE. YOU'RE SAFE.
EXIT
MY GOD! THAT DANCER! WHERE'D THEY FIND HER? SHE'S TOO GOOD TO BE TRUE!
HAVEN'T SEEN A BEAUTY LIKE THAT SINCE...
...SINCE DELIA...
IDIOT! THIS IS NO TIME TO THINK ABOUT DELIA!
IDIOT! GET YOURSELF A DRINK!

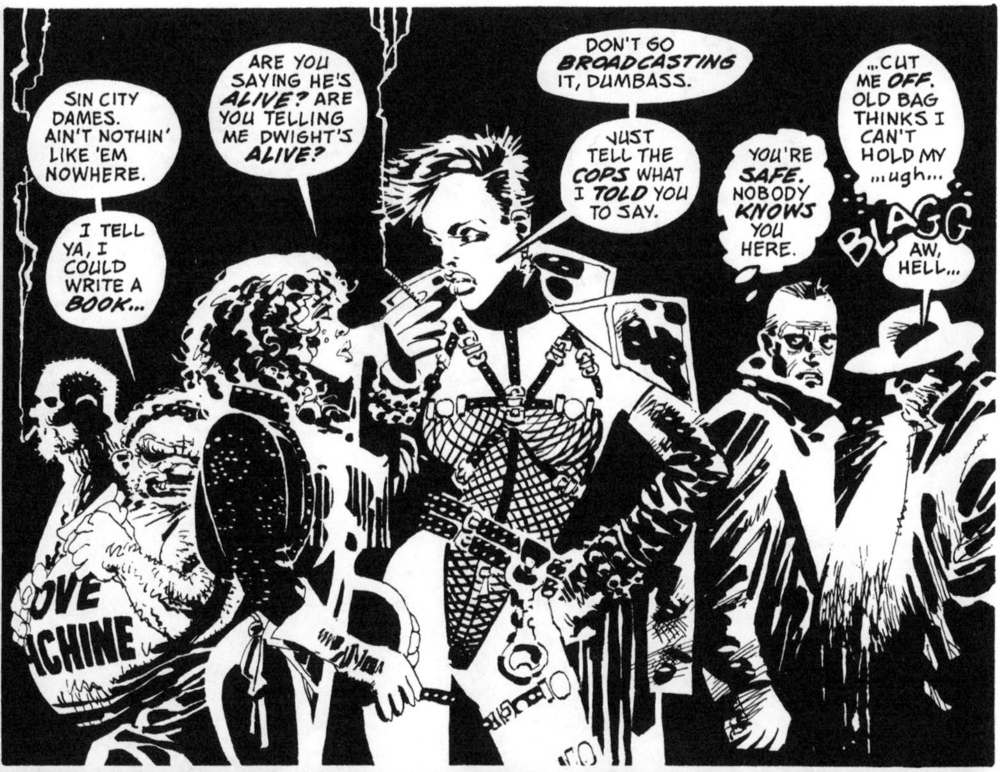
SIN CITY DAMES. AIN'T NOTHIN' LIKE 'EM NOWHERE.
I TELL YA, I COULD WRITE A BOOK...
ARE YOU SAYING HE'S ALIVE? ARE YOU TELLING ME DWIGHT'S ALIVE?
DON'T GO BROADCASTING IT, DUMBASS.
JUST TELL THE COPS WHAT I TOLD YOU TO SAY.
YOU'RE SAFE. NOBODY KNOWS YOU HERE.
...CUT ME OFF. OLD BAG THINKS I CAN'T HOLD MY ...ugh...
BLAGG
AW, HELL...

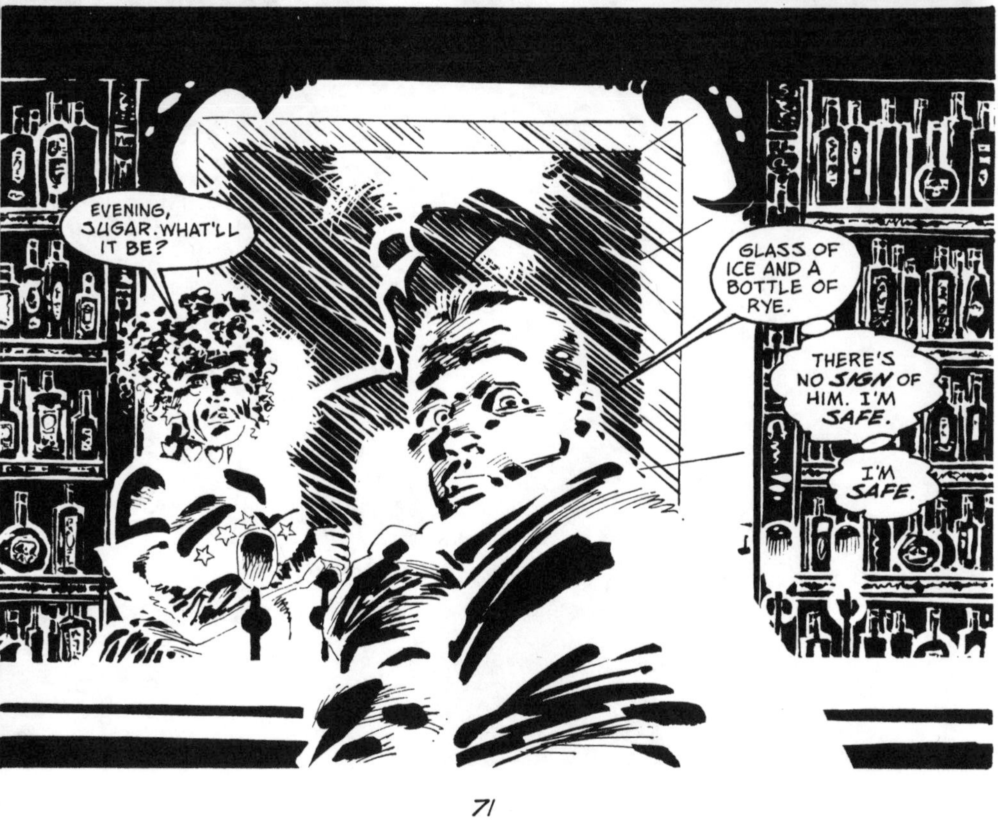
EVENING, SUGAR. WHAT'LL IT BE?
GLASS OF ICE AND A BOTTLE OF RYE.
THERE'S NO SIGN OF HIM. I'M SAFE.
I'M SAFE.

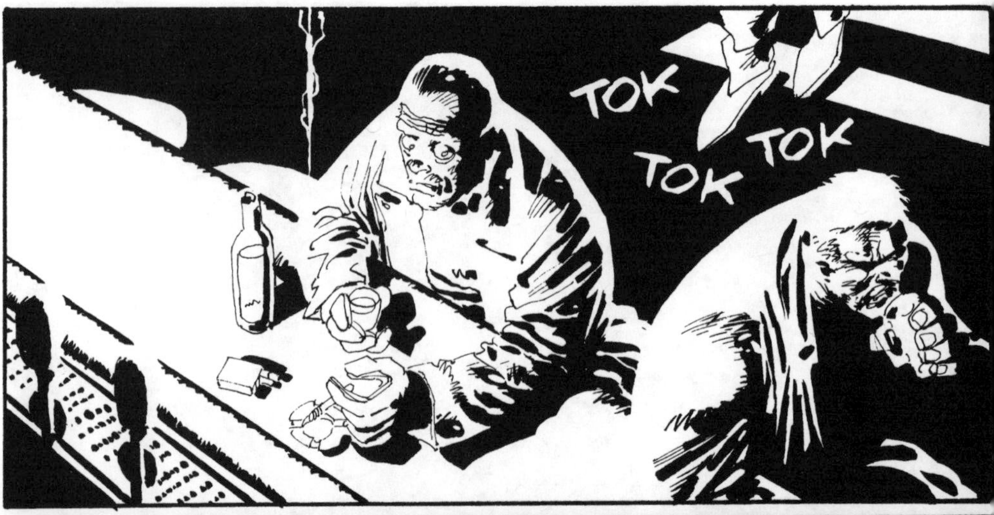
TOK
TOK TOK
TOK

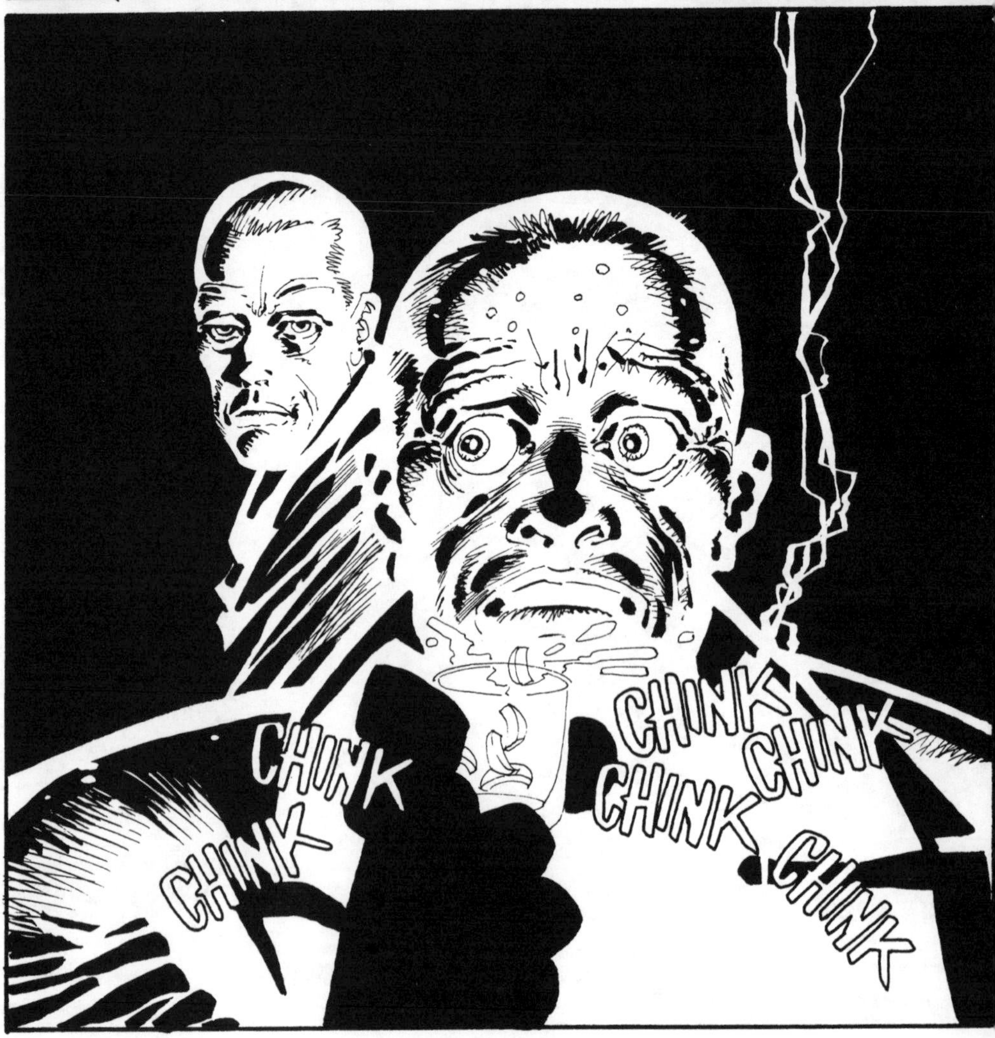
CHINK
CHINK
CHINK
CHINK
CHINK
CHINK

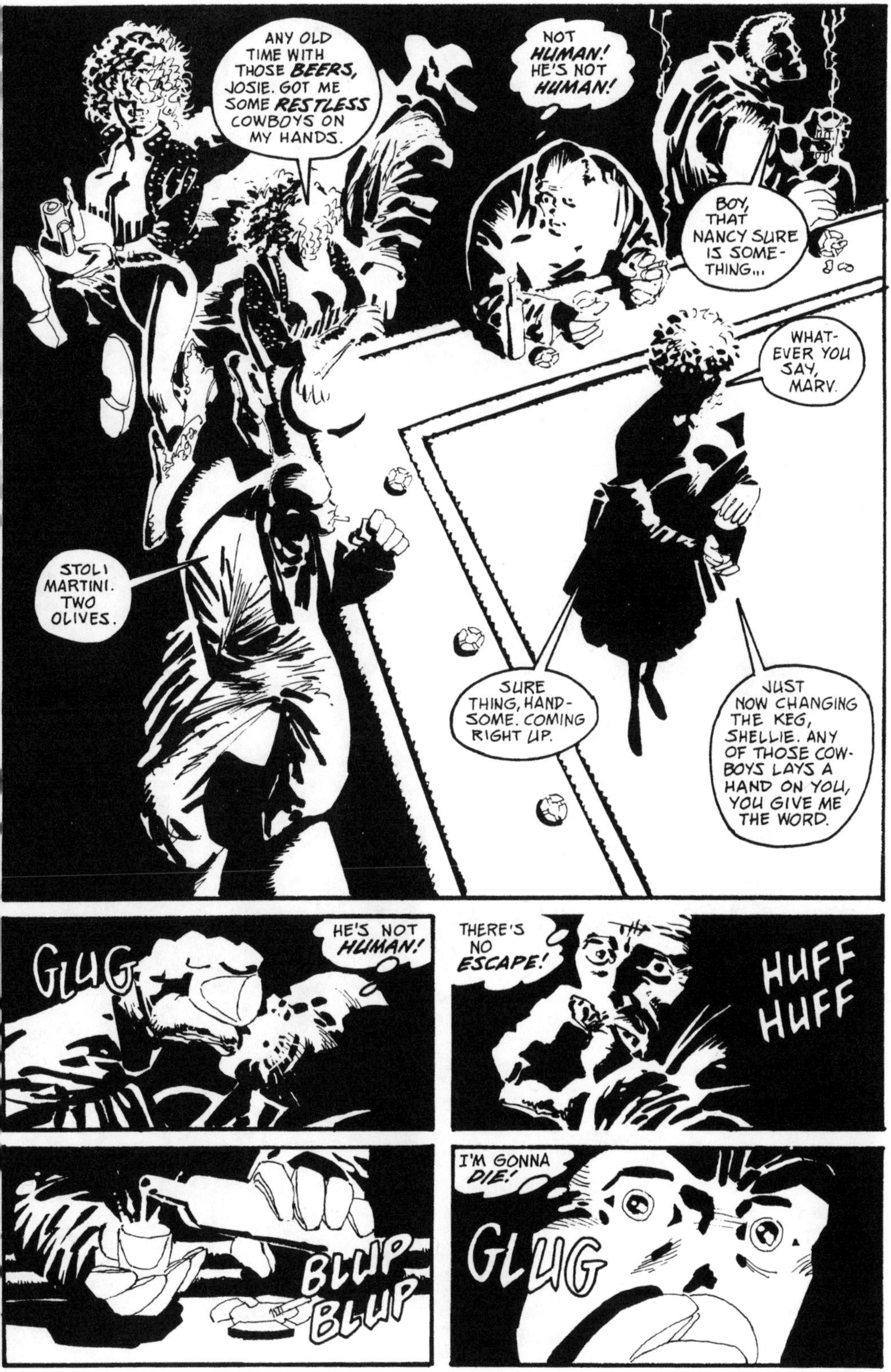
ANY OLD TIME WITH THOSE BEERS, JOSIE. GOT ME SOME RESTLESS COWBOYS ON MY HANDS.
NOT HUMAN! HE'S NOT HUMAN!
BOY, THAT NANCY SURE IS SOME-THING...
WHAT-EVER YOU SAY, MARV.
STOLI MARTINI. TWO OLIVES.
SURE THING, HAND-SOME. COMING RIGHT UP.
JUST NOW CHANGING THE KEG, SHELLIE. ANY OF THOSE COW-BOYS LAYS A HAND ON YOU, YOU GIVE ME THE WORD.
GLUG
HE'S NOT HUMAN!
THERE'S NO ESCAPE!
HUFF HUFF
BLUP BLUP
I'M GONNA DIE!
GLUG

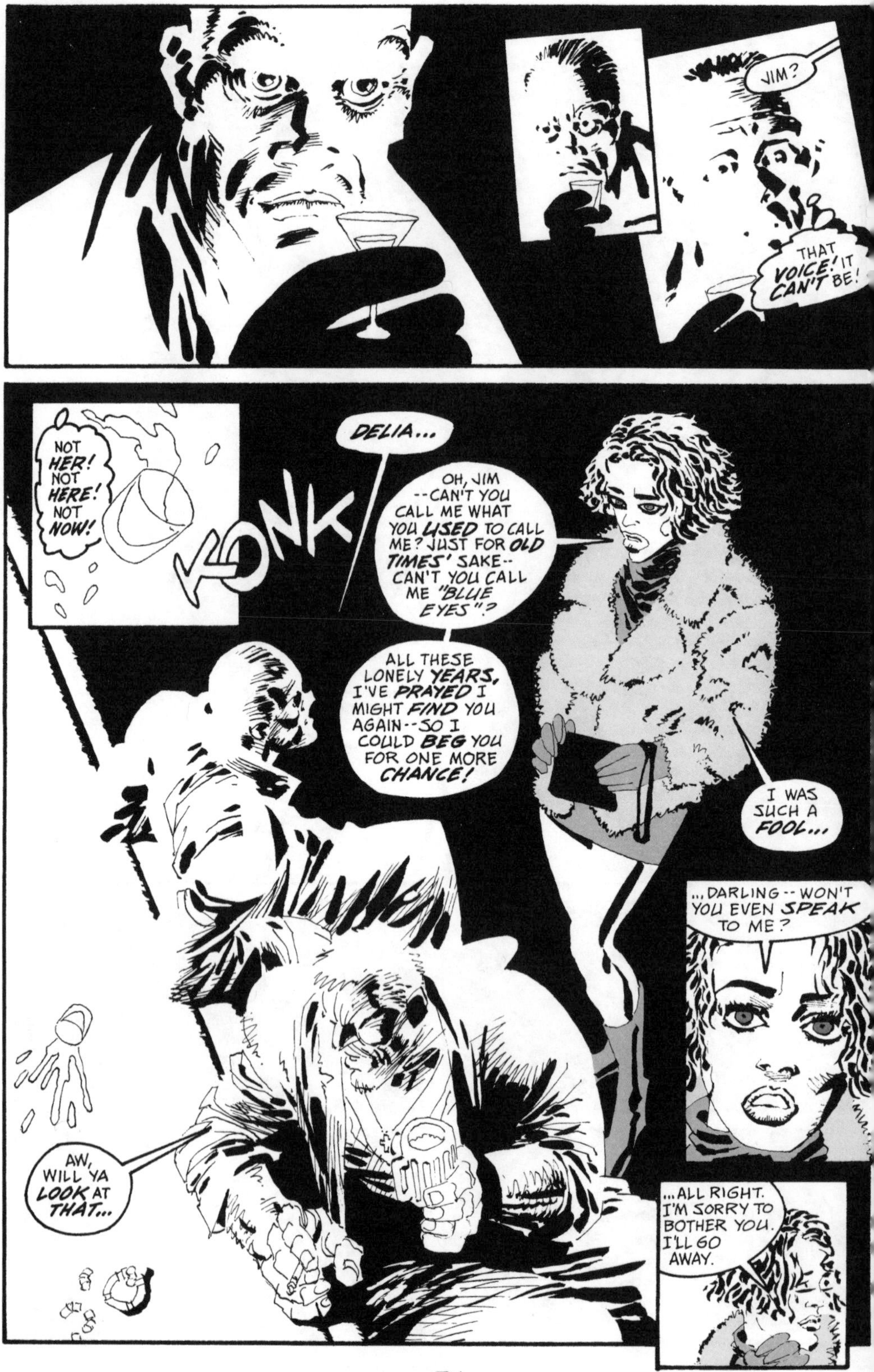
JIM?
THAT VOICE! IT CAN'T BE!
NOT HER! NOT HERE! NOT NOW!
KONK
DELIA...
OH, JIM --CAN'T YOU CALL ME WHAT YOU USED TO CALL ME? JUST FOR OLD TIMES' SAKE-- CAN'T YOU CALL ME "BLUE EYES"?
ALL THESE LONELY YEARS, I'VE PRAYED I MIGHT FIND YOU AGAIN--SO I COULD BEG YOU FOR ONE MORE CHANCE!
I WAS SUCH A FOOL...
...DARLING--WON'T YOU EVEN SPEAK TO ME?
AW, WILL YA LOOK AT THAT...
...ALL RIGHT. I'M SORRY TO BOTHER YOU. I'LL GO AWAY.

75

76

77

THE END

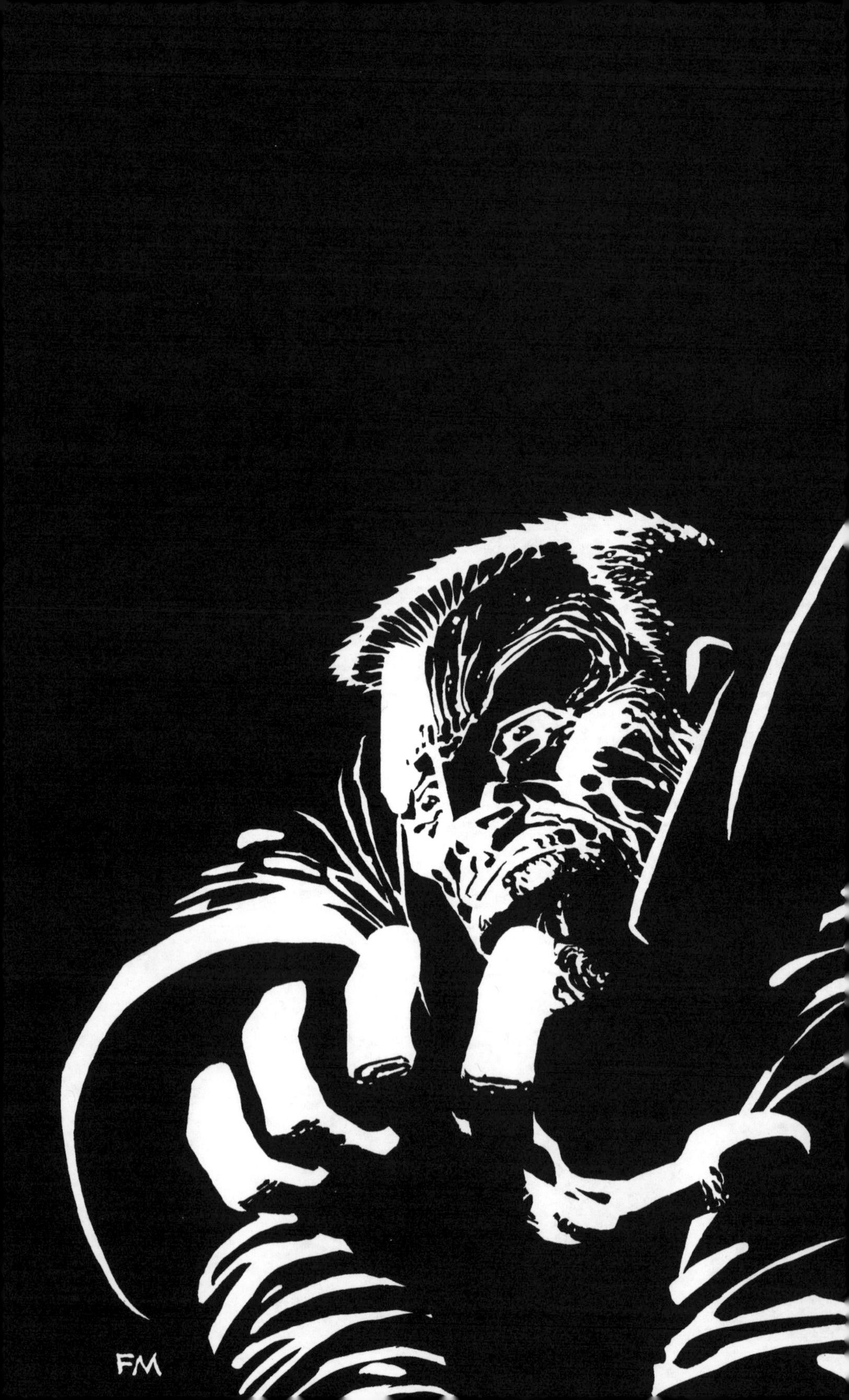
FM

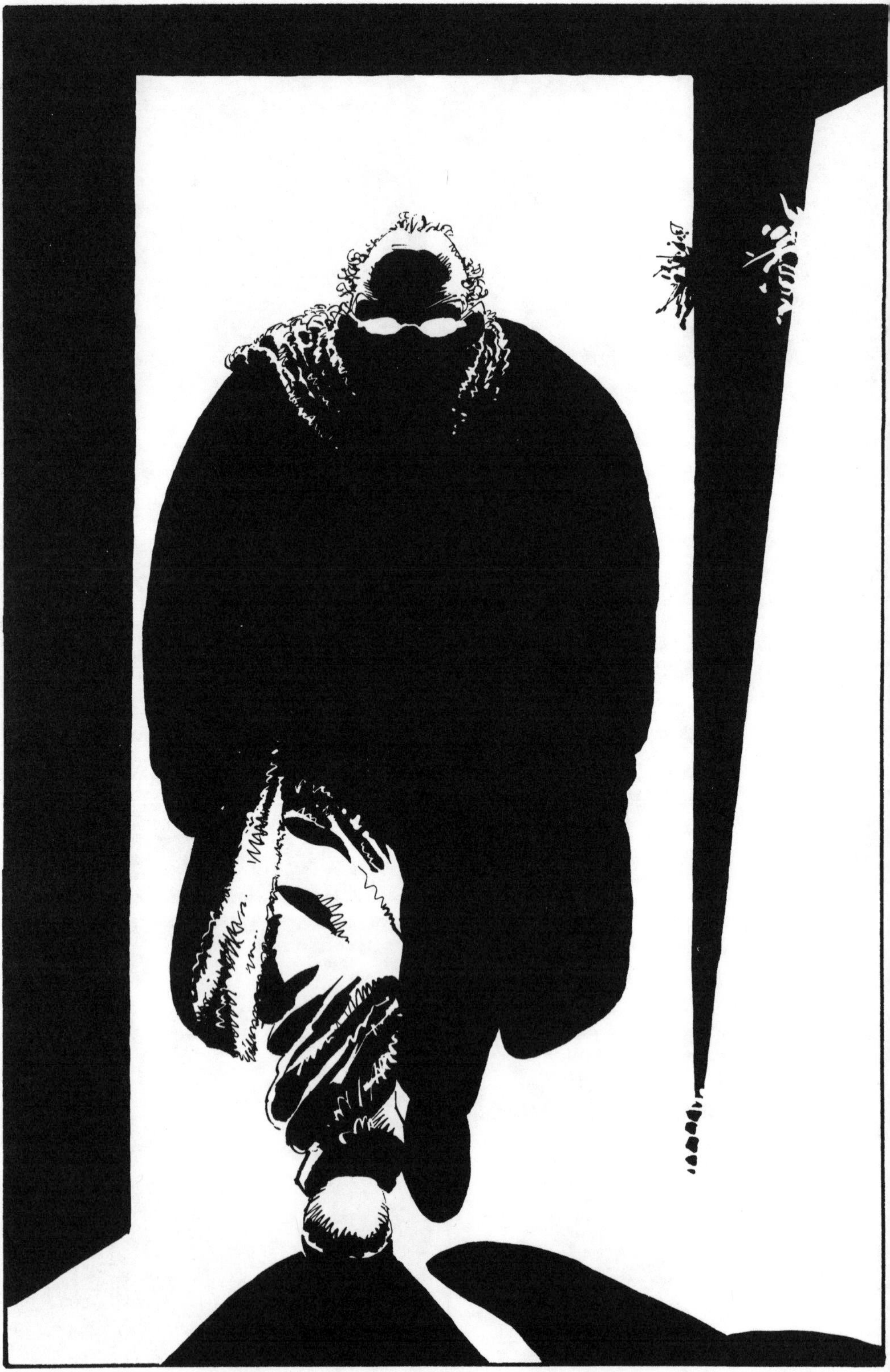

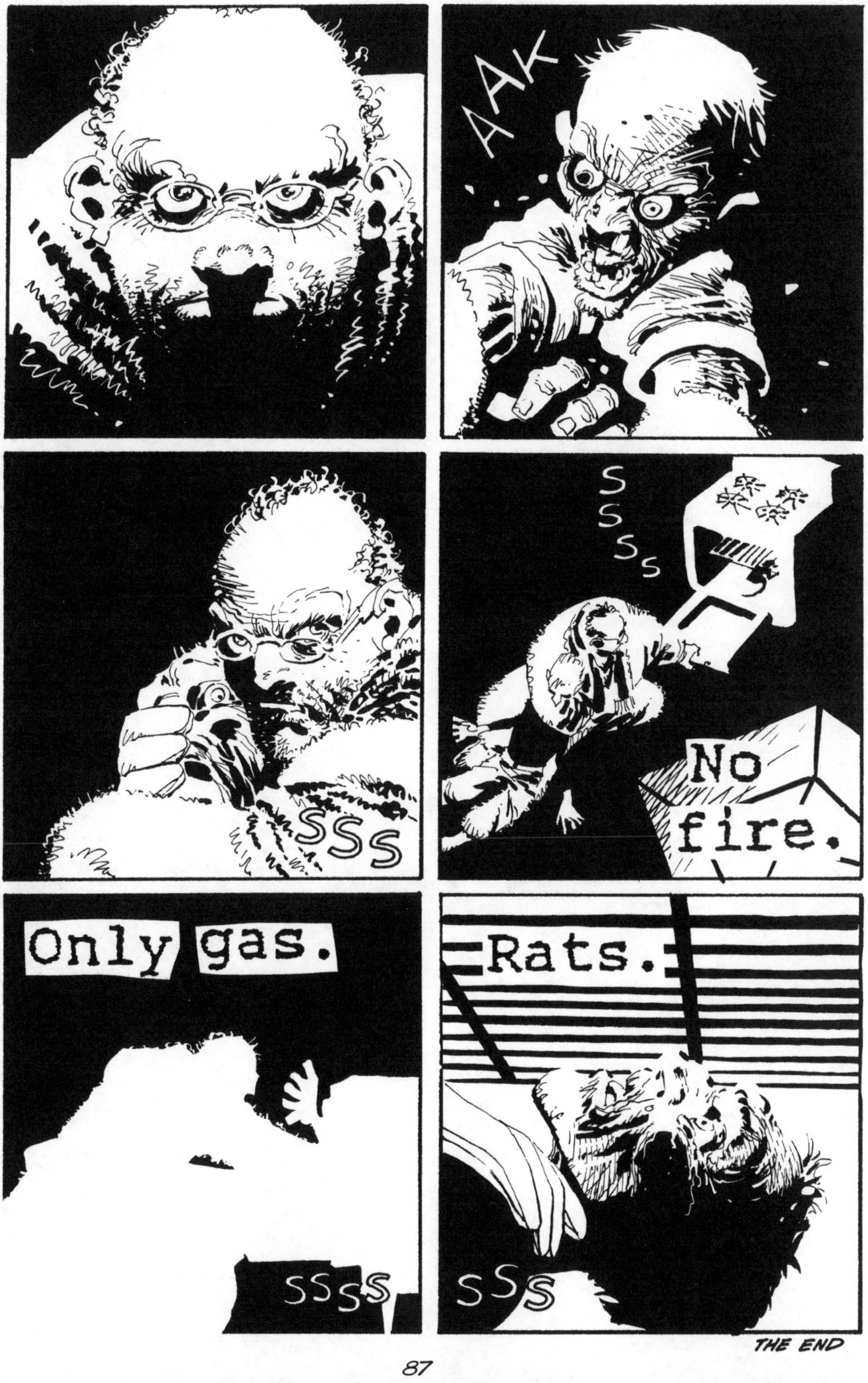
AAK
SSSS
SSS
No fire.
Only gas.
SSSS
Rats.
SSS
THE END

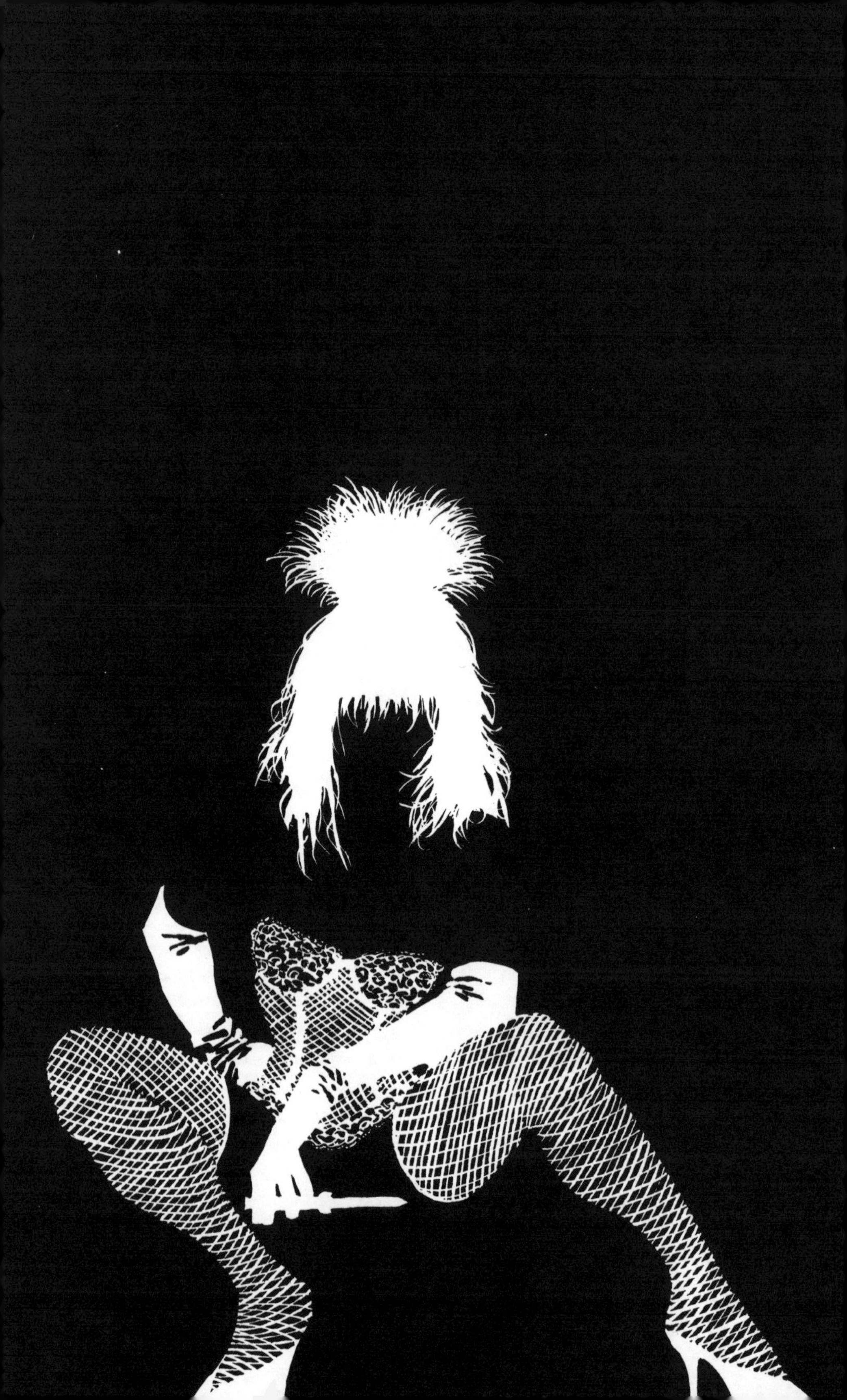

90

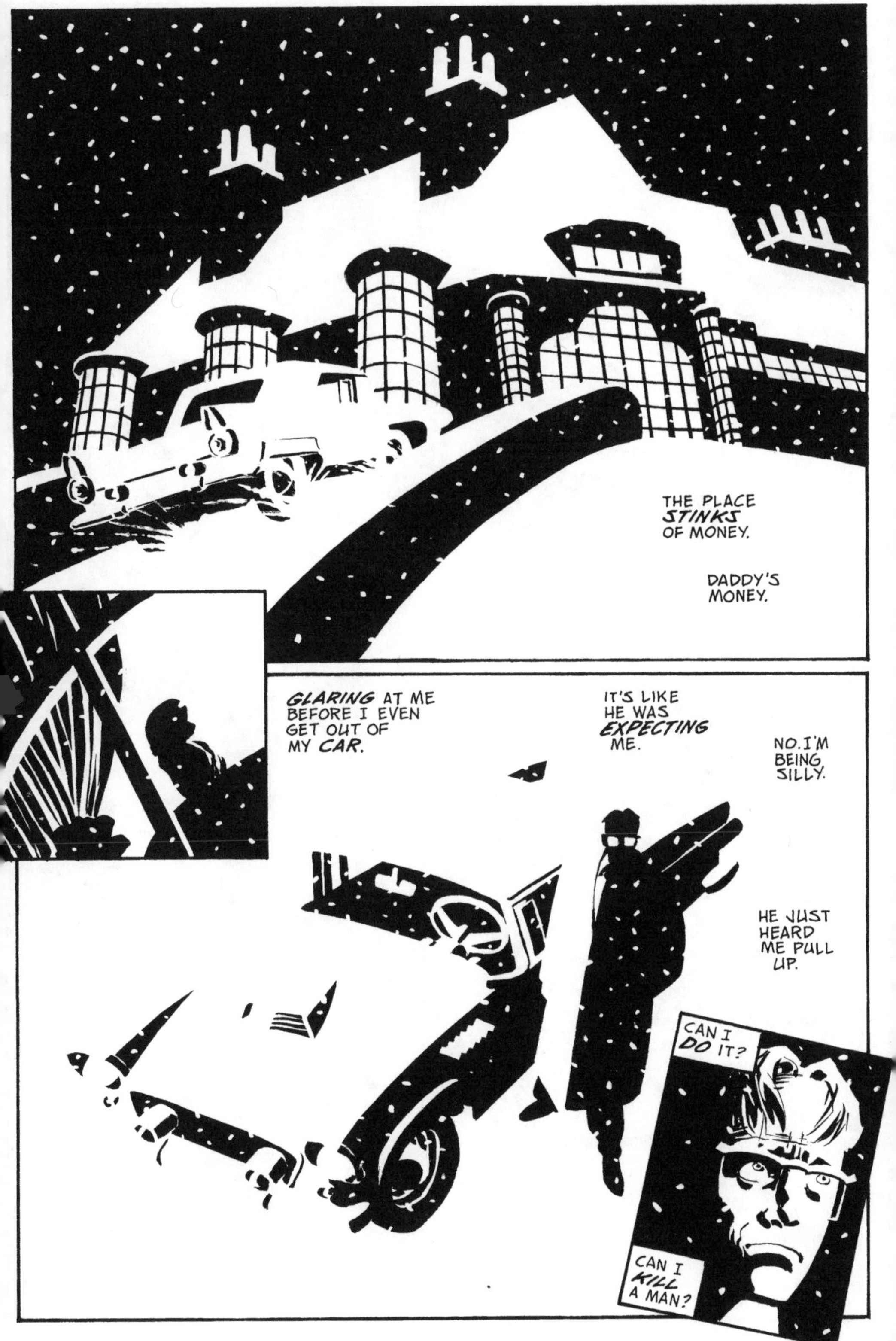
THE PLACE STINKS OF MONEY.
DADDY'S MONEY.
GLARING AT ME BEFORE I EVEN GET OUT OF MY CAR.
IT'S LIKE HE WAS EXPECTING ME.
NO. I'M BEING SILLY.
HE JUST HEARD ME PULL UP.
CAN I DO IT?
CAN I KILL A MAN?

92

94

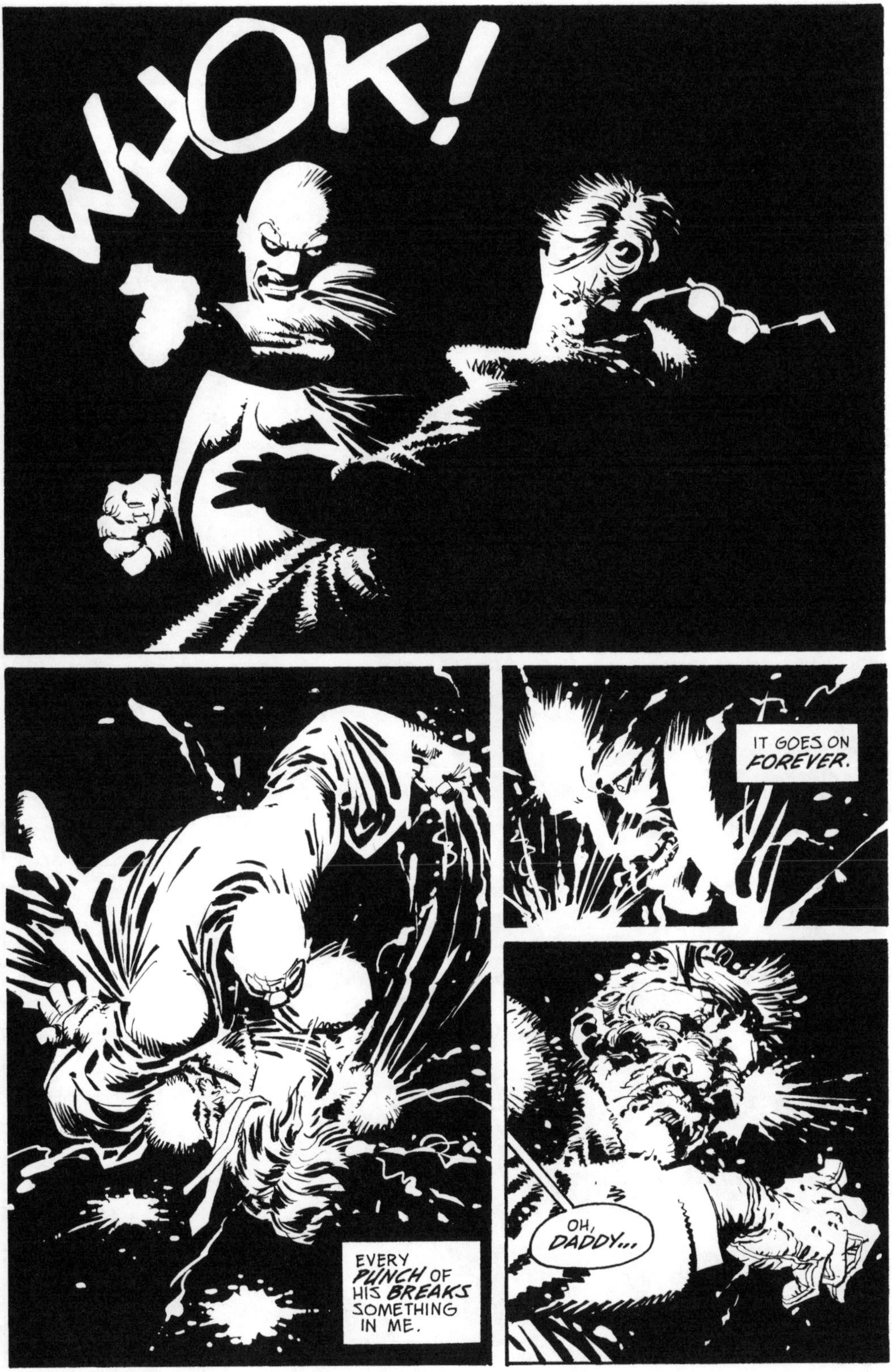
WHOK!
EVERY PUNCH OF HIS BREAKS SOMETHING IN ME.
IT GOES ON FOREVER.
OH, DADDY...

THE END

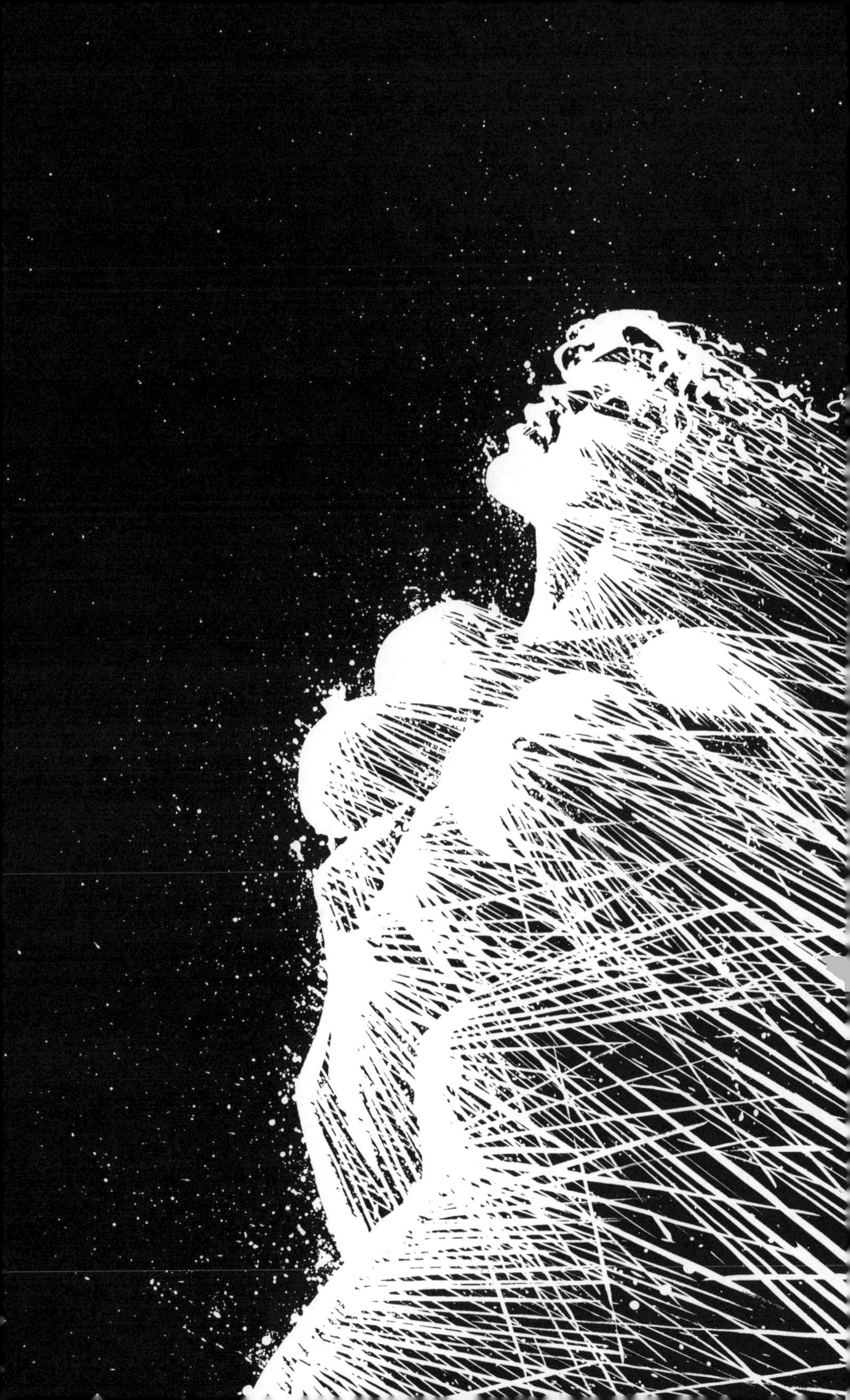

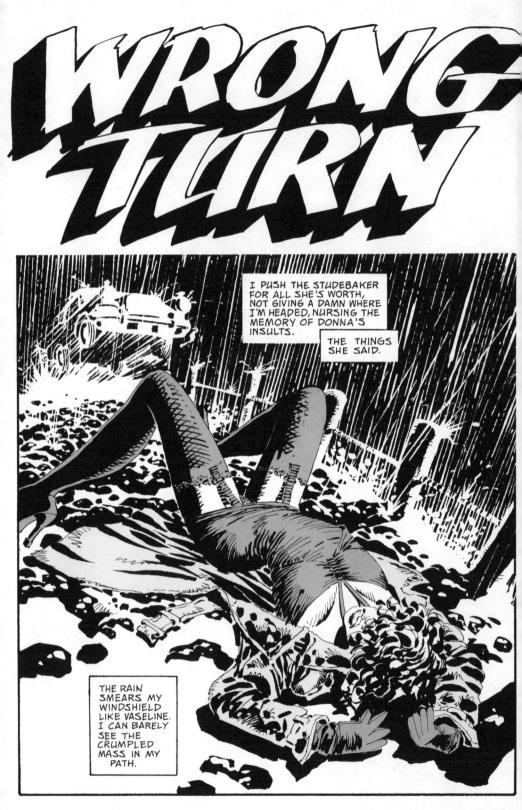

WRONG TURN

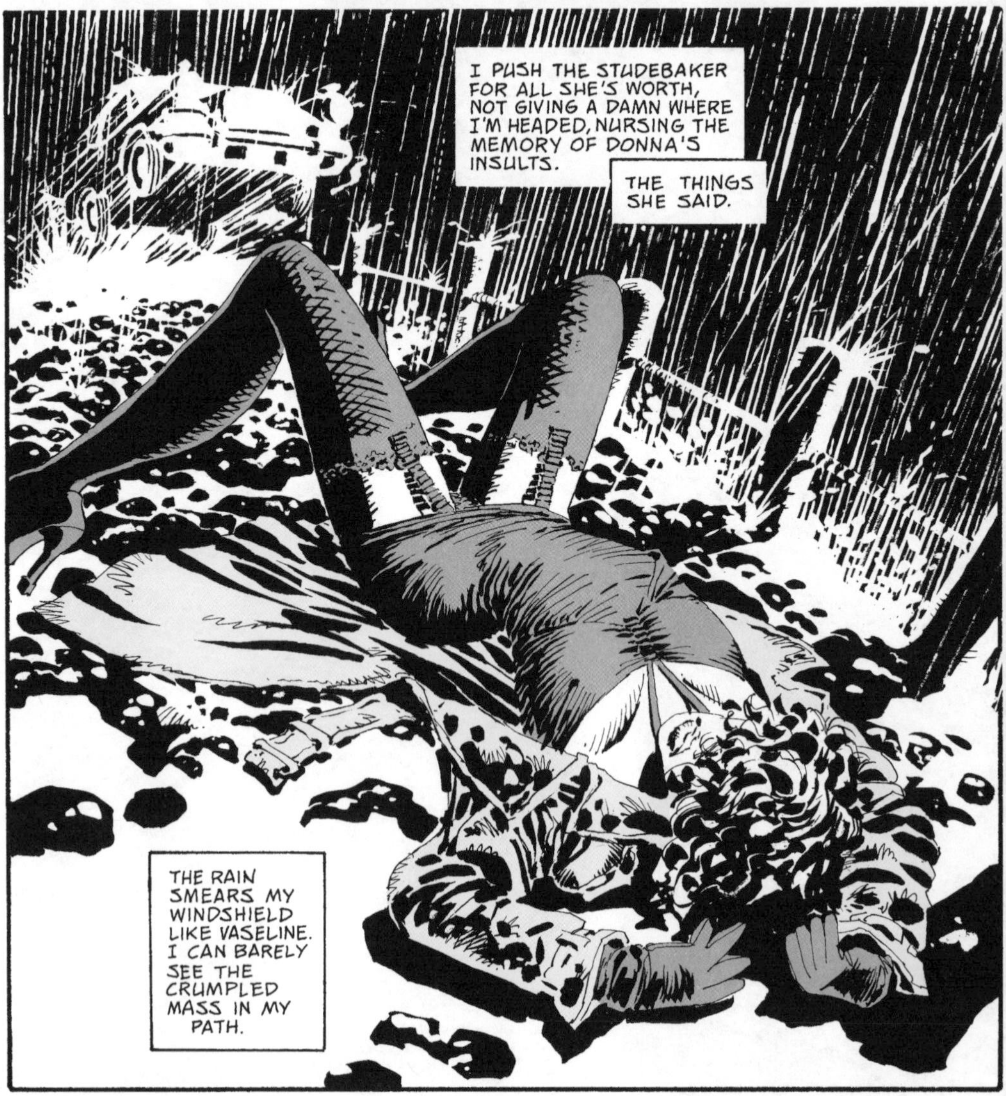
I PUSH THE STUDEBAKER FOR ALL SHE'S WORTH, NOT GIVING A DAMN WHERE I'M HEADED, NURSING THE MEMORY OF DONNA'S INSULTS.
THE THINGS SHE SAID.
THE RAIN SMEARS MY WINDSHIELD LIKE VASELINE. I CAN BARELY SEE THE CRUMPLED MASS IN MY PATH.

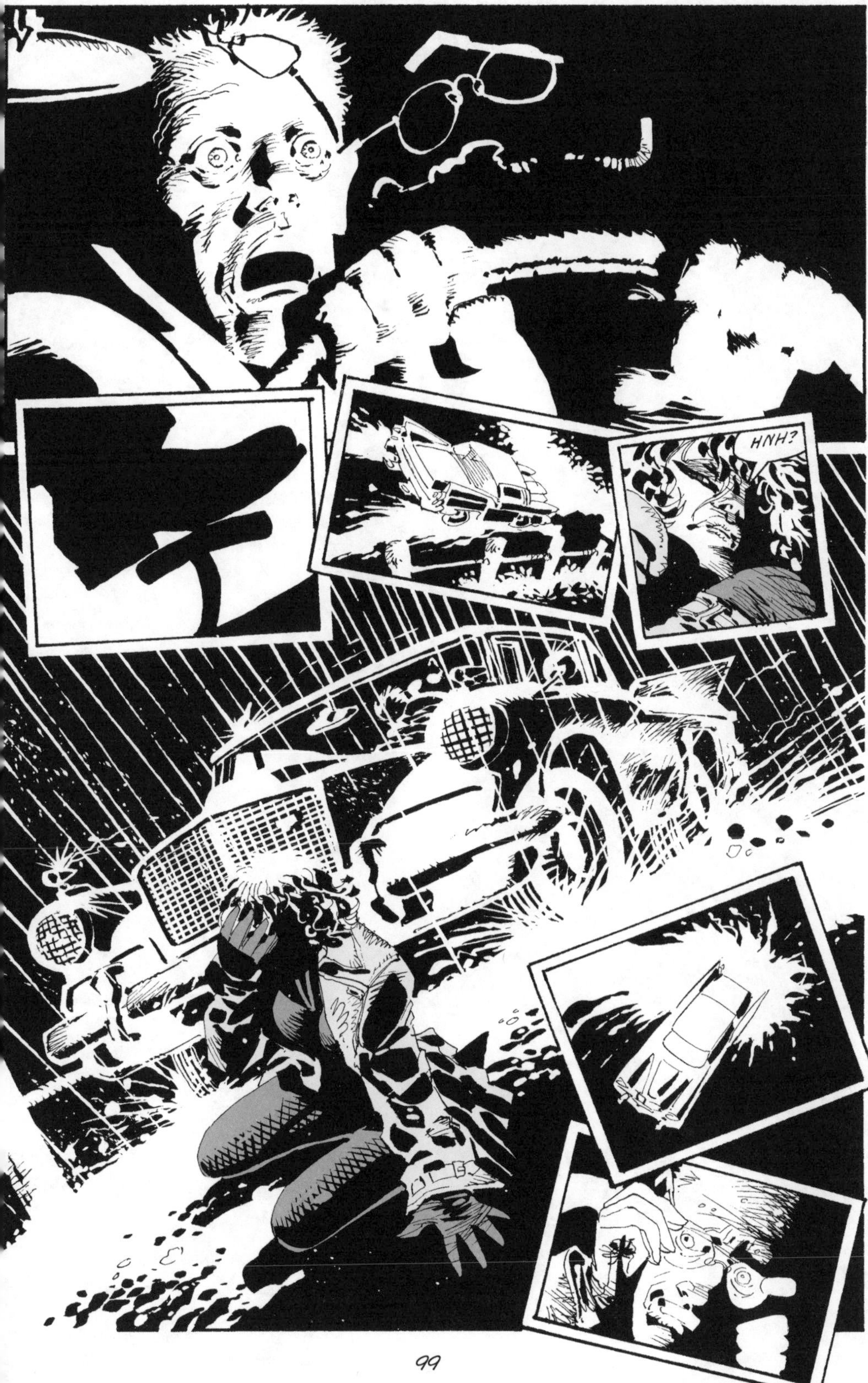
HNH?

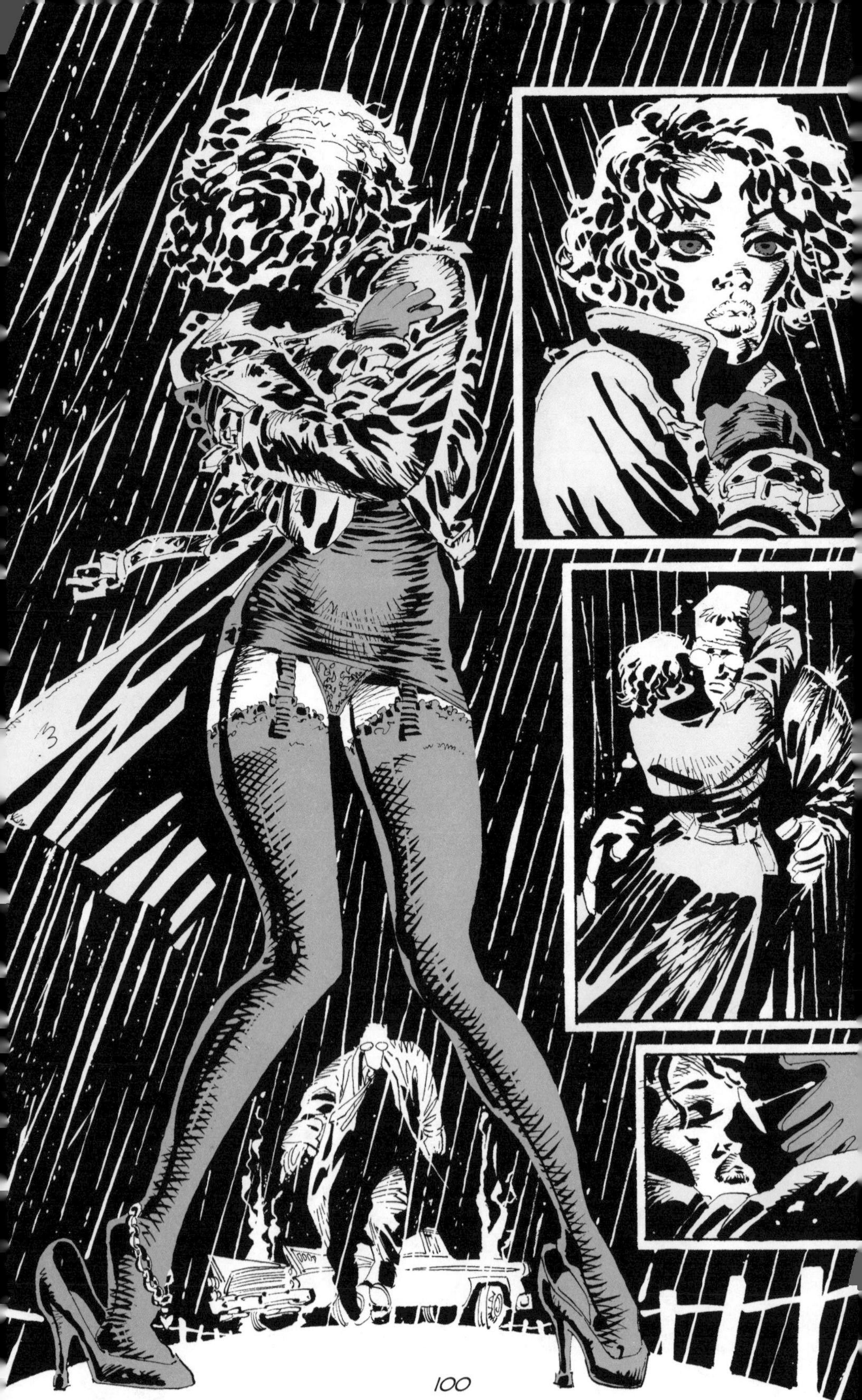

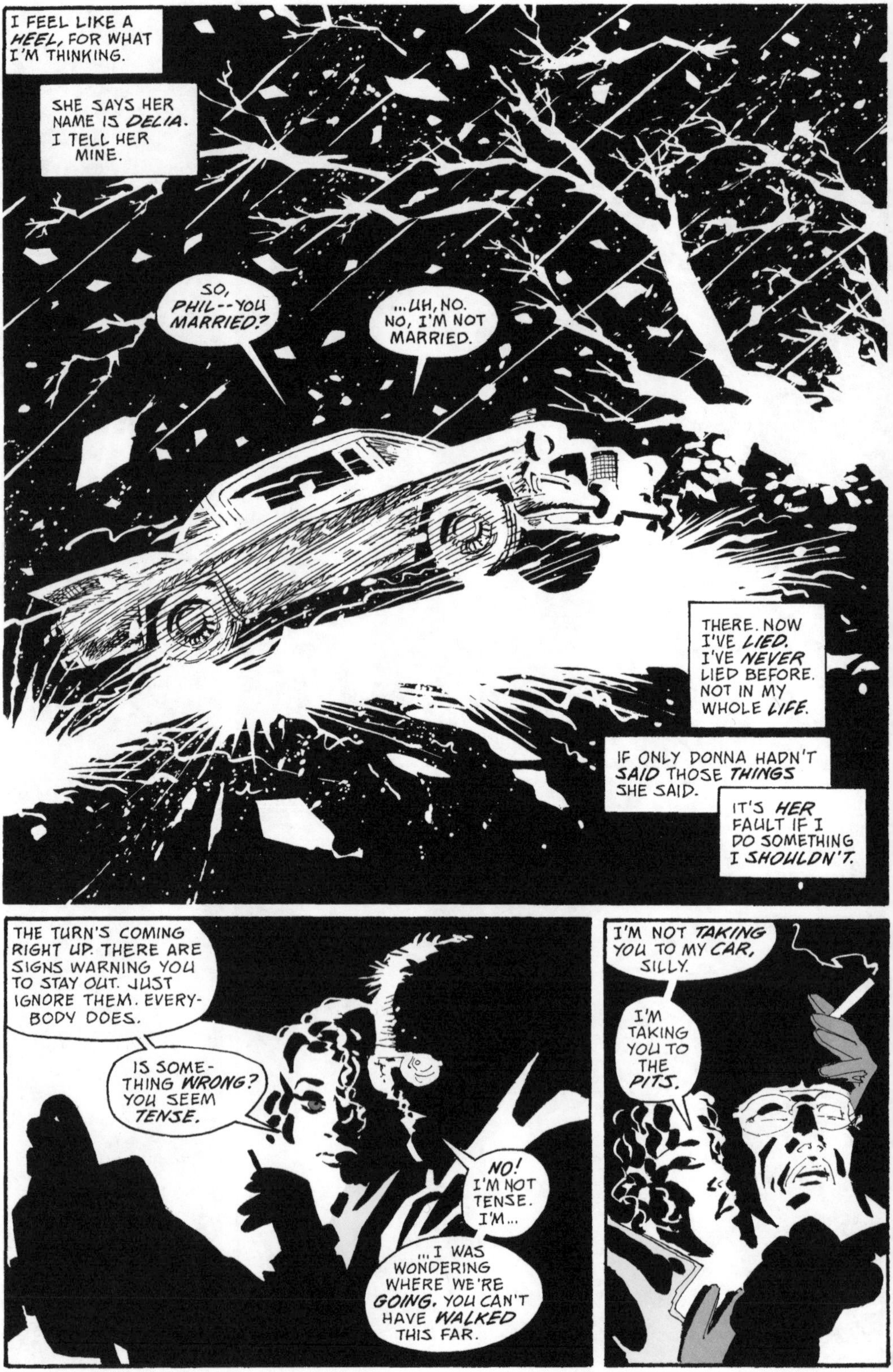
I FEEL LIKE A HEEL, FOR WHAT I'M THINKING.
SHE SAYS HER NAME IS DELIA. I TELL HER MINE.
SO, PHIL--YOU MARRIED?
...UH, NO. NO, I'M NOT MARRIED.
THERE. NOW I'VE LIED. I'VE NEVER LIED BEFORE. NOT IN MY WHOLE LIFE.
IF ONLY DONNA HADN'T SAID THOSE THINGS SHE SAID.
IT'S HER FAULT IF I DO SOMETHING I SHOULDN'T.
THE TURN'S COMING RIGHT UP. THERE ARE SIGNS WARNING YOU TO STAY OUT. JUST IGNORE THEM. EVERY-BODY DOES.
IS SOME-THING WRONG? YOU SEEM TENSE.
NO! I'M NOT TENSE. I'M...
...I WAS WONDERING WHERE WE'RE GOING. YOU CAN'T HAVE WALKED THIS FAR.
I'M NOT TAKING YOU TO MY CAR, SILLY.
I'M TAKING YOU TO THE PITS.

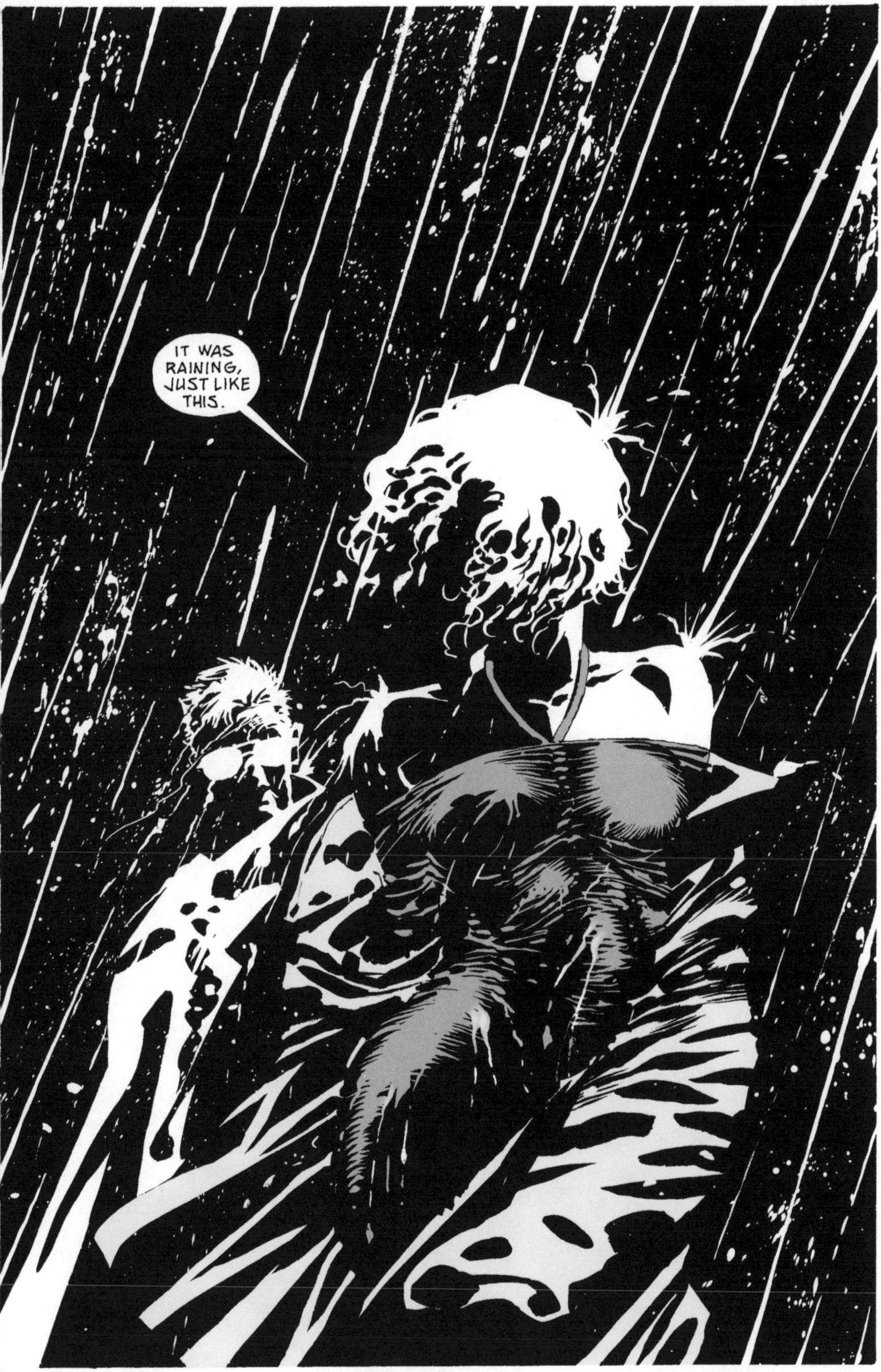
IT WAS RAINING, JUST LIKE THIS.

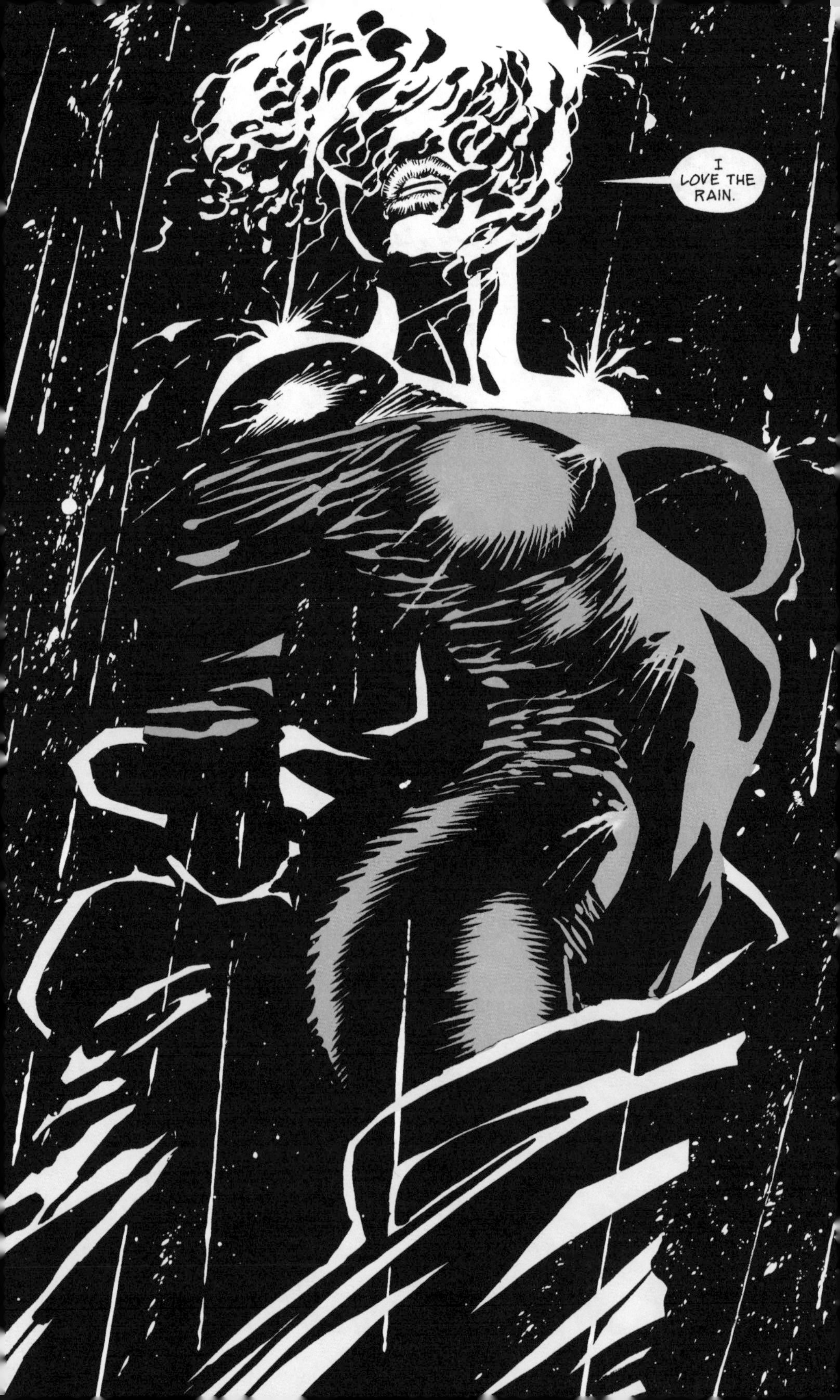
I LOVE THE RAIN.

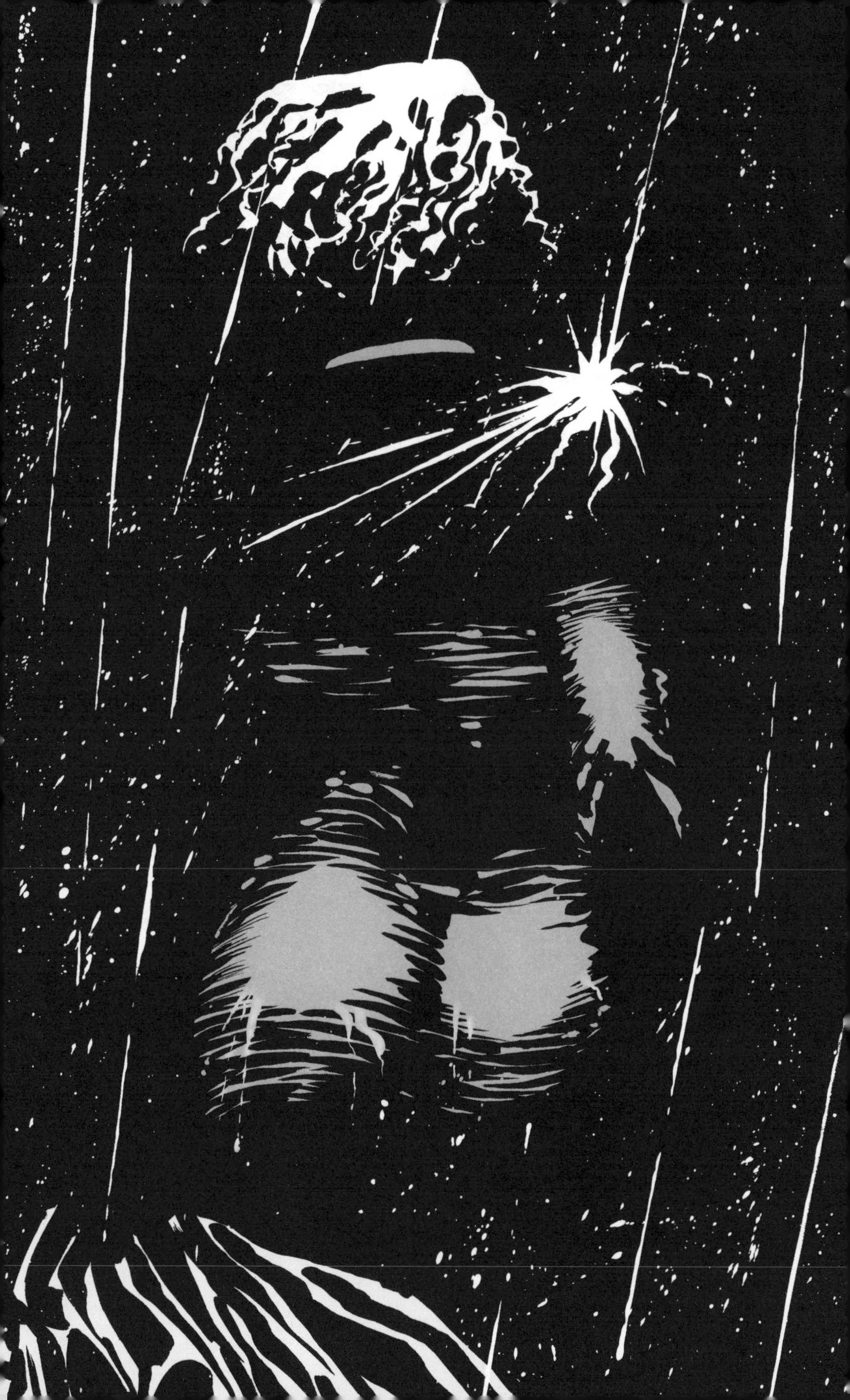

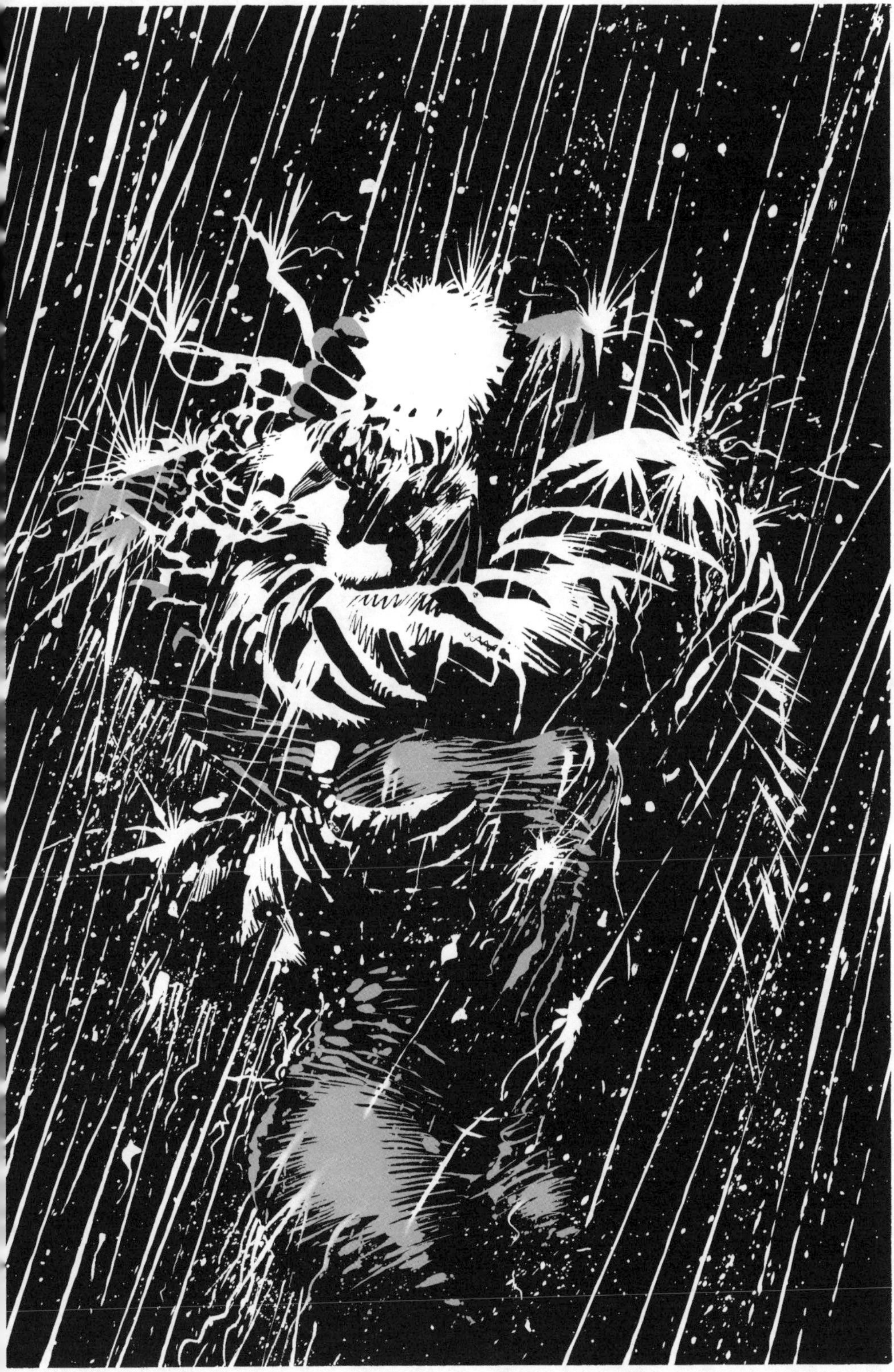

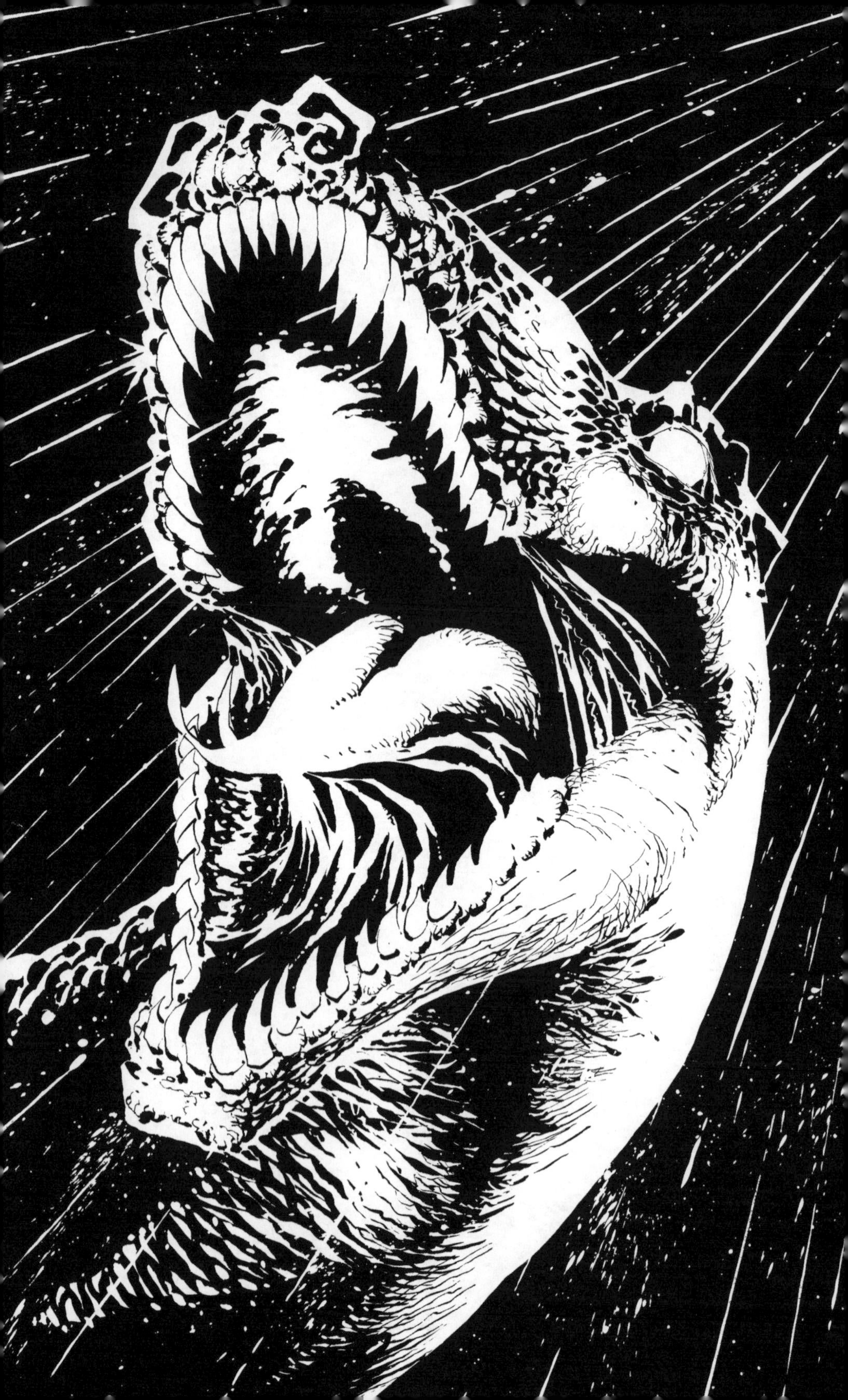

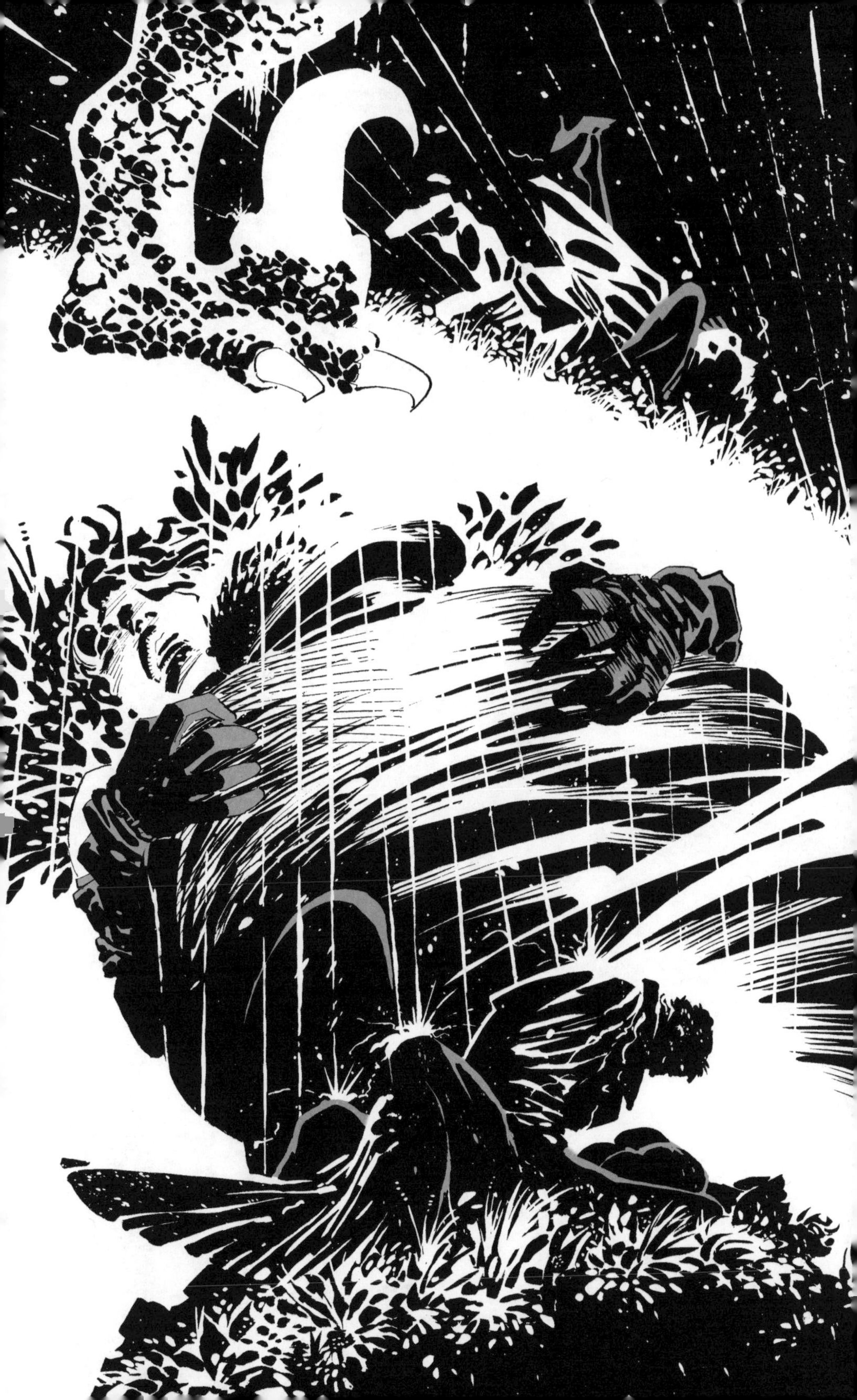

118

119

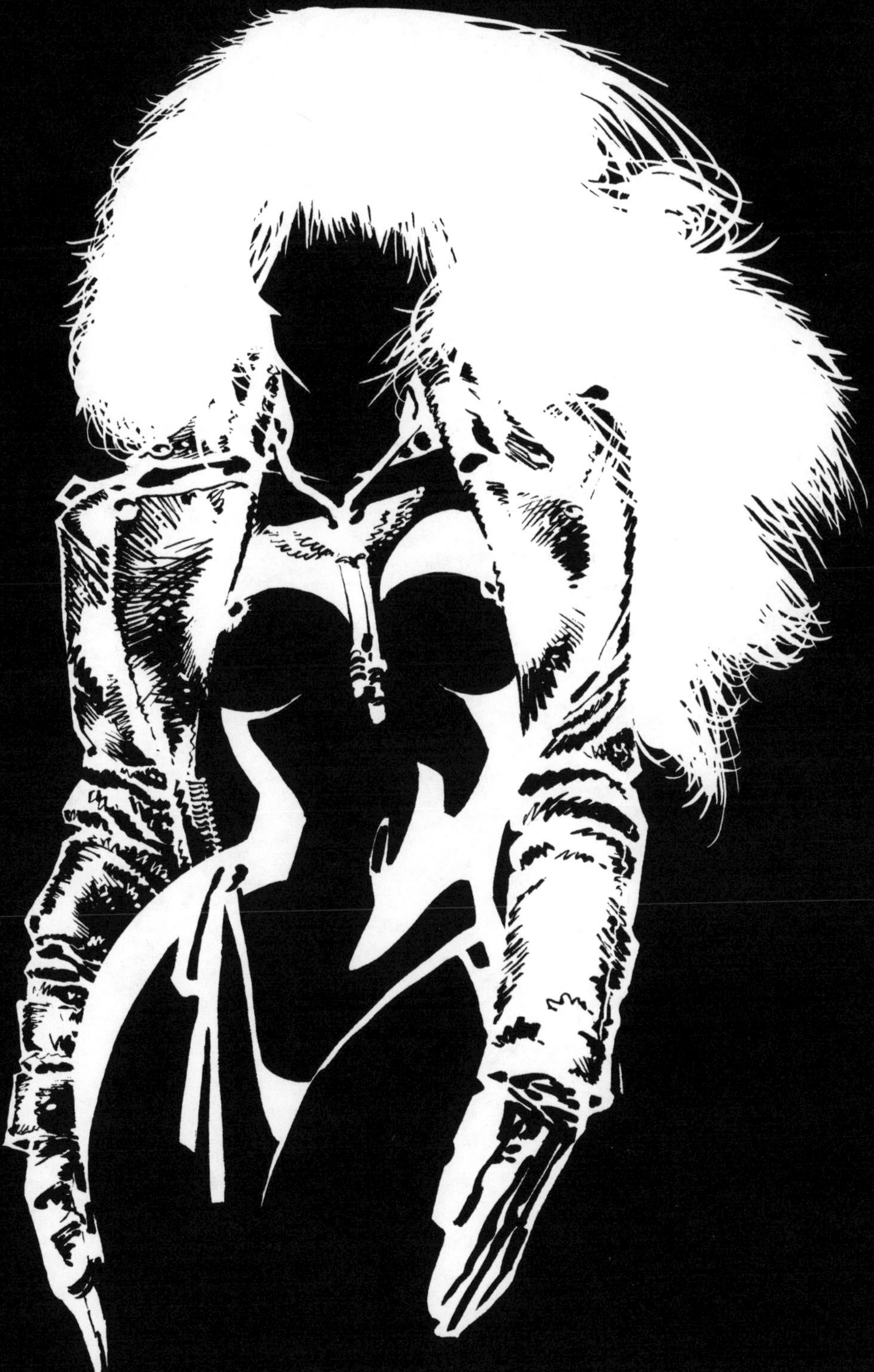

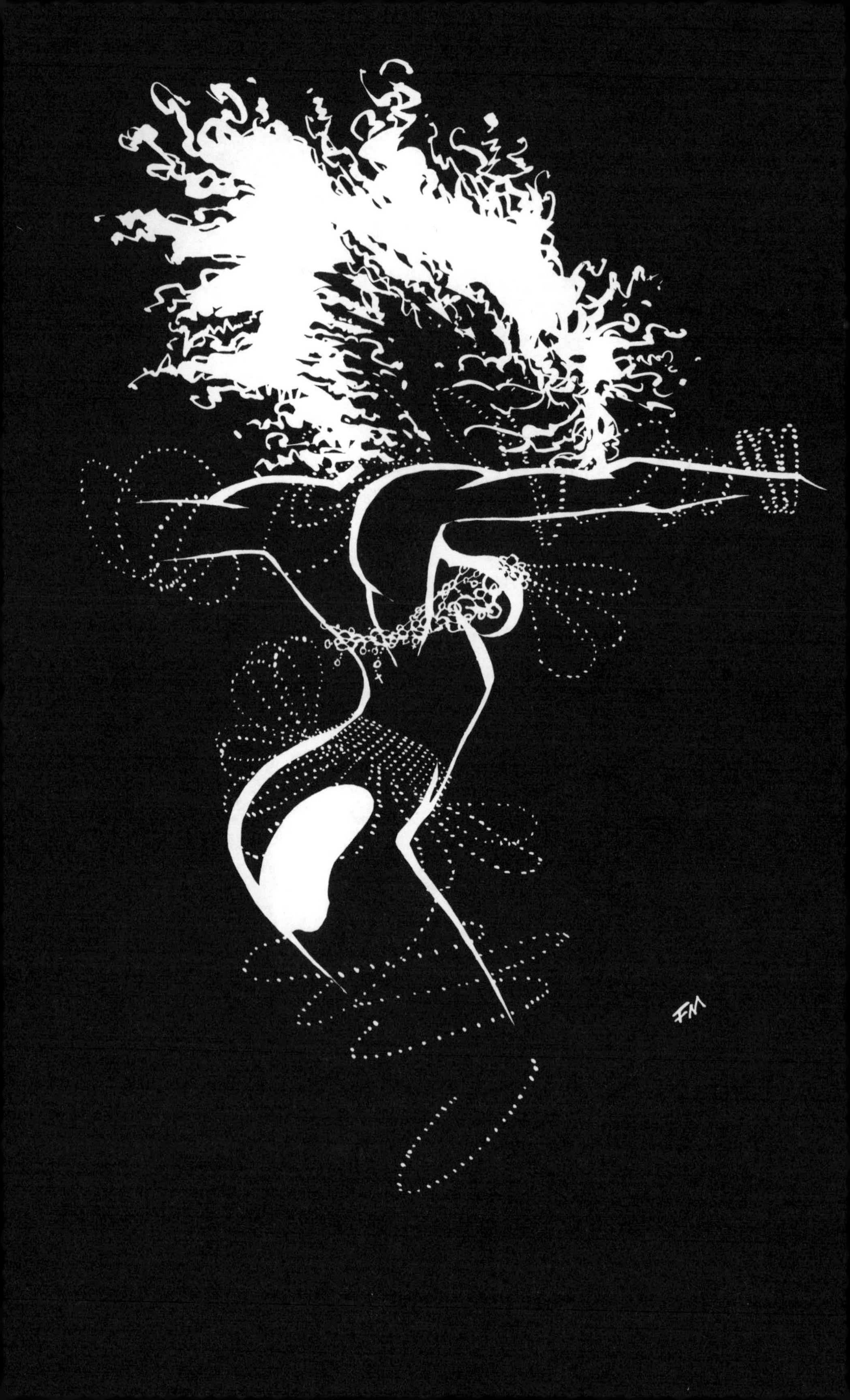

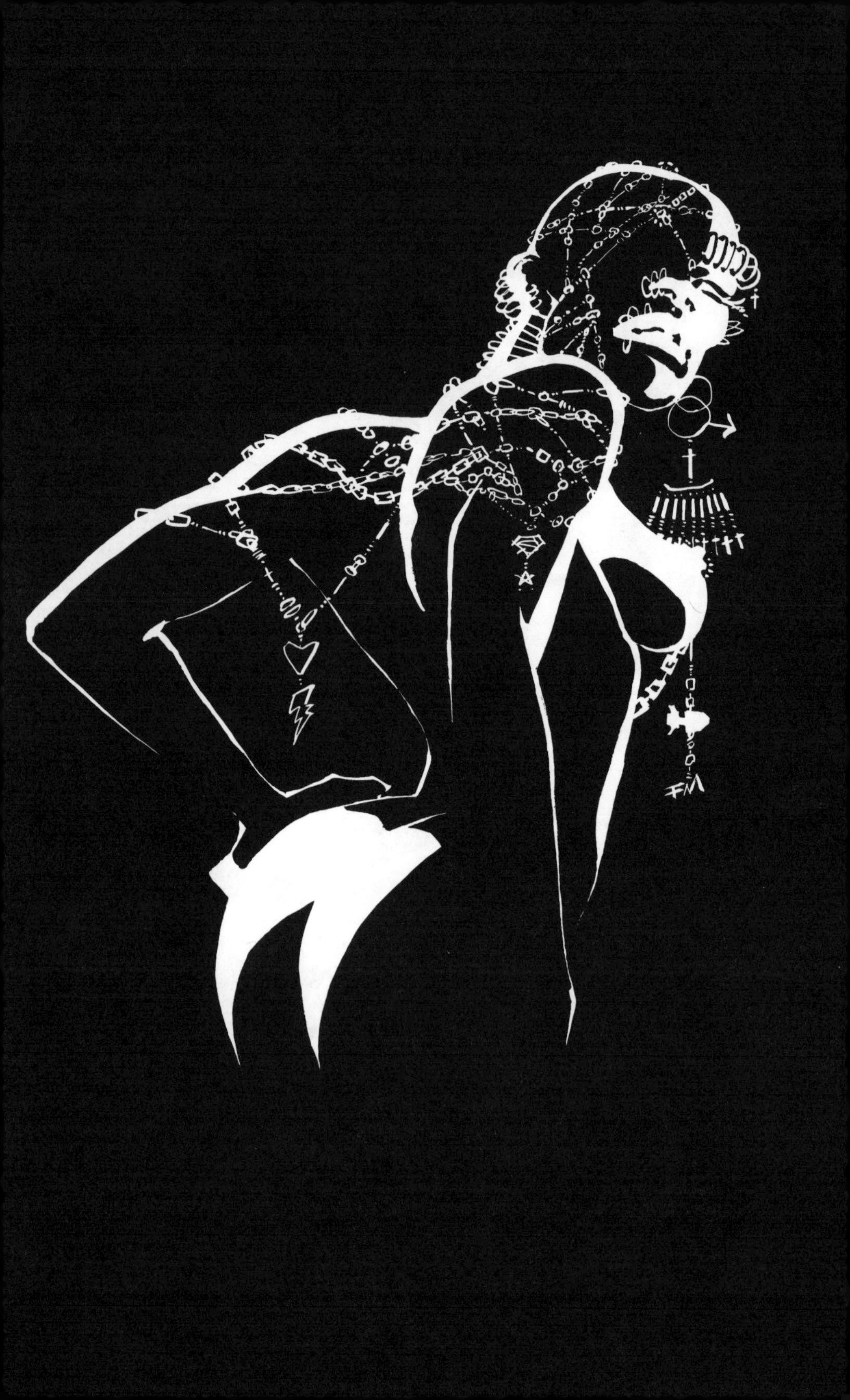
FM

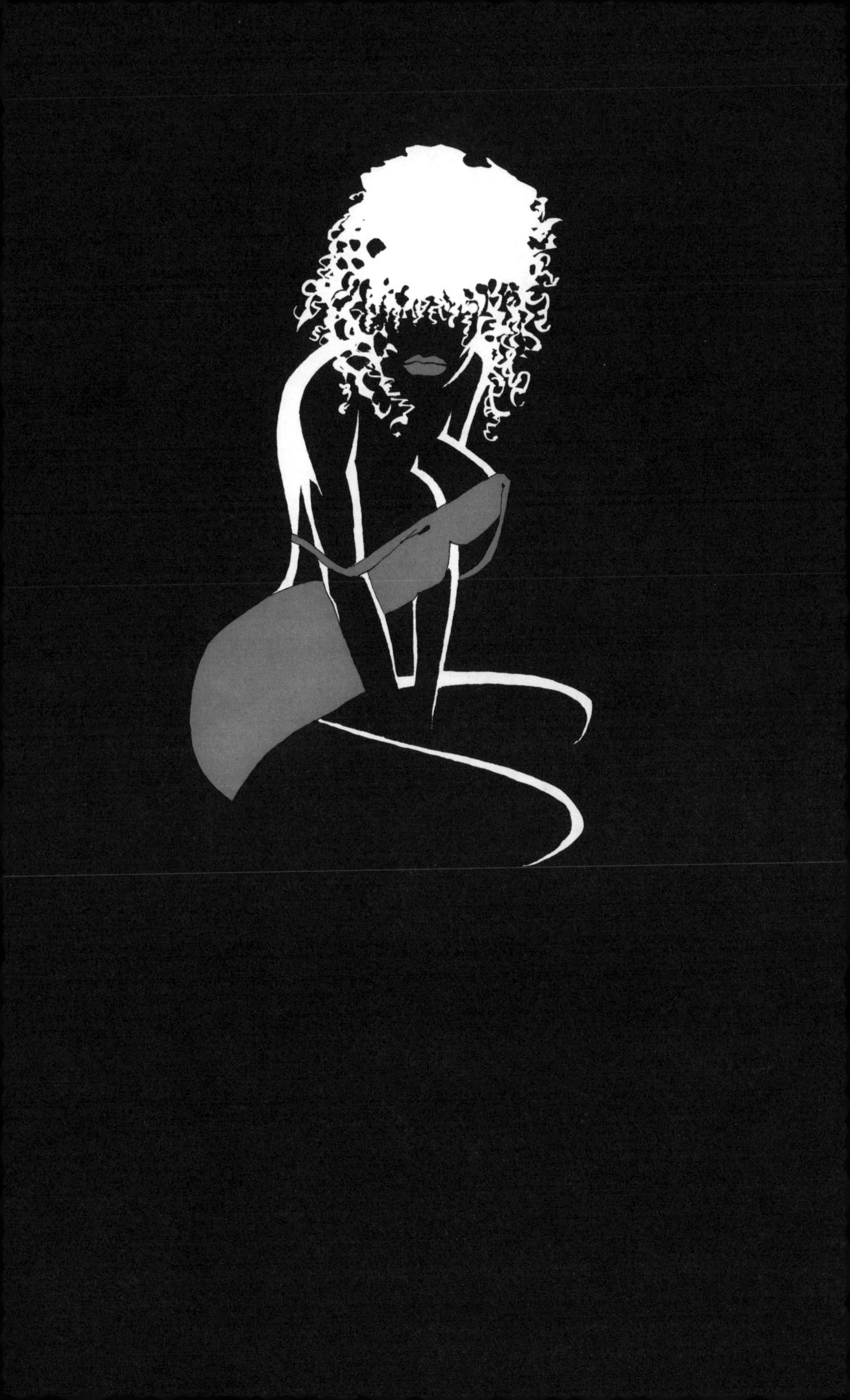

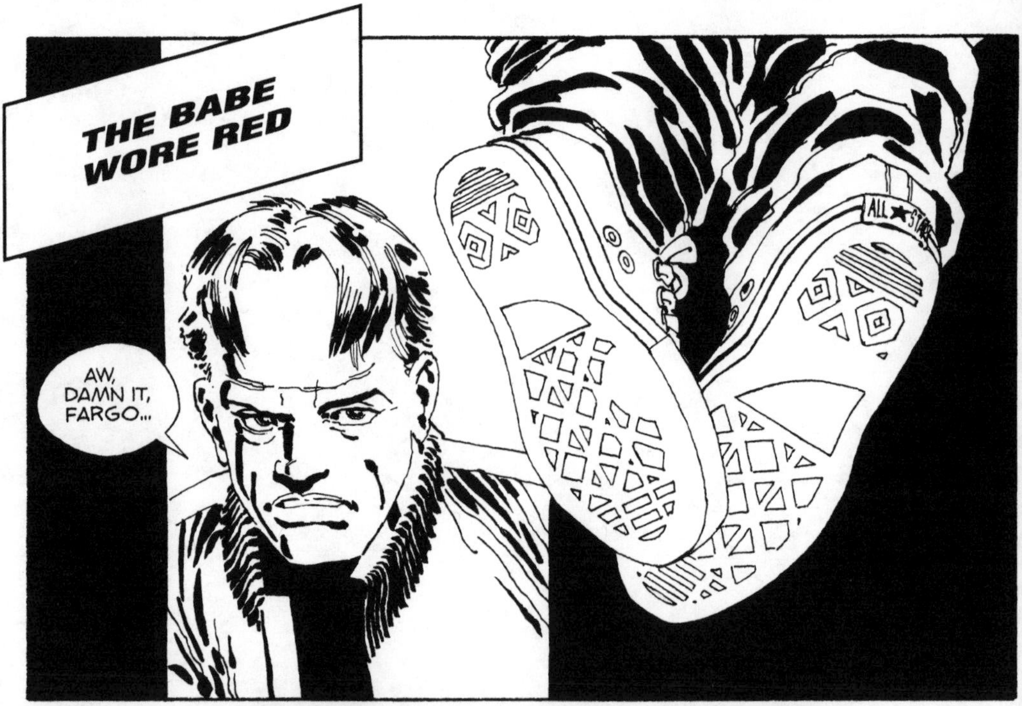
THE BABE WORE RED
AW, DAMN IT, FARGO...
ALL STARS

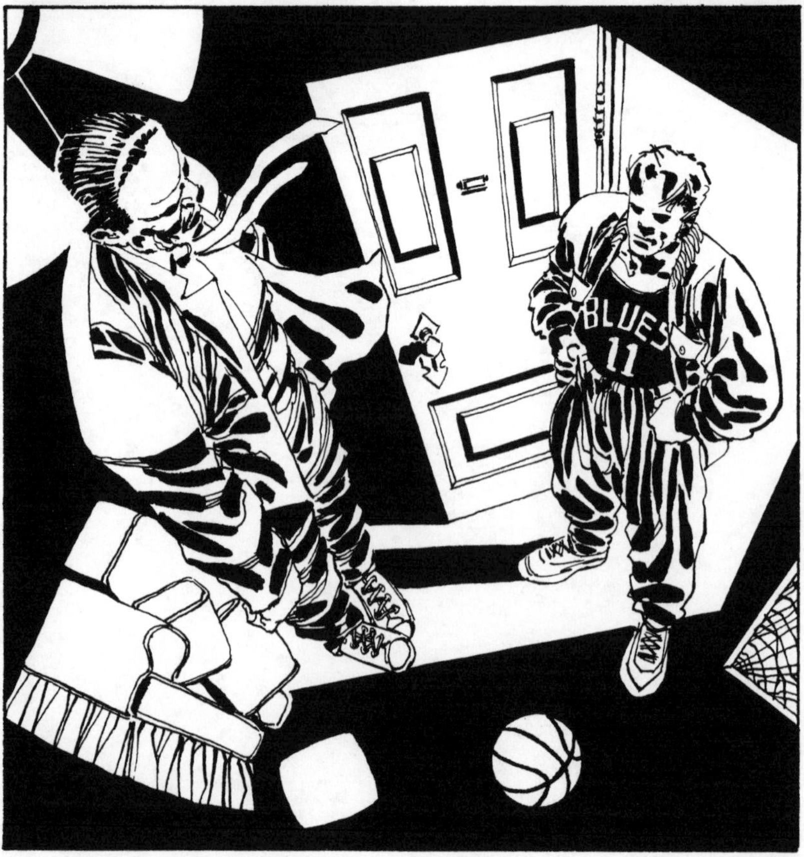
BLUES
11

HALF PAST MIDNIGHT AND MY PHONE RINGS. IT'S FARGO, IN TROUBLE AGAIN. HE WON'T SAY WHAT KIND.

I PULL MY PANTS ON AND GET TO HIS FLOP IN TEN MINUTES FLAT.

BUT BY THEN FARGO'S TROUBLES ARE OVER.

AND IT'S A SAFE BET MINE ARE JUST GETTING STARTED.

FOR A WHILE I JUST STAND THERE LIKE AN IDIOT, WATCHING HIM SPIN. THE POOR SCHMUCK ...

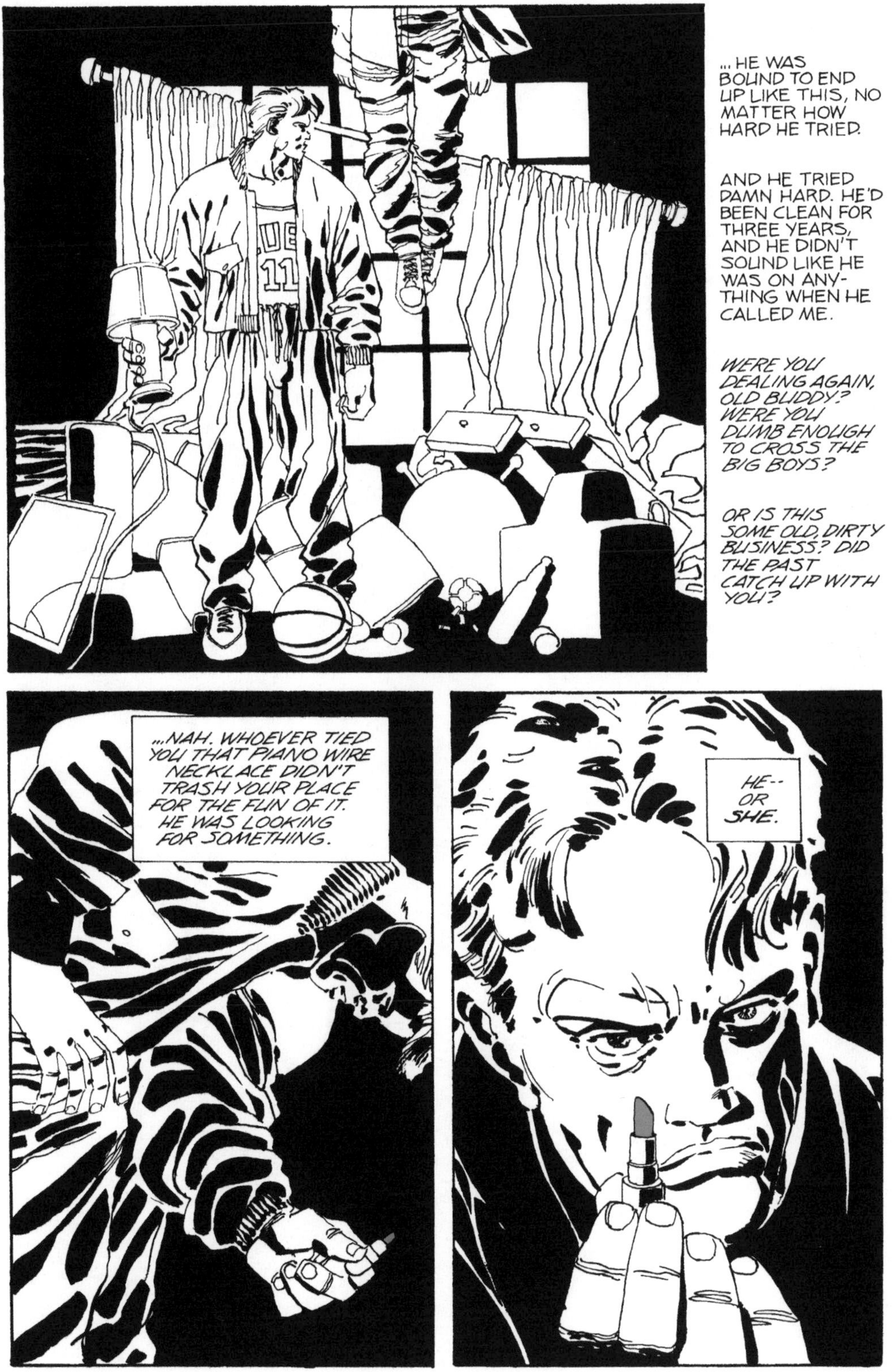
...HE WAS BOUND TO END UP LIKE THIS, NO MATTER HOW HARD HE TRIED.
AND HE TRIED DAMN HARD. HE'D BEEN CLEAN FOR THREE YEARS, AND HE DIDN'T SOUND LIKE HE WAS ON ANYTHING WHEN HE CALLED ME.
WERE YOU DEALING AGAIN, OLD BUDDY? WERE YOU DUMB ENOUGH TO CROSS THE BIG BOYS?
OR IS THIS SOME OLD, DIRTY BUSINESS? DID THE PAST CATCH UP WITH YOU?
...NAH. WHOEVER TIED YOU THAT PIANO WIRE NECKLACE DIDN'T TRASH YOUR PLACE FOR THE FUN OF IT. HE WAS LOOKING FOR SOMETHING.
HE-- OR SHE.

...NAH. THERE MAY HAVE BEEN A DAME HERE, BUT LIFTING FARGO AND STRINGING HIM UP LIKE THAT, THAT'S MAN'S WORK.

I WISH HE'D STOP SPINNING.

I'D TURN THE FAN OFF IF I WASN'T AFRAID THE MOMENTUM WOULD MAKE THE WIRE LOB OFF HIS HEAD.

NO HARM IN HAVING A LOOK AROUND BEFORE I CALL THE COPS.

131

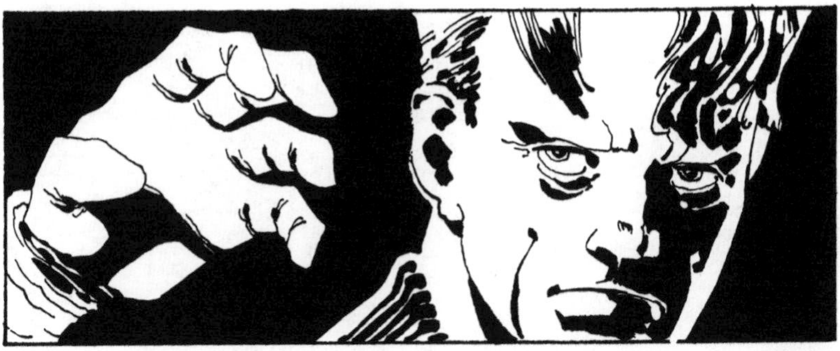

IT'S NOT THAT THE JERK SNEAKING UP ON ME MAKES ANY *NOISE*. IT'S WHAT HE HAD FOR *DINNER*.

HE *STINKS* OF *EGG SALAD*.

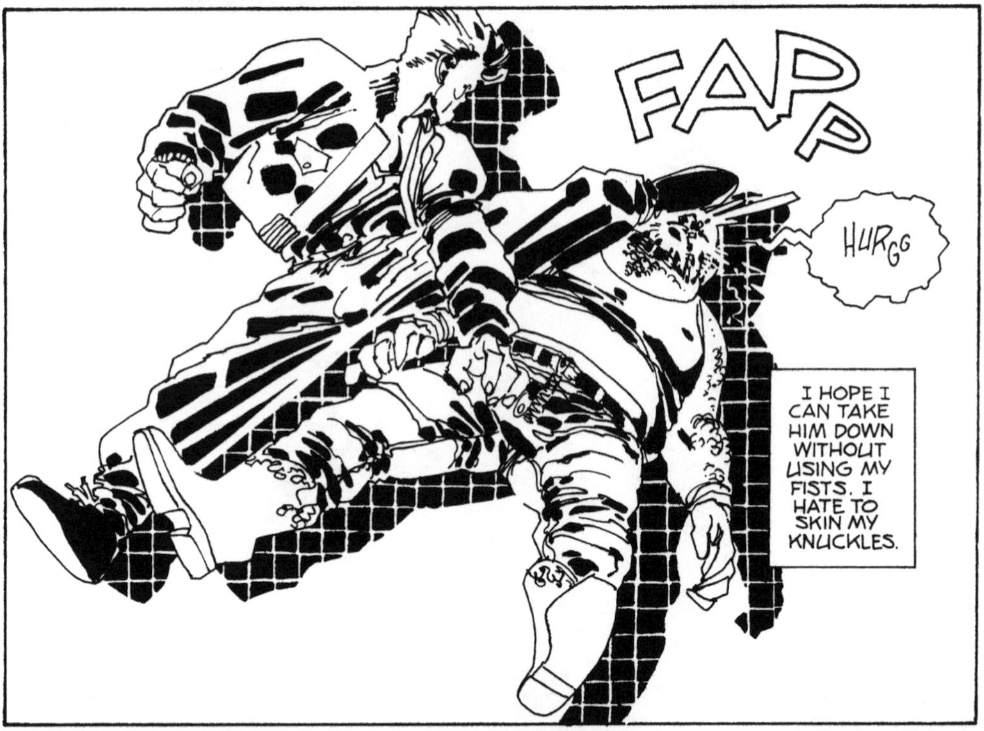
FAPP
HURGG
I HOPE I CAN TAKE HIM DOWN WITHOUT USING MY FISTS. I HATE TO SKIN MY KNUCKLES.

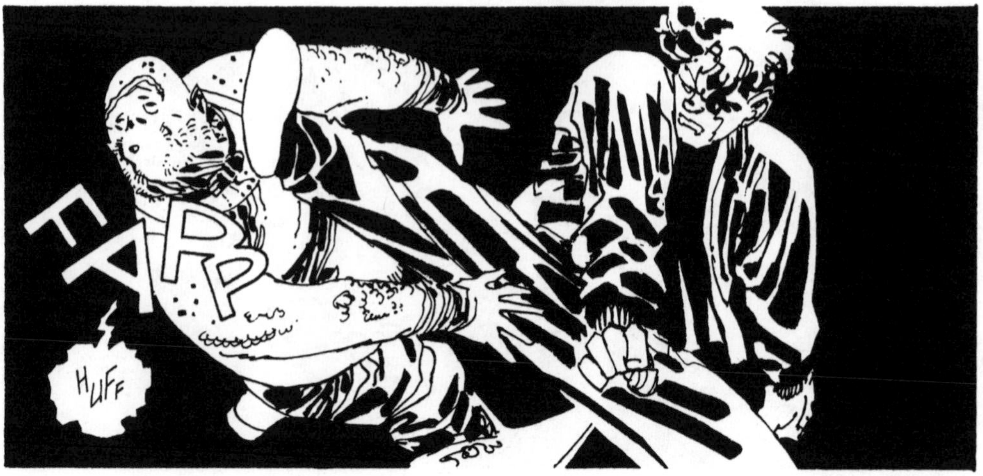
FAPP
HUFF

133

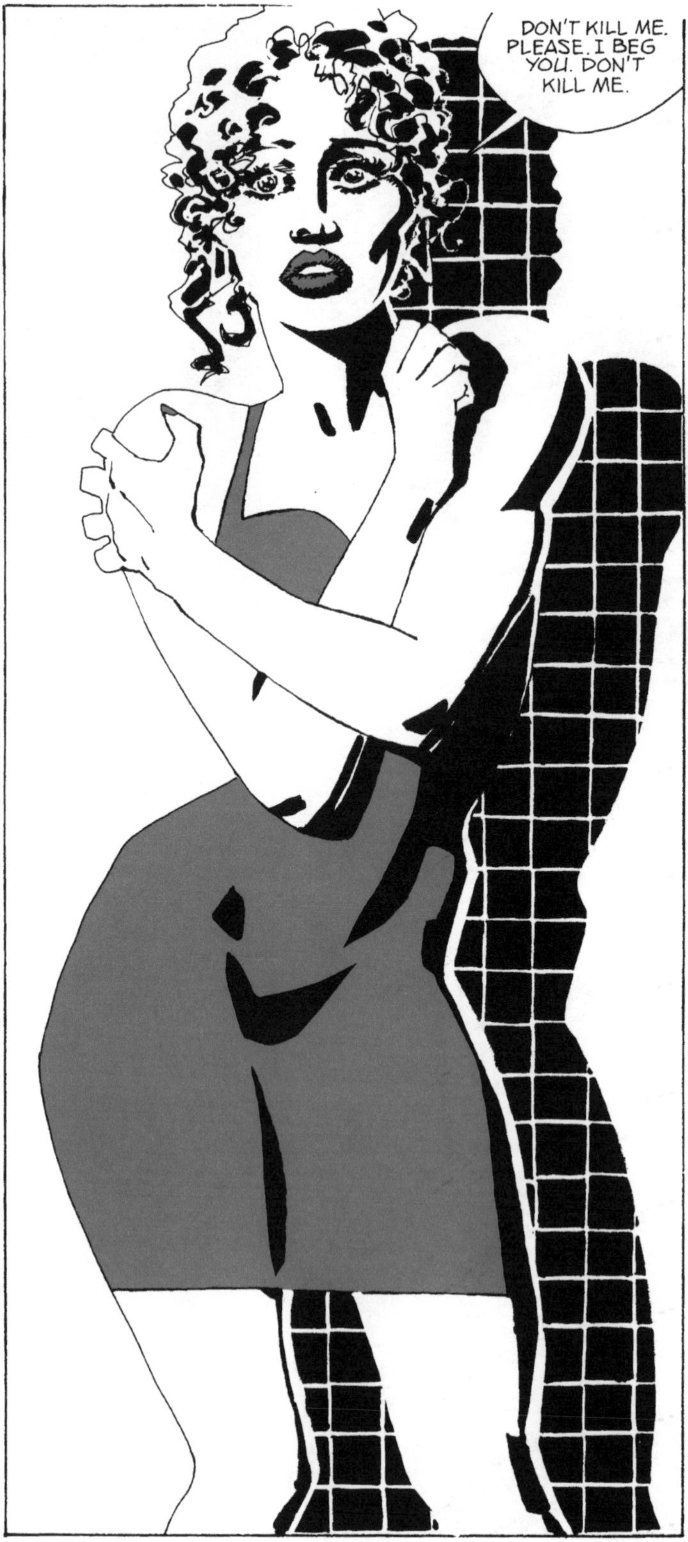
DON'T KILL ME. PLEASE. I BEG YOU. DON'T KILL ME.

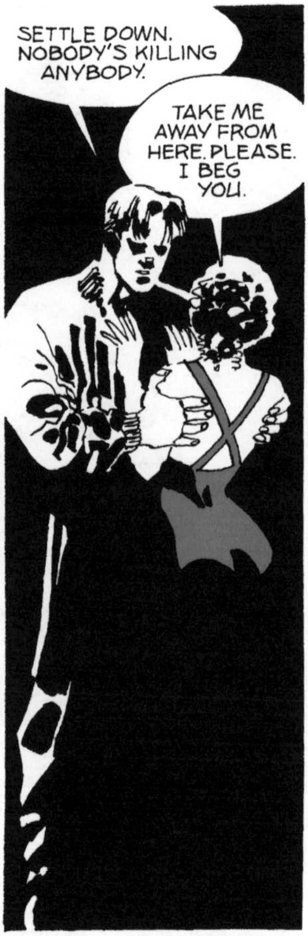
SETTLE DOWN. NOBODY'S KILLING ANYBODY.
TAKE ME AWAY FROM HERE. PLEASE. I BEG YOU.

WHAT IS IT ABOUT SOME WOMEN? THE ONE-IN-A-MILLION KIND, WHO MAKE YOUR HEAD GO LIGHT AND YOUR MOUTH GO DRY AND YOUR HEART CLIMB UP YOUR THROAT? IT'S NOT JUST THEIR LOOKS. IT'S SOMETHING ELSE-- SOMETHING YOU CAN FEEL FROM ACROSS THE ROOM.

WHATEVER IT IS, THIS BABE HAS IT IN SPADES.

BE CAREFUL, THE SMART PART OF ME SAYS. *BE DAMN CAREFUL. REMEMBER THAT OLD ENEMY. HOW SHE SMILED AND TOLD YOU THAT SEX ALWAYS MAKES YOU STUPID.*

SHE WAS RIGHT.

BE CAREFUL.

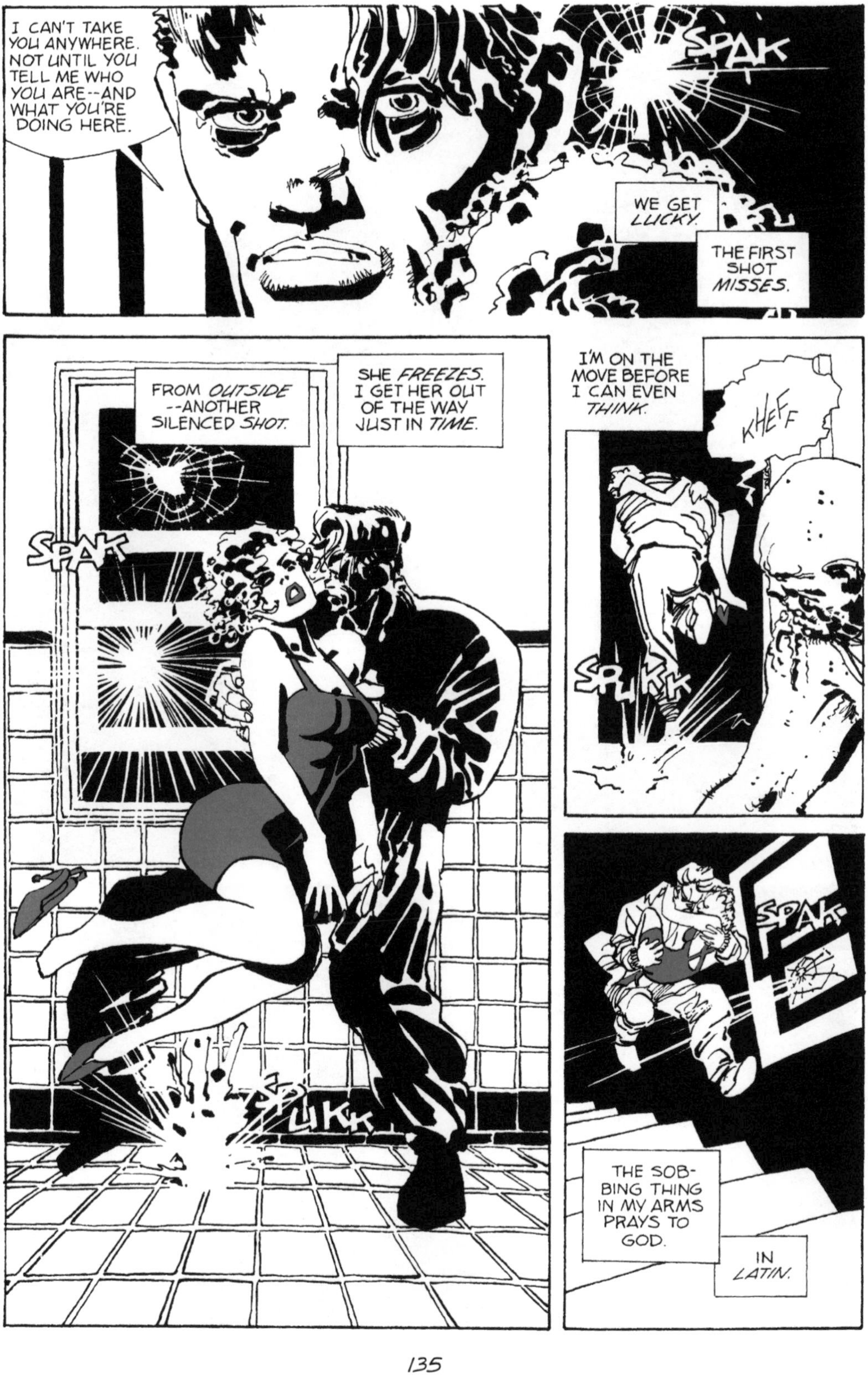
I CAN'T TAKE YOU ANYWHERE. NOT UNTIL YOU TELL ME WHO YOU ARE--AND WHAT YOU'RE DOING HERE.
SPAK
WE GET LUCKY.
THE FIRST SHOT MISSES.
FROM OUTSIDE --ANOTHER SILENCED SHOT.
SHE FREEZES. I GET HER OUT OF THE WAY JUST IN TIME.
SPAK
SPLUKK
I'M ON THE MOVE BEFORE I CAN EVEN THINK.
KHEFF
SPLUKK
SPAK
THE SOB-BING THING IN MY ARMS PRAYS TO GOD.
IN LATIN.

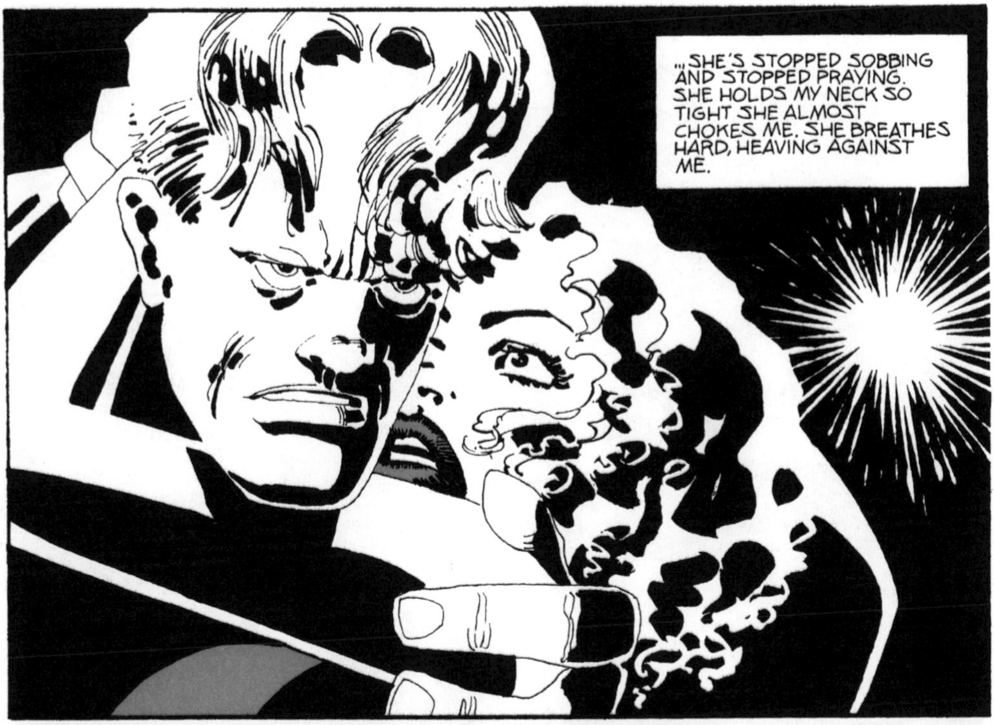
...SHE'S STOPPED SOBBING AND STOPPED PRAYING. SHE HOLDS MY NECK SO TIGHT SHE ALMOST CHOKES ME. SHE BREATHES HARD, HEAVING AGAINST ME.

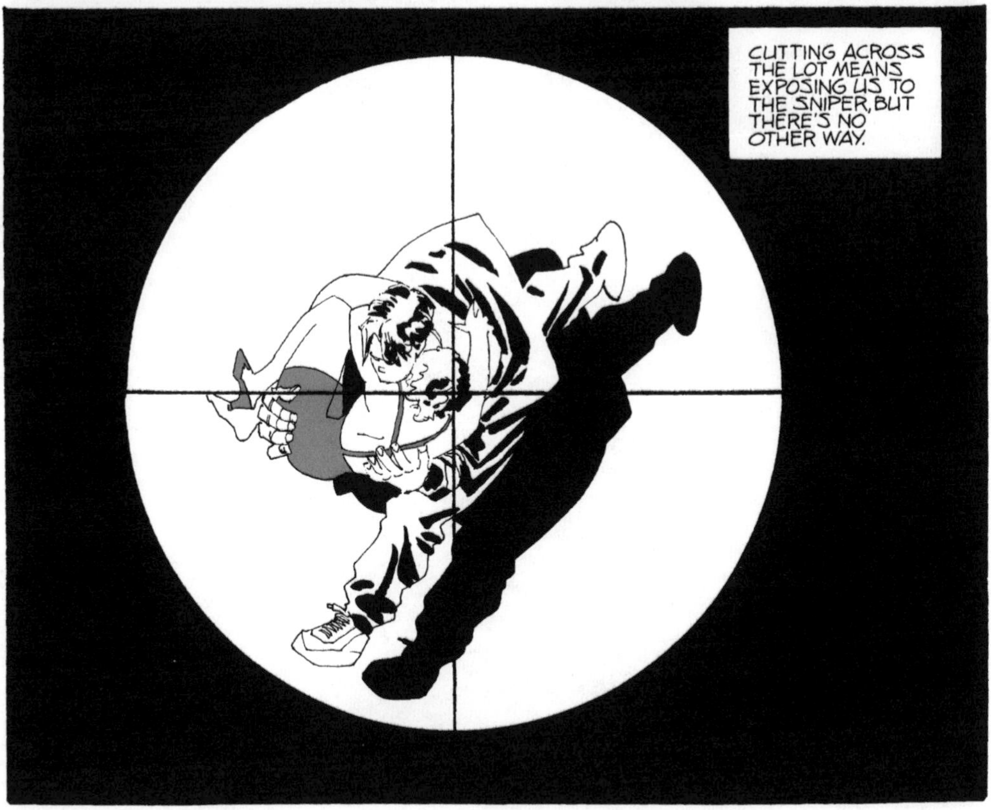
CUTTING ACROSS THE LOT MEANS EXPOSING US TO THE SNIPER, BUT THERE'S NO OTHER WAY.

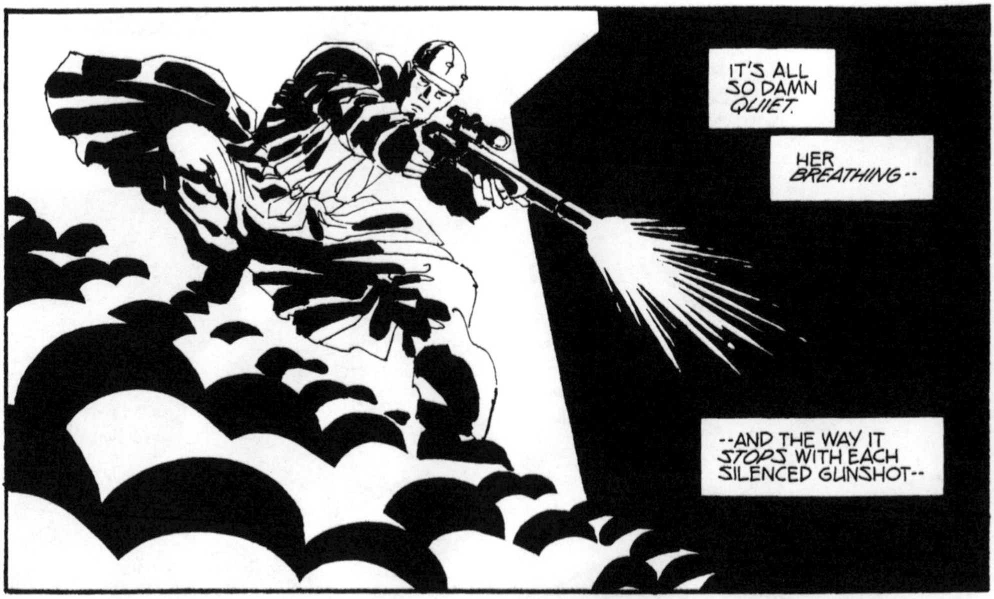
IT'S ALL SO DAMN *QUIET.*
HER *BREATHING*--
--AND THE WAY IT *STOPS* WITH EACH SILENCED GUNSHOT--

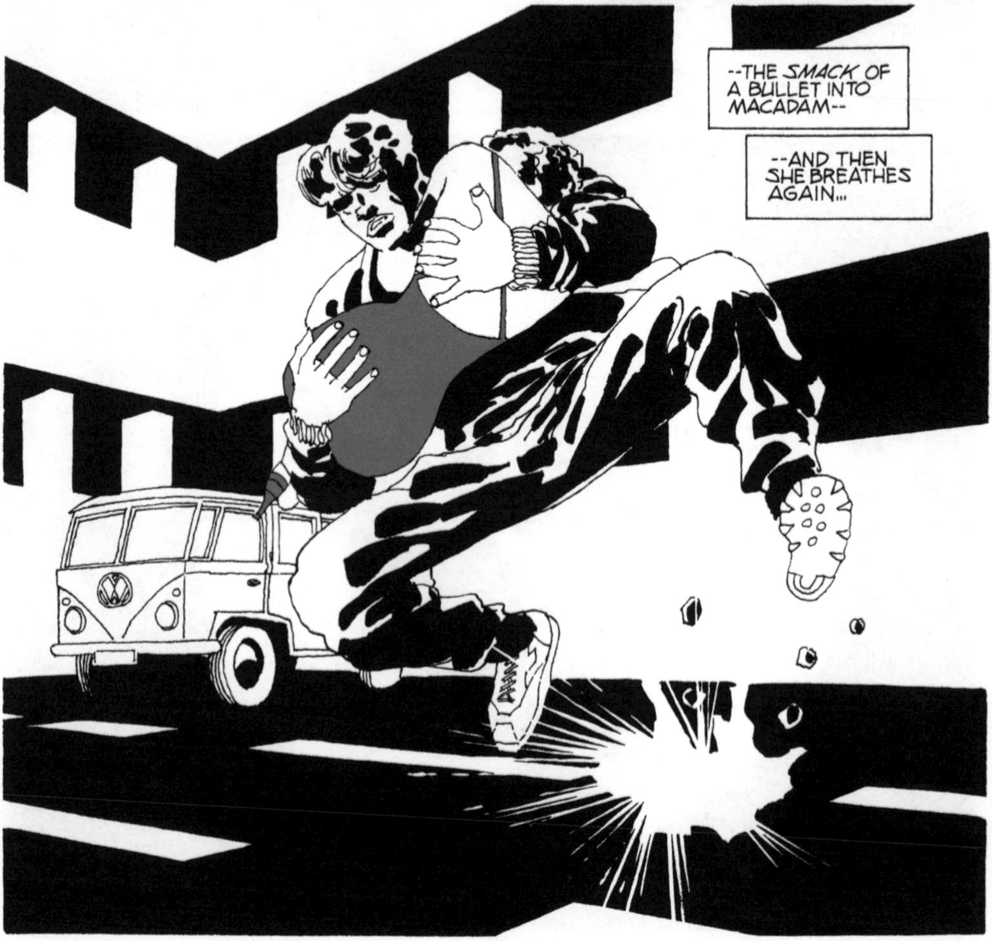
--THE *SMACK* OF A BULLET INTO MACADAM--
--AND THEN SHE BREATHES AGAIN...

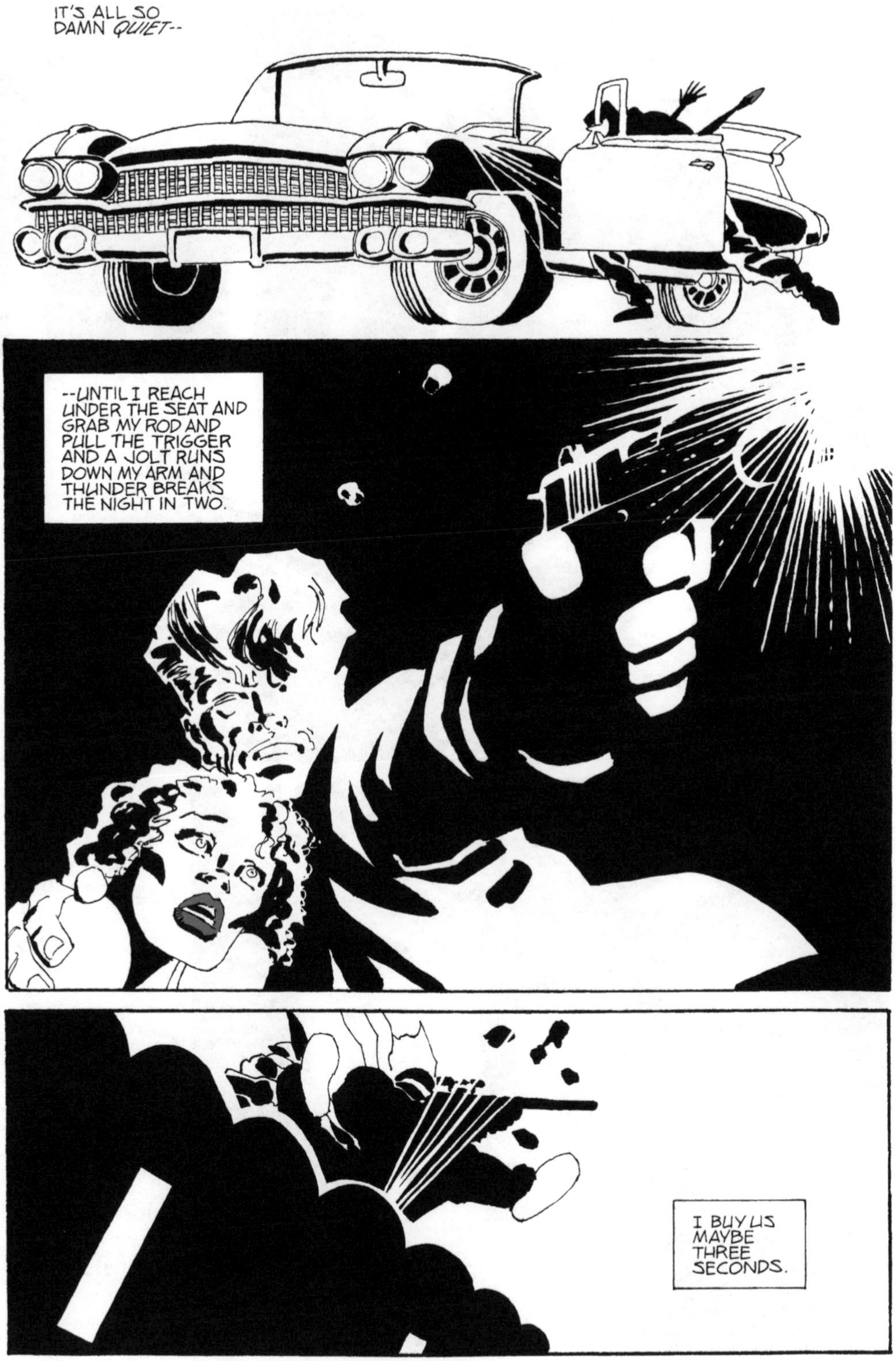
IT'S ALL SO DAMN QUIET--
--UNTIL I REACH UNDER THE SEAT AND GRAB MY ROD AND PULL THE TRIGGER AND A JOLT RUNS DOWN MY ARM AND THUNDER BREAKS THE NIGHT IN TWO.
I BUY US MAYBE THREE SECONDS.

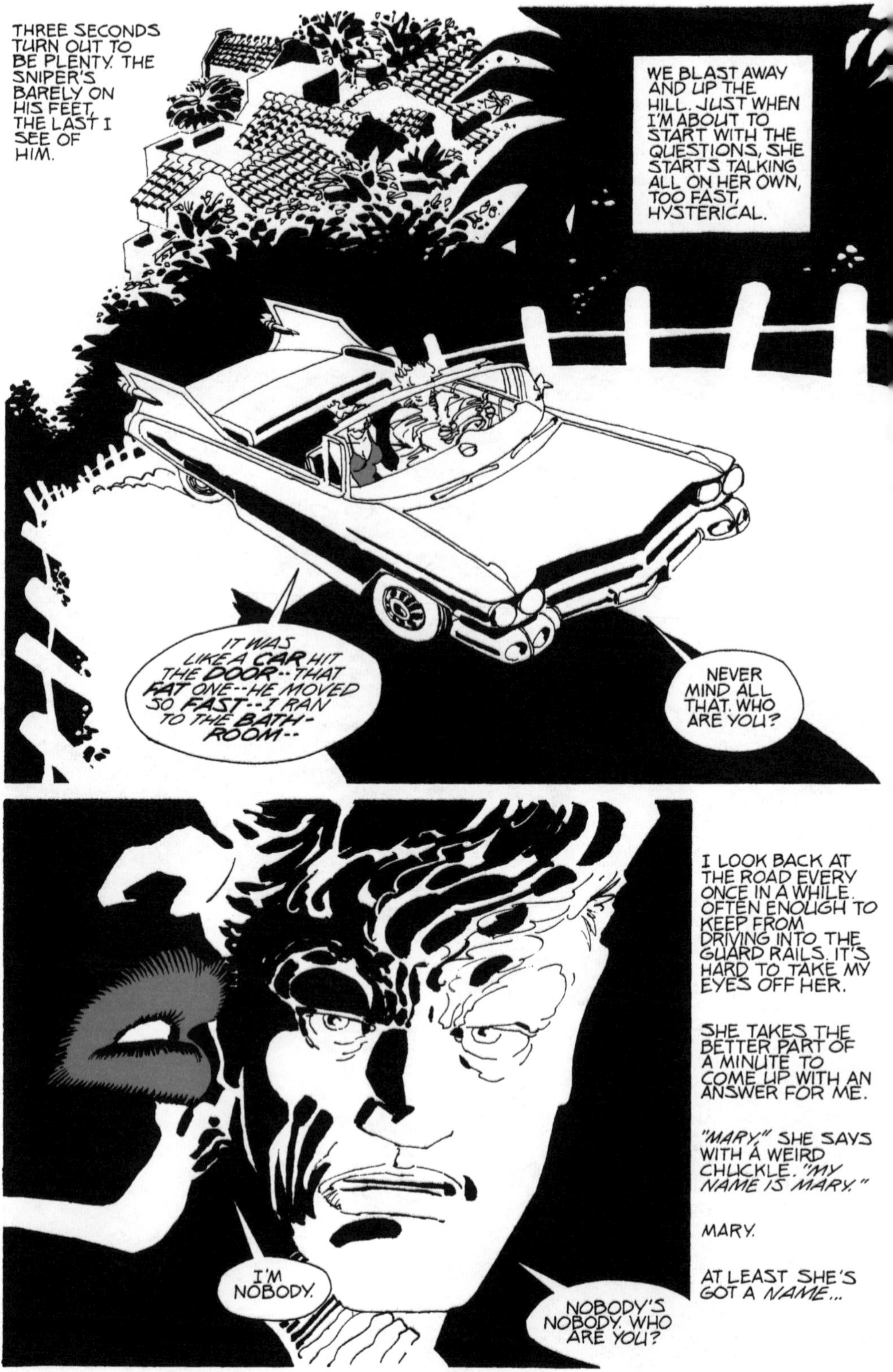
THREE SECONDS TURN OUT TO BE PLENTY. THE SNIPER'S BARELY ON HIS FEET, THE LAST I SEE OF HIM.
WE BLAST AWAY AND UP THE HILL. JUST WHEN I'M ABOUT TO START WITH THE QUESTIONS, SHE STARTS TALKING ALL ON HER OWN, TOO FAST, HYSTERICAL.
IT WAS LIKE A CAR HIT THE DOOR-- THAT FAT ONE-- HE MOVED SO FAST-- I RAN TO THE BATH-ROOM--
NEVER MIND ALL THAT. WHO ARE YOU?
I LOOK BACK AT THE ROAD EVERY ONCE IN A WHILE. OFTEN ENOUGH TO KEEP FROM DRIVING INTO THE GUARD RAILS. IT'S HARD TO TAKE MY EYES OFF HER.
SHE TAKES THE BETTER PART OF A MINUTE TO COME UP WITH AN ANSWER FOR ME.
"MARY," SHE SAYS WITH A WEIRD CHUCKLE. "MY NAME IS MARY."
MARY.
AT LEAST SHE'S GOT A NAME...
I'M NOBODY.
NOBODY'S NOBODY. WHO ARE YOU?

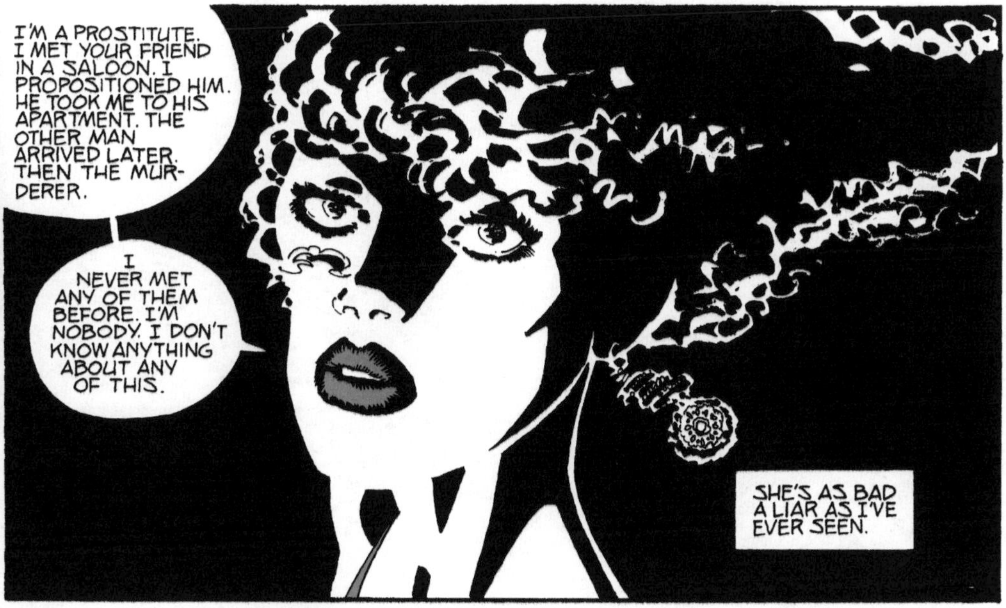
I'M A PROSTITUTE. I MET YOUR FRIEND IN A SALOON. I PROPOSITIONED HIM. HE TOOK ME TO HIS APARTMENT. THE OTHER MAN ARRIVED LATER. THEN THE MURDERER.
I NEVER MET ANY OF THEM BEFORE. I'M NOBODY. I DON'T KNOW ANYTHING ABOUT ANY OF THIS.
SHE'S AS BAD A LIAR AS I'VE EVER SEEN.

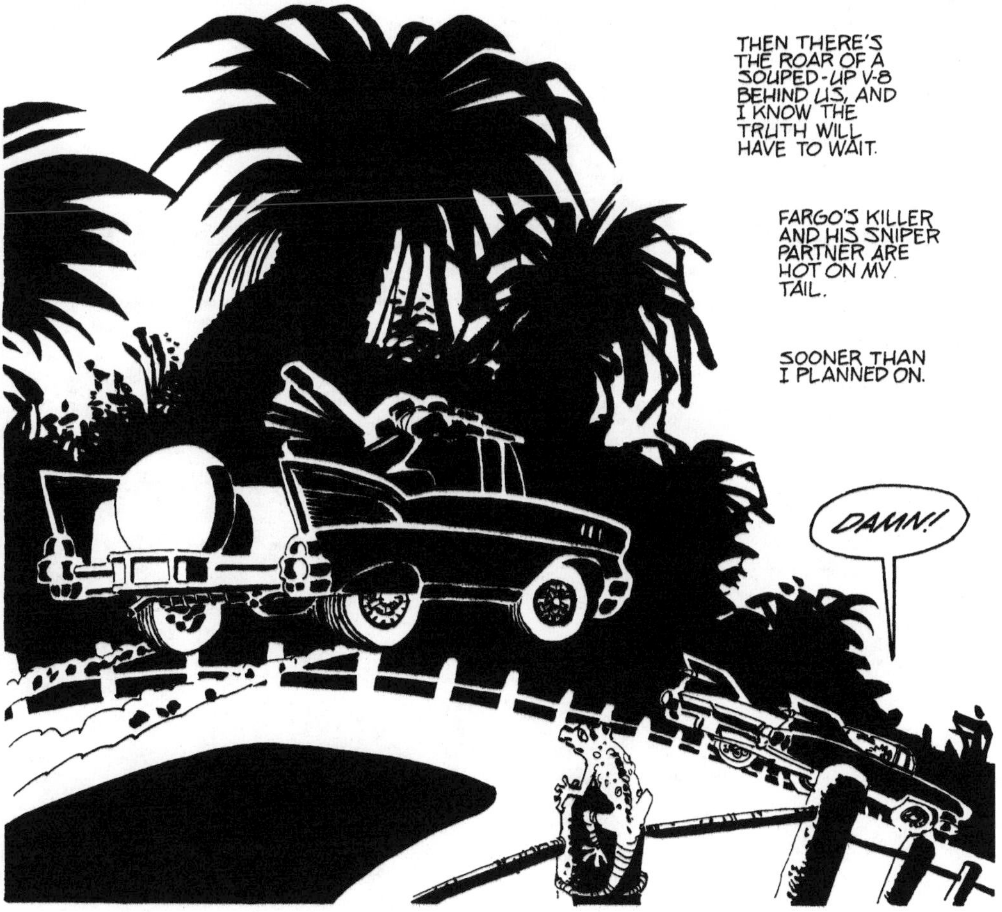
THEN THERE'S THE ROAR OF A SOUPED-UP V-8 BEHIND US, AND I KNOW THE TRUTH WILL HAVE TO WAIT.
FARGO'S KILLER AND HIS SNIPER PARTNER ARE HOT ON MY TAIL.
SOONER THAN I PLANNED ON.
DAMN!

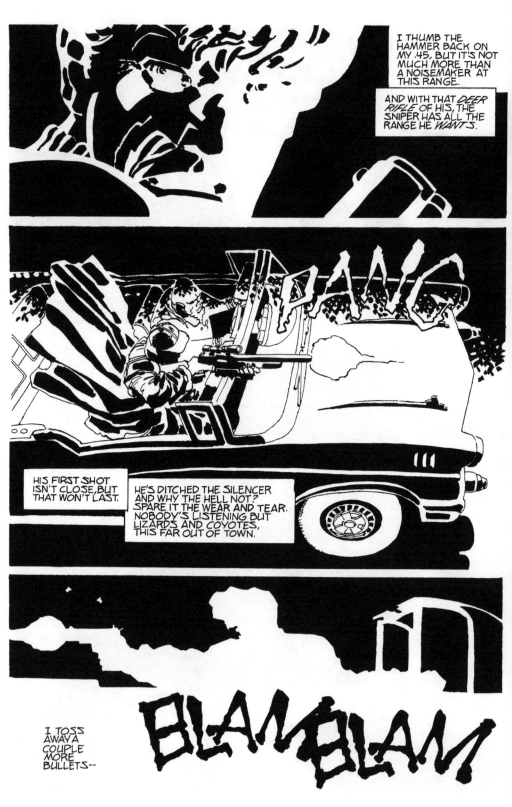

I THUMB THE HAMMER BACK ON MY .45, BUT IT'S NOT MUCH MORE THAN A NOISEMAKER AT THIS RANGE.

AND WITH THAT *DEER RIFLE* OF HIS, THE SNIPER HAS ALL THE RANGE HE *WANTS.*

PANG

HIS FIRST SHOT ISN'T CLOSE, BUT THAT WON'T LAST.

HE'S DITCHED THE SILENCER AND WHY THE HELL NOT? SPARE IT THE WEAR AND TEAR. NOBODY'S LISTENING BUT LIZARDS AND COYOTES, THIS FAR OUT OF TOWN.

I TOSS AWAY A COUPLE MORE BULLETS--

BLAM BLAM

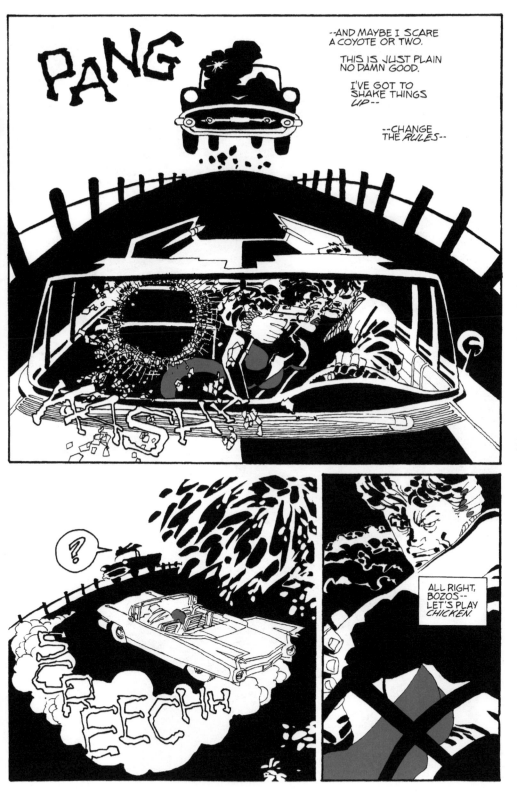

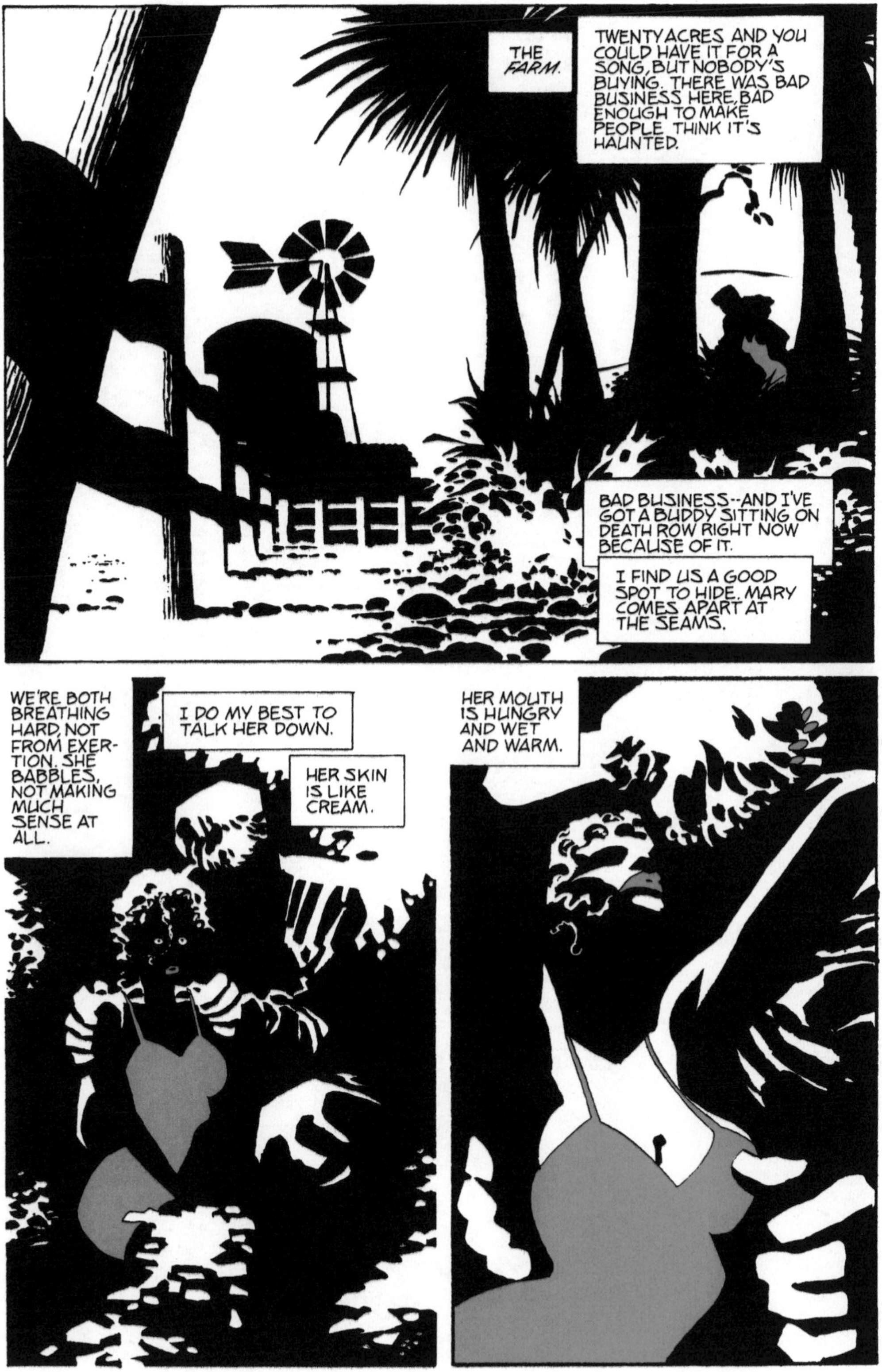
THE *FARM*.
TWENTY ACRES AND YOU COULD HAVE IT FOR A SONG, BUT NOBODY'S BUYING. THERE WAS BAD BUSINESS HERE, BAD ENOUGH TO MAKE PEOPLE THINK IT'S HAUNTED.
BAD BUSINESS--AND I'VE GOT A BUDDY SITTING ON DEATH ROW RIGHT NOW BECAUSE OF IT.
I FIND US A GOOD SPOT TO HIDE. MARY COMES APART AT THE SEAMS.
WE'RE BOTH BREATHING HARD, NOT FROM EXERTION. SHE BABBLES, NOT MAKING MUCH SENSE AT ALL.
I DO MY BEST TO TALK HER DOWN.
HER SKIN IS LIKE CREAM.
HER MOUTH IS HUNGRY AND WET AND WARM.

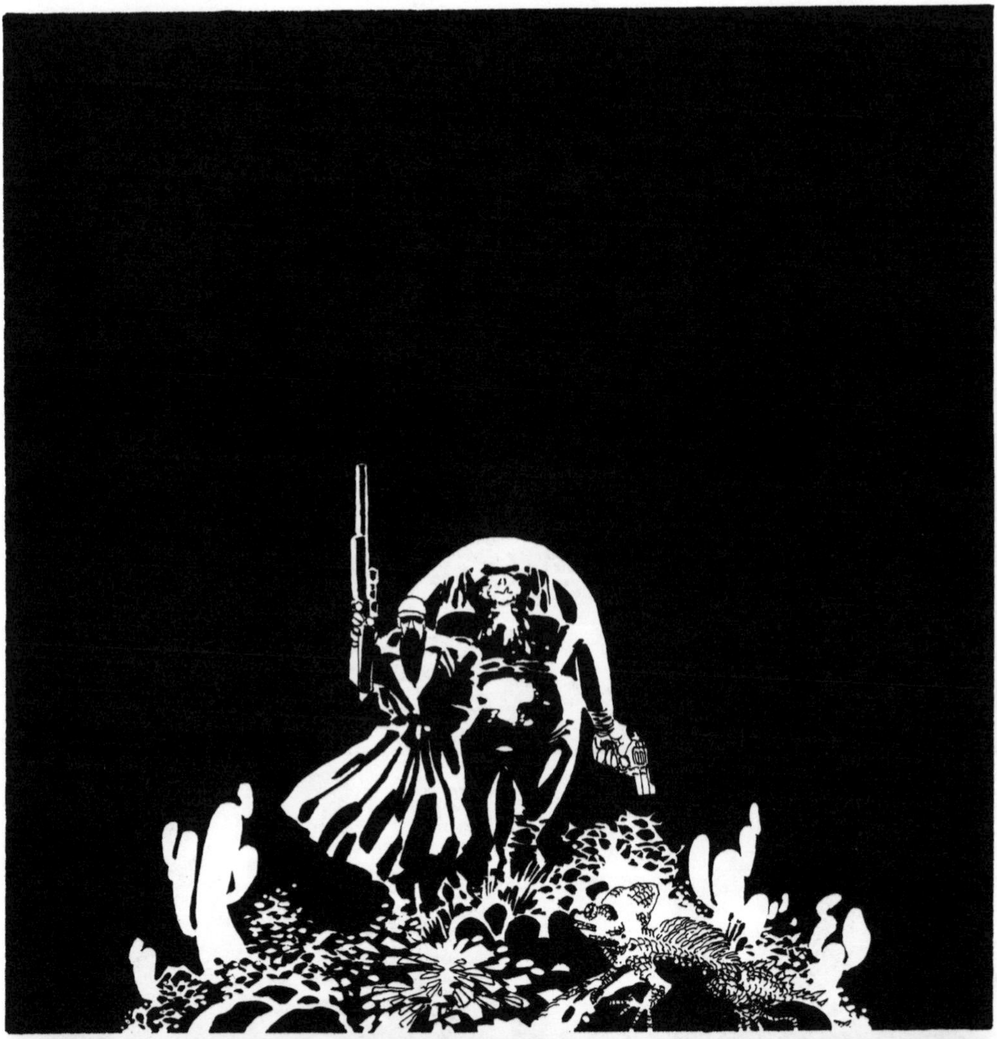

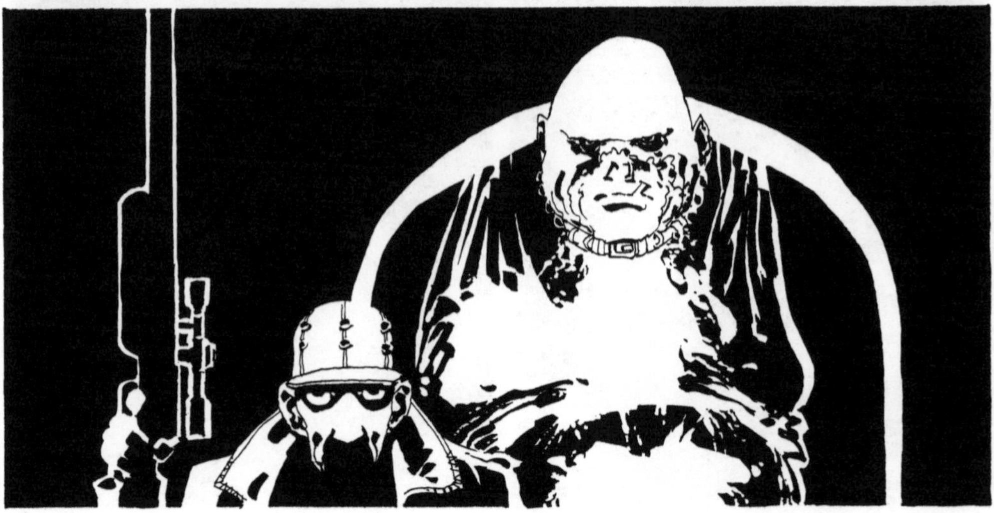

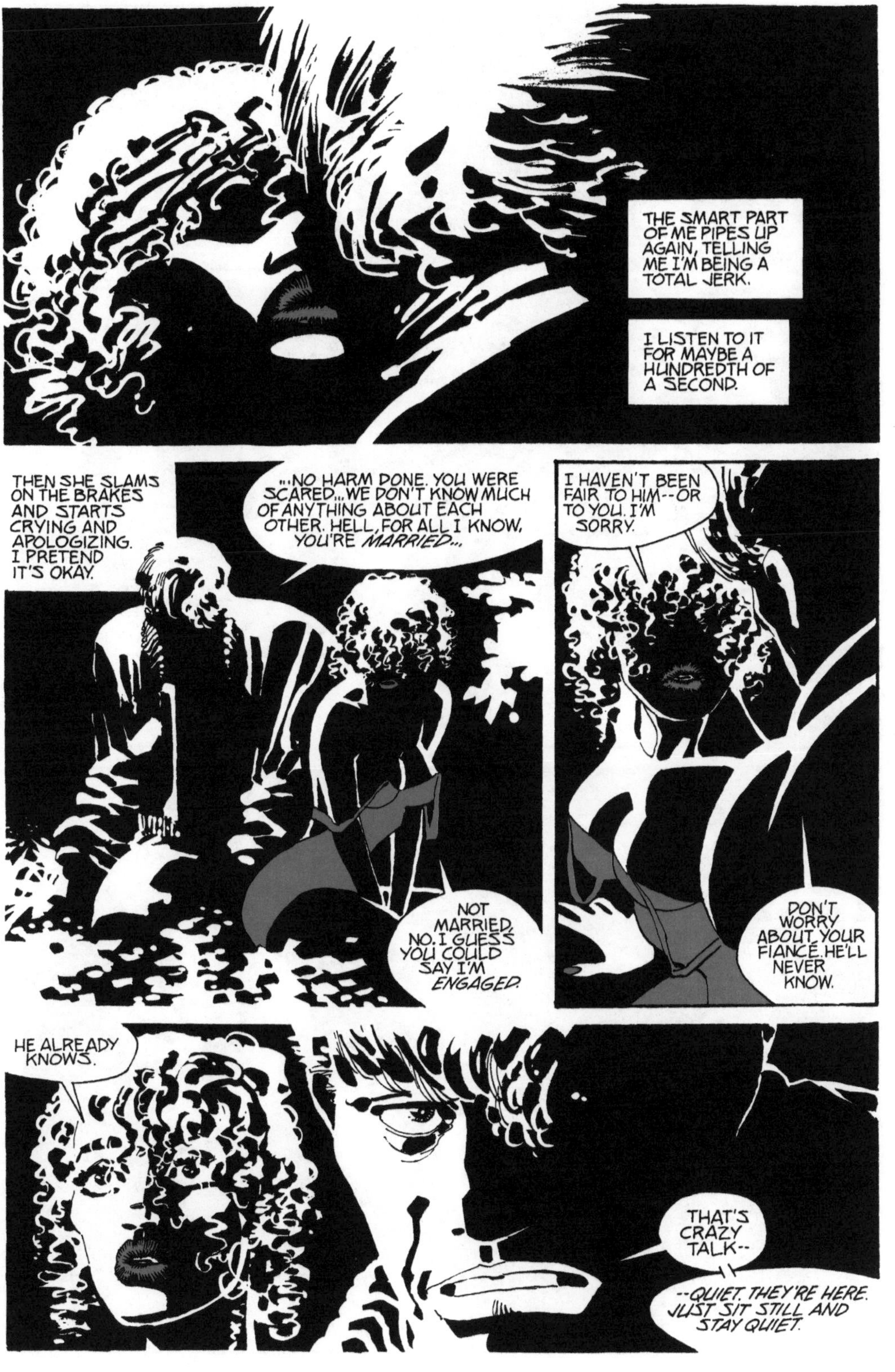
THE SMART PART OF ME PIPES UP AGAIN, TELLING ME I'M BEING A TOTAL JERK.
I LISTEN TO IT FOR MAYBE A HUNDREDTH OF A SECOND.
THEN SHE SLAMS ON THE BRAKES AND STARTS CRYING AND APOLOGIZING. I PRETEND IT'S OKAY.
...NO HARM DONE. YOU WERE SCARED... WE DON'T KNOW MUCH OF ANYTHING ABOUT EACH OTHER. HELL, FOR ALL I KNOW, YOU'RE *MARRIED*...
NOT MARRIED, NO. I GUESS YOU COULD SAY I'M *ENGAGED*.
I HAVEN'T BEEN FAIR TO HIM--OR TO YOU. I'M SORRY.
DON'T WORRY ABOUT YOUR FIANCÉ. HE'LL NEVER KNOW.
HE ALREADY KNOWS.
THAT'S CRAZY TALK--
--QUIET. THEY'RE HERE. JUST SIT STILL AND STAY QUIET.

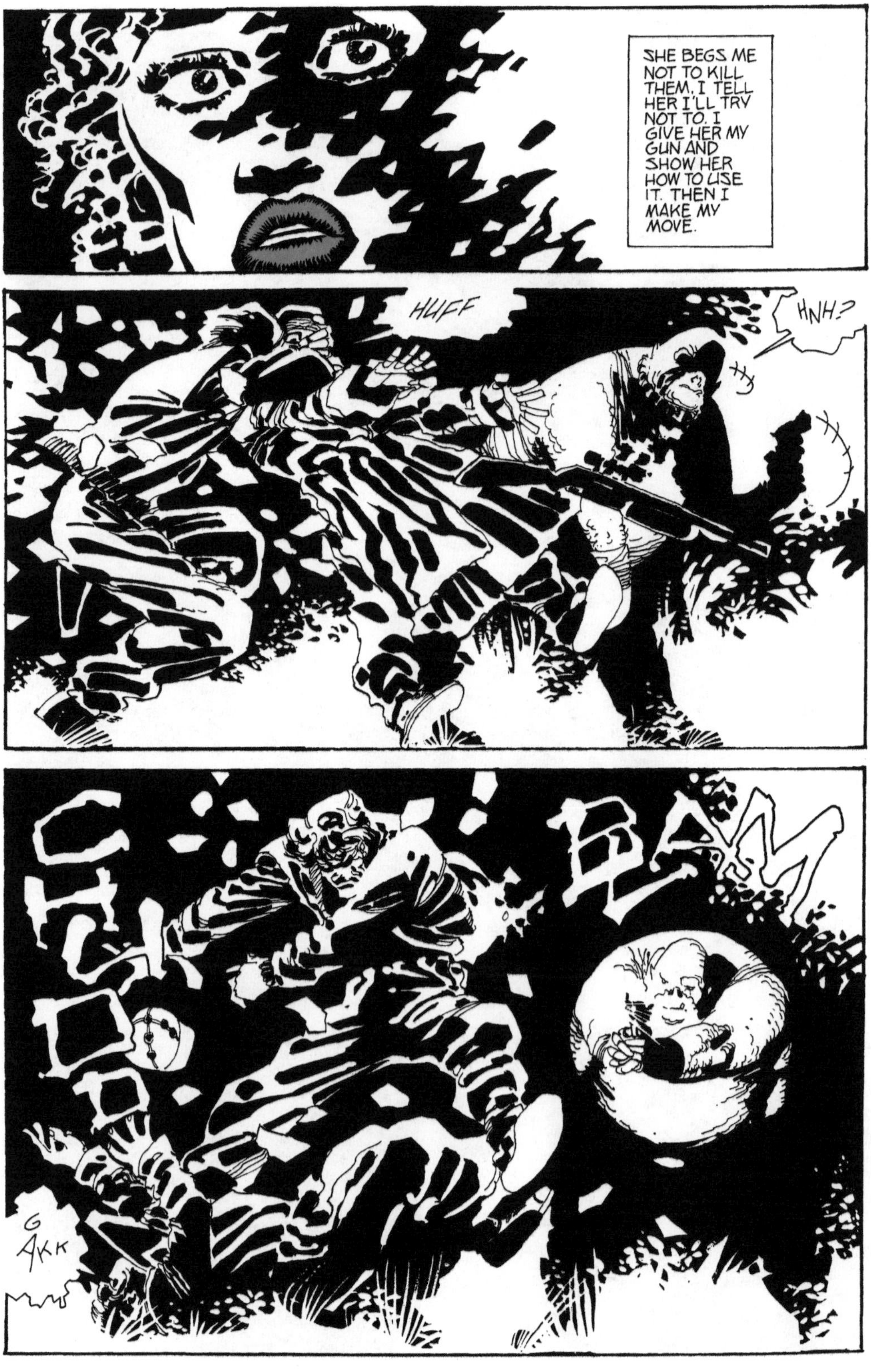
SHE BEGS ME NOT TO KILL THEM. I TELL HER I'LL TRY NOT TO. I GIVE HER MY GUN AND SHOW HER HOW TO USE IT. THEN I MAKE MY MOVE.
HUFF
HNH?
BAM
GAKK

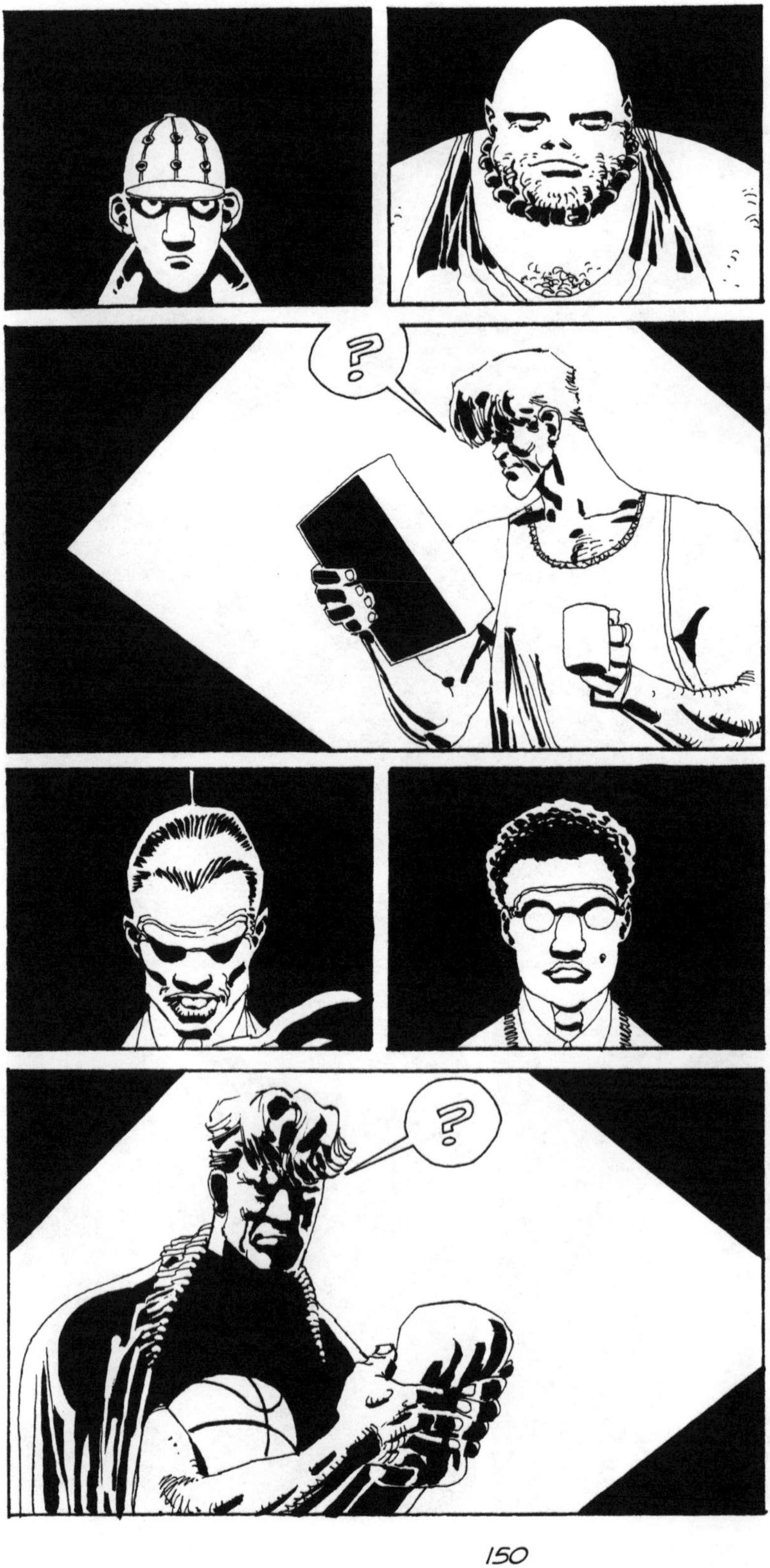
?
?

THE *ANSWERS*. SOME OF THEM COME WITH THE MORNING *PAPER*.

THE GOONS TURN OUT TO BE *DOUGLAS KLUMP* AND *BURT SHLUBB*, A PAIR OF LOW-RENT *HIT MEN* WHO GO BY THE NAMES OF *"FAT MAN AND LITTLE BOY."*

I'M ON MY SECOND CUP OF COFFEE WHEN A *PACKAGE* ARRIVES. BEING OFFICIALLY *DEAD*, I'M ALWAYS SURPRISED WHEN I GET *MAIL*.

FARGO SHIPPED IT OFF TO ME BEFORE THEY GOT TO HIM. IT'S *EVIDENCE*.

MY OLD PAL WAS WORKING WITH PRIVATE EYE *BERNARD ZIMMER*--

--ON A *DRUG TRAFFICKING EXPOSÉ* THAT SENDS *SHIVERS* DOWN THE SPINES OF THE *MAYOR* AND THE *DISTRICT ATTORNEY*, AND SENDS BOSS *WALLENQUIST'S* LIEUTENANTS SCRAMBLING TO FIND SOMEBODY TO PIN IT ON.

A FEW DAYS LATER I'M JUST BACK FROM A DECENT WORKOUT AND I FIND *ANOTHER* PACKAGE.

FROM *MARY*, THIS TIME.

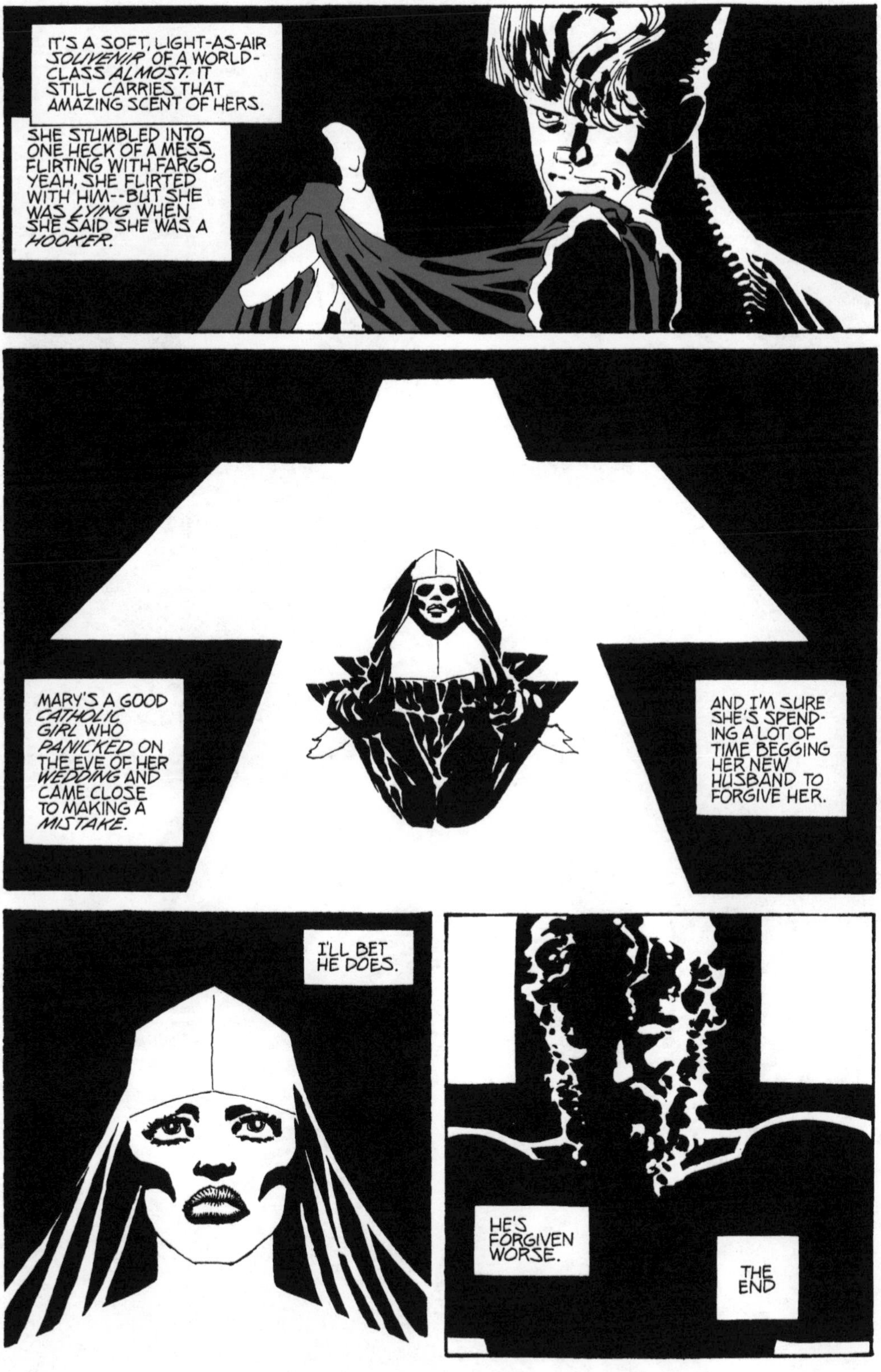
IT'S A SOFT, LIGHT-AS-AIR SOUVENIR OF A WORLD-CLASS ALMOST. IT STILL CARRIES THAT AMAZING SCENT OF HERS.
SHE STUMBLED INTO ONE HECK OF A MESS, FLIRTING WITH FARGO. YEAH, SHE FLIRTED WITH HIM--BUT SHE WAS LYING WHEN SHE SAID SHE WAS A HOOKER.
MARY'S A GOOD CATHOLIC GIRL WHO PANICKED ON THE EVE OF HER WEDDING AND CAME CLOSE TO MAKING A MISTAKE.
AND I'M SURE SHE'S SPENDING A LOT OF TIME BEGGING HER NEW HUSBAND TO FORGIVE HER.
I'LL BET HE DOES.
HE'S FORGIVEN WORSE.
THE END

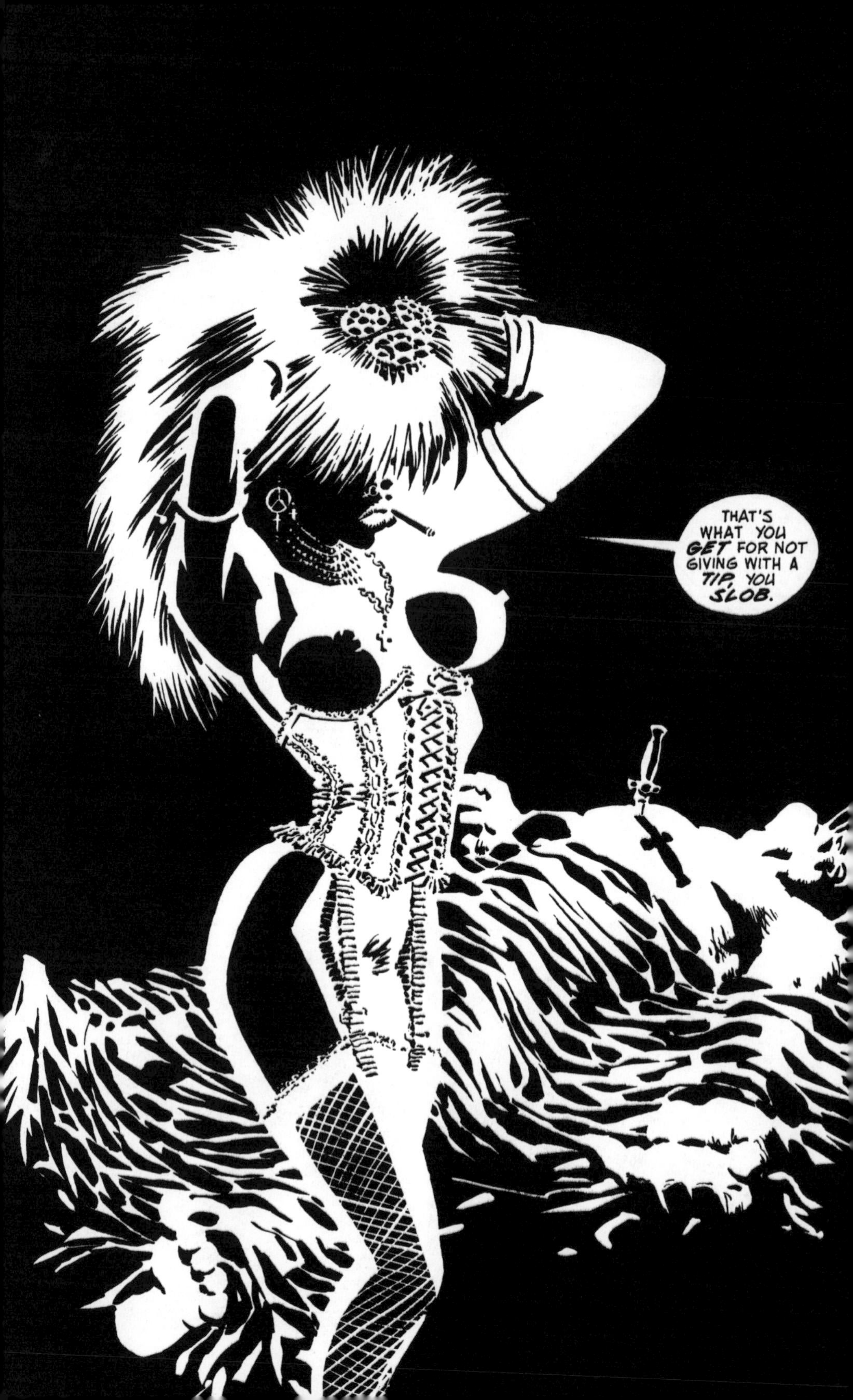
THAT'S WHAT YOU GET FOR NOT GIVING WITH A TIP, YOU SLOB.

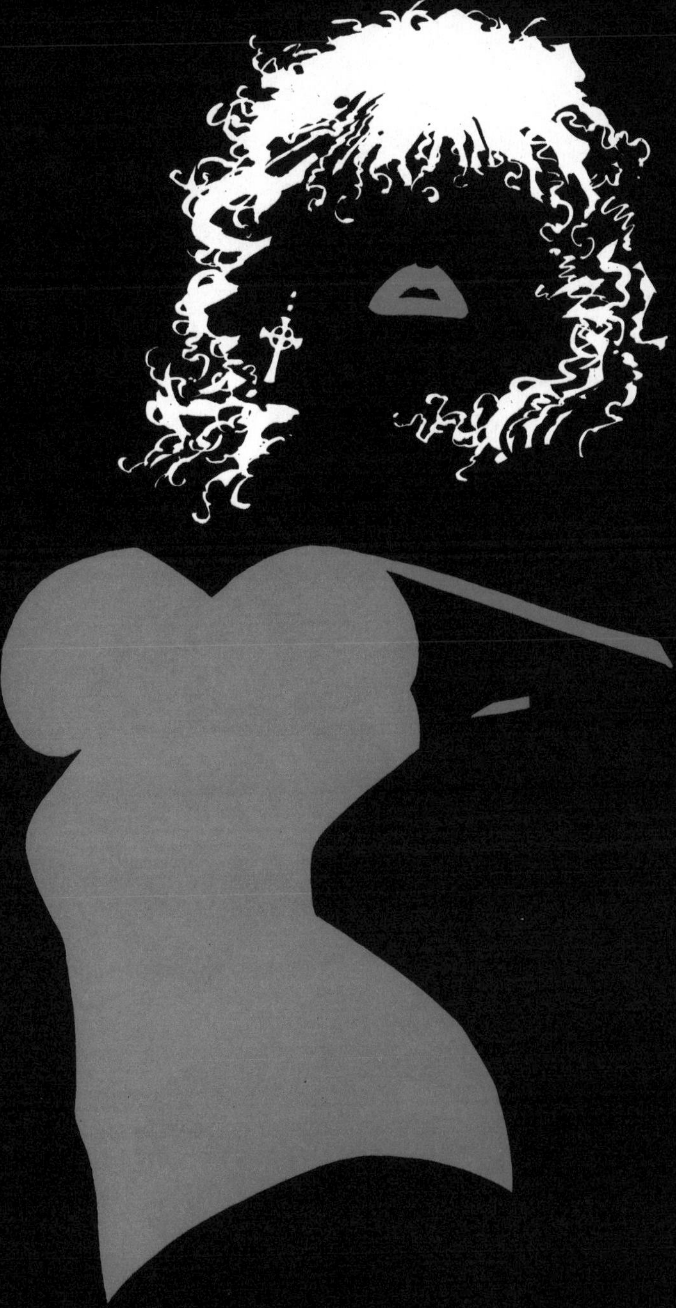

COVER GALLERY

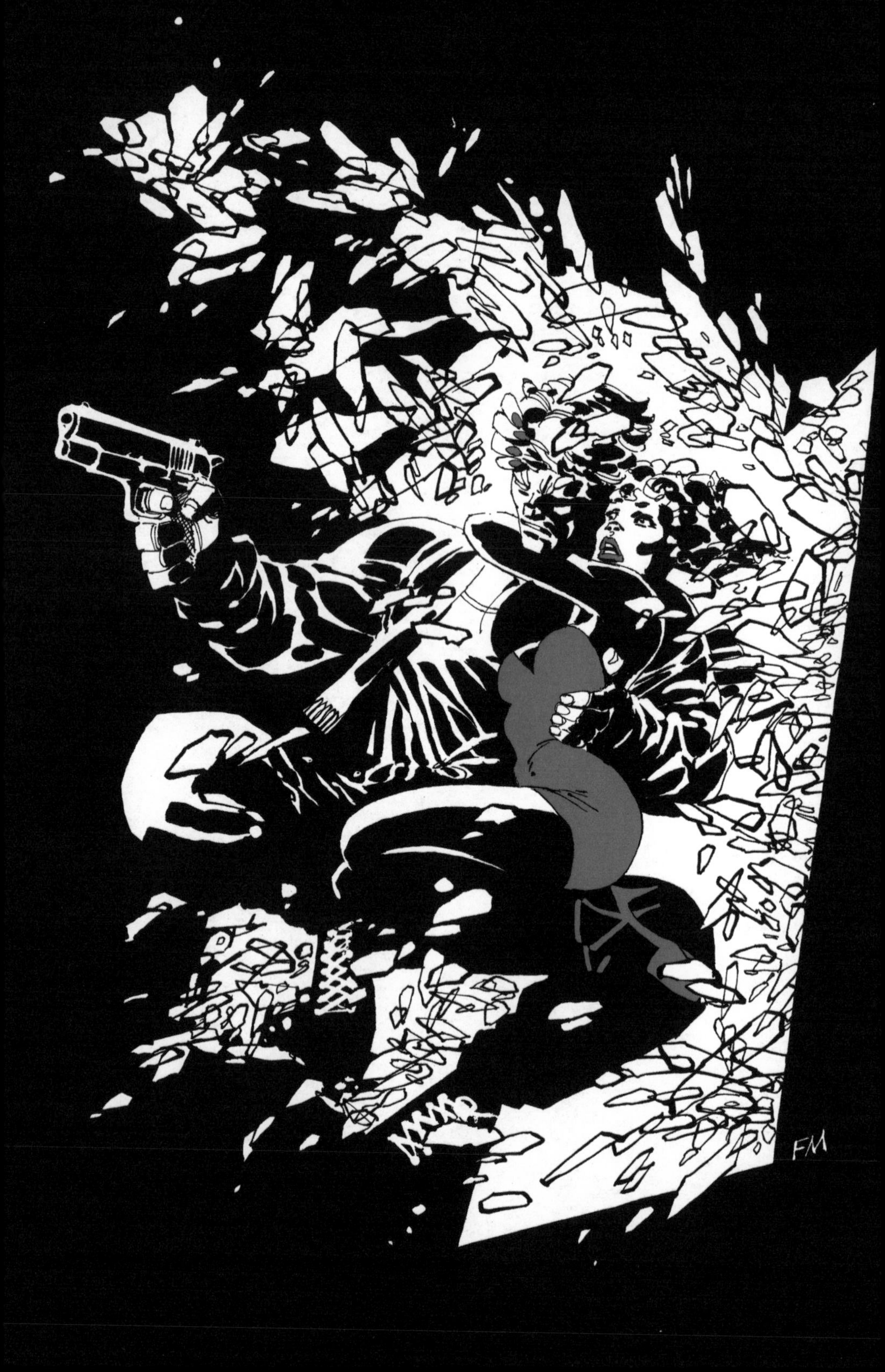
FM

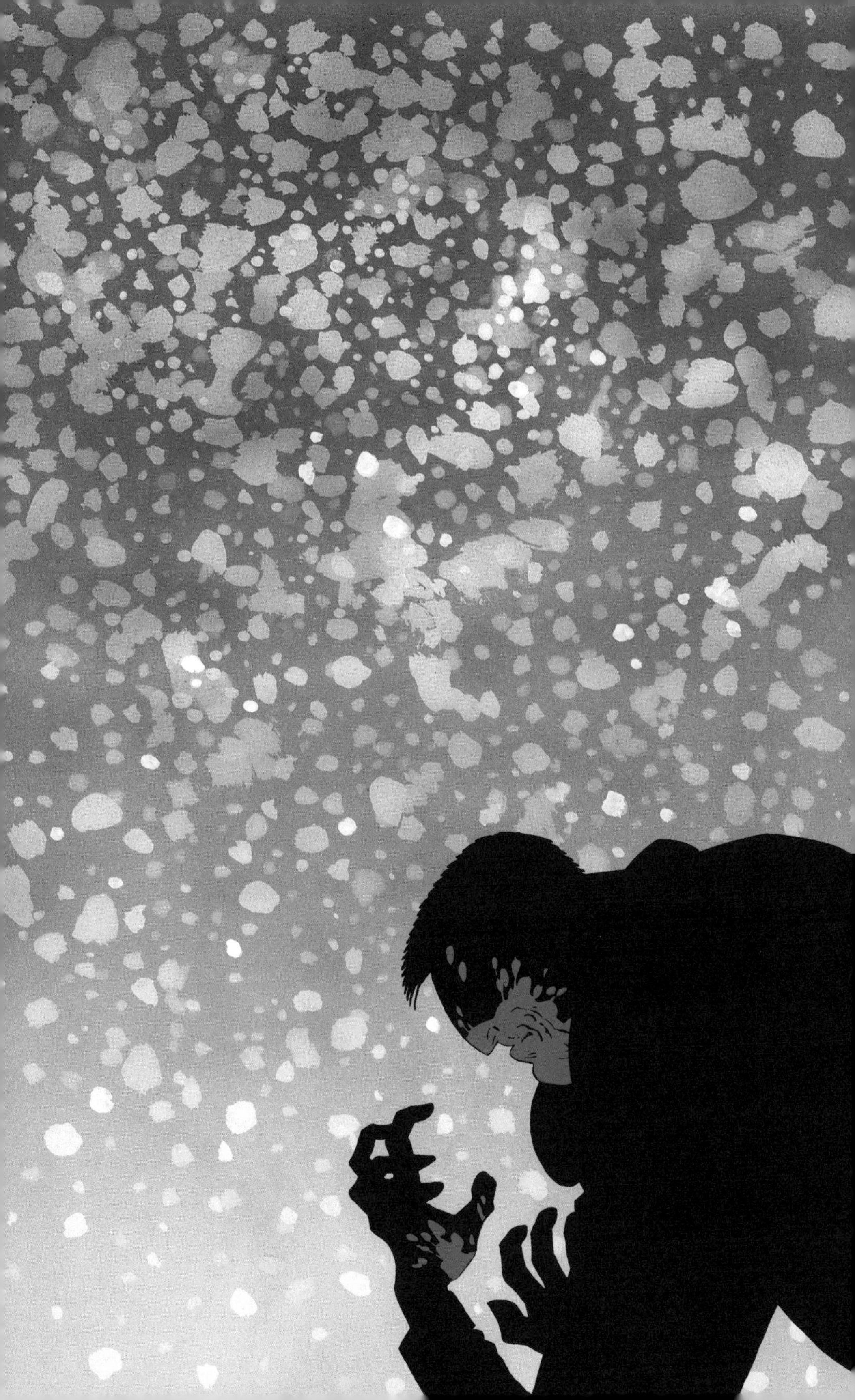

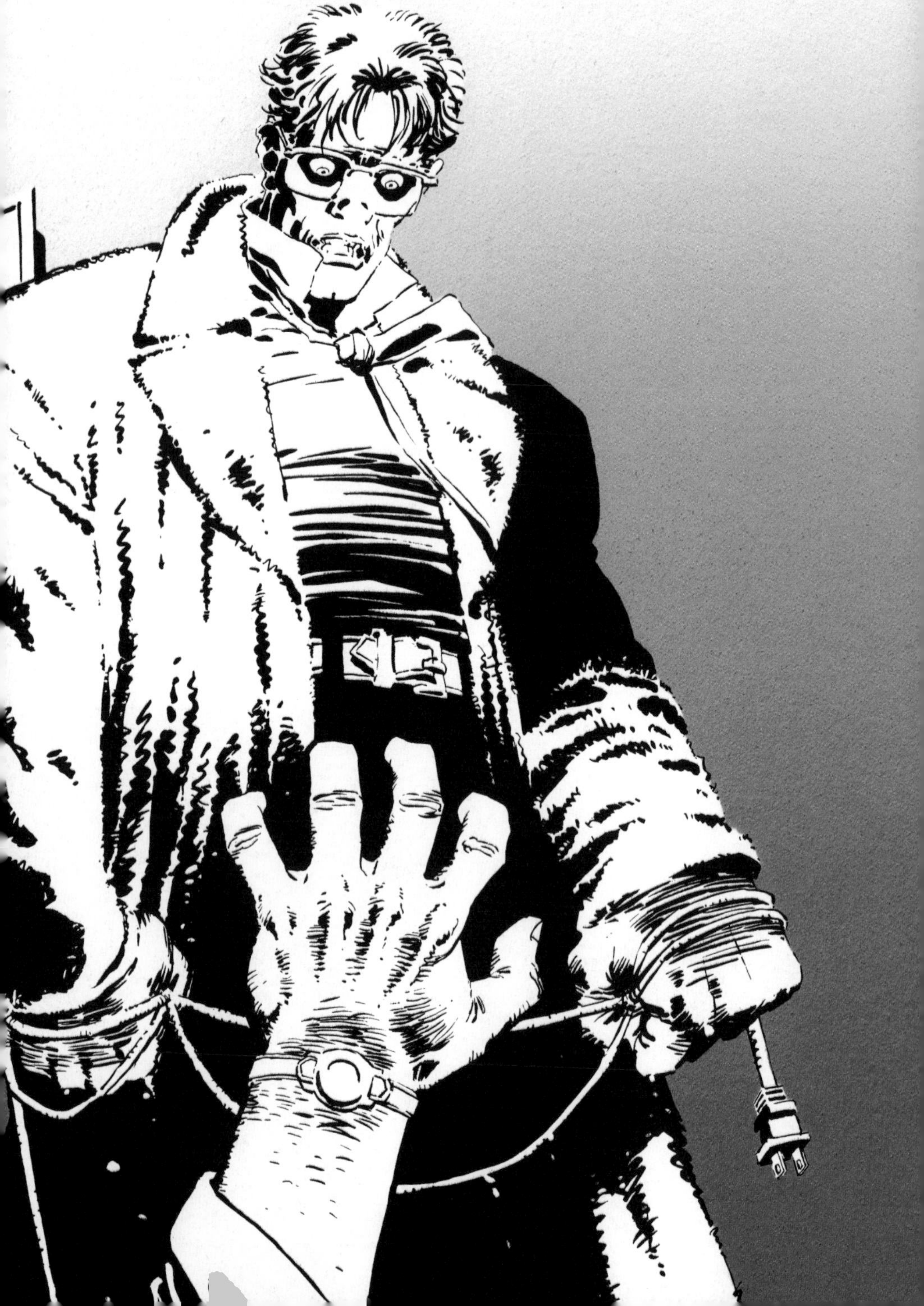

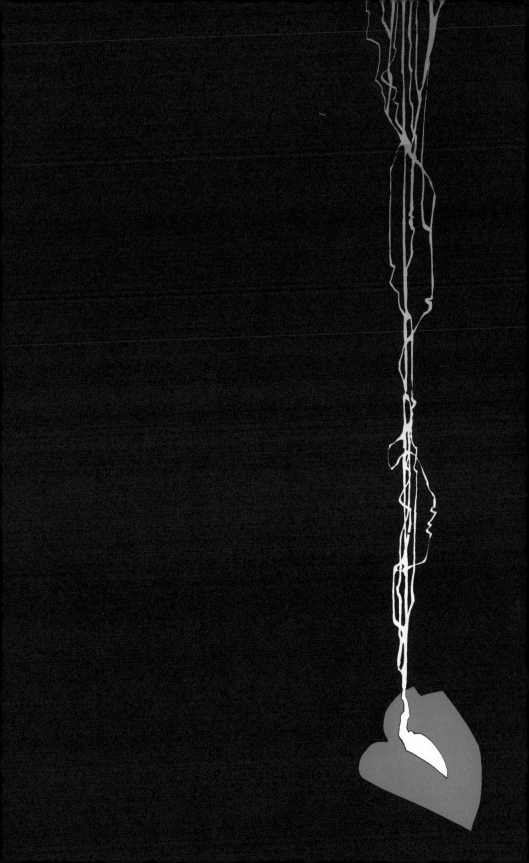

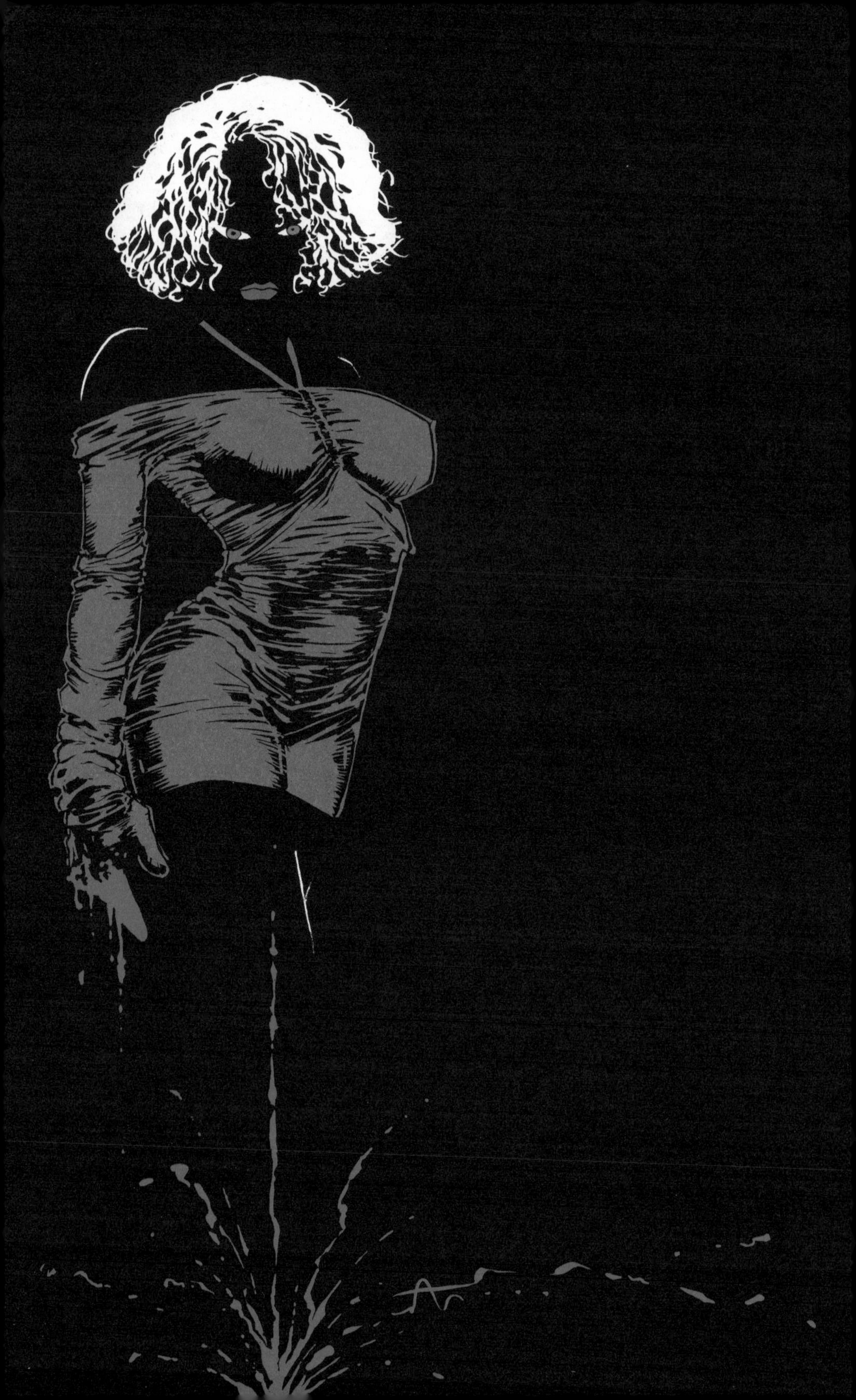